D1505252

How to Make Money
in Commercial Real Estate

FOR THE SMALL INVESTOR

How to Make Money in Commercial Real Estate

FOR THE SMALL INVESTOR

Second Edition

Nicholas Masters

WILEY

John Wiley & Sons, Inc.

Published by John Wiley & Sons, Inc., Hoboken, New Jersey.
Published simultaneously in Canada.

No part of this publication may be reproduced, stored in a retrieval system, or transmitted in any form or by any means, electronic, mechanical, photocopying, recording, scanning, or otherwise, except as permitted under Section 107 or 108 of the 1976 United States Copyright Act, without either the prior written permission of the Publisher, or authorization through payment of the appropriate per-copy fee to the Copyright Clearance Center, Inc., 222 Rosewood Drive, Danvers, MA 01923, (978) 750-8400, fax (978) 646-8600, or on the web at www.copyright.com. Requests to the Publisher for permission should be addressed to the Permissions Department, John Wiley & Sons, Inc., 111 River Street, Hoboken, NJ 07030, (201) 748-6011, fax (201) 748-6008, or online at http://www.wiley.com/go/permissions.

Limit of Liability/Disclaimer of Warranty: While the publisher and author have used their best efforts in preparing this book, they make no representations or warranties with respect to the accuracy or completeness of the contents of this book and specifically disclaim any implied warranties of merchantability or fitness for a particular purpose. No warranty may be created or extended by sales representatives or written sales materials. The advice and strategies contained herein may not be suitable for your situation. The publisher is not engaged in rendering professional services, and you should consult a professional where appropriate. Neither the publisher nor author shall be liable for any loss of profit or any other commercial damages, including but not limited to special, incidental, consequential, or other damages.

For general information on our other products and services please contact our Customer Care Department within the United States at (800) 762-2974, outside the United States at (317) 572-3993 or fax (317) 572-4002.

Wiley also publishes its books in a variety of electronic formats. Some content that appears in print may not be available in electronic books. For more information about Wiley products, visit our web site at www.Wiley.com.

Library of Congress Cataloging-in-Publication Data:

Sfouggatakis, Nicholas, 1947–
  How to make money in commercial real estate for the small investor / Nicholas Masters.—2nd ed.
      p. cm.
    Includes index.
    ISBN-13: 978-0-471-75261-5 (cloth)
    ISBN-10: 0-471-75261-4 (cloth)
    1. Real estate investment.   2. Commercial real estate—Management.
  3. Real estate management.   I. Title.

  HD1382.5.M286 2006
  332.63'24—dc22

                                                                2005043649

Printed in the United States of America.

10 9 8 7 6 5 4 3 2 1

To all aspiring real estate investors,
and to the many people who have helped me
throughout my career in real estate.

CONTENTS

PART II
INVESTING IN REAL ESTATE

PREFACE

Nicholas Masters is a retired certified public accountant, a professor of accounting and finance, and a licensed real estate broker. He has had over 30 years of experience in accounting, finance, and real estate investing.

Masters has turned a $35,000 initial investment in 1966 into a $10 million real estate debt-free portfolio. The purpose of this book is to impart some of his accumulated knowledge and experience to the general public.

This book is geared toward the small and inexperienced investor. It is written in layman's terms and the author has attempted to simplify terminology as much as possible.

The author suggests that you prepare yourself to read this book as follows:

1. Read it once to get an overview of real estate.
2. Study the definitions.
3. Reread it carefully.
4. Use it as needed for future reference.

ACKNOWLEDGMENTS

Thanks to Barbara Hanson, Janice Borzendowski, for a most comprehensive edit; and to Mike Hamilton, who saw the value in this book.

How to Make Money
in Commercial Real Estate

Part I

Preparing to Invest in Real Estate

1

Introduction

Traditionally, though real estate has been the major source of wealth worldwide, most how-to investment books focus on securities (stocks, bonds, mutual funds), insurance policies, and the like. This book was written to fill that gap.

All investment professionals agree that it is best to take a twofold approach to accumulating wealth: (1) to save as much as possible and (2) to embark on a long-term investment program. Real estate is superior as a long-term investment because:

- It is not subject to daily price fluctuations, as stocks are.
- The relative difficulty of buying and selling encourages investors to hold on for the long run.
- An investment in real estate other than land initially provides a return of 5 to 10 percent per year, plus amortization (paydown) of loans, and some tax benefits.

In addition, as real estate appreciates and/or an equity buildup is achieved by paying down outstanding mortgages, the opportunity of refinancing the property presents itself. Refinancing an appreciated property for more than the mortgage would pay off the existing debt and provide cash to the owner, a measure of liquidity.

What compelled me to write *How to Make Money in Commercial Real Estate* was the obvious absence from the real estate book offerings in bookstores everywhere of a realistic how-to publication on real estate investing in income-producing properties. The only books available in this area fell essentially into two categories: those designated for the professional and the "get-rich-quick" infomercial types.

How to Make Money in Commercial Real Estate is designed to help small investors get started in creating a real estate portfolio. The book is organized to facilitate a gradual and logical process of understanding, as delineated in this chapter outline. The book takes a step-by-step approach to explain to you, the neophyte investor, the ins and outs of real estate investments. All aspects of the process, from how to get started to finding and evaluating properties to negotiating, financing, closing the deal, and managing the property are covered—in layperson's terms. To facilitate the learning process and to minimize the amount of money any one person risks at the beginning, while at the same time ensuring that you have enough capital to make suitable investments, I apply the investment club concept to real estate. (More about that in Chapter 6.)

Let me assure you, what I preach here is what I practice. By making methodical investments in income-producing real estate over the years—as I illustrate in this book—I have built up a real estate portfolio of more than $10 million from a small $35,000 initial investment 35 years ago. I started my real estate investment program before I turned 20, and with very little money.

The simple truth is, real estate investment can give you excellent long-term profits. For example, assuming a 20 percent down payment, the following will result:

Return:

Net cash flow on 20% down payment   8%

Amortization of loan (20-year, 8% mortgage):

$$2\tfrac{1}{2}\% \text{ of } 80 = \frac{2\%}{20\% \text{ down payment}} \qquad = 10\%$$

Appreciation (say, 5% of 100% = 5% on 20% invested)= 25%

Total return on down payment   43%

That's a long-term total return of 43 percent—yes! 43 percent—annual return.

HOW THIS BOOK IS ORGANIZED

You, too, can achieve similar results! The purpose of this book is to show you a realistic approach to doing just that. Here's how it's set up. The book is divided into two parts: Part I, comprising Chapters 1 through 5, provides background information you need to know before you venture into this potentially lucrative, but somewhat complex, investment arena. Part II is the nitty-gritty of the book. In Chapters 6 through 9, you'll learn all the details of the process, from finding properties to closing deals. The following gives a brief overview of the contents of each of the chapters.

- *Part I: Preparing to Invest in Real Estate*

  Chapter 1, "Introduction." The remainder of this chapter is devoted to recommendations for general financial planning that all investors should have in place before becoming involved in real estate investing.

  Chapter 2, "Comparing Real Estate to Other Investments." Following a brief explanation of the development of real estate as a viable investment strategy, this chapter overviews the advantages and disadvantages of cash, savings, debt instruments, stocks, collectibles, and more, in comparison to the advantages and disadvantages of investing in real estate.

  Chapter 3, "Evaluating Types of Real Estate." Here you will learn about the various types of real estate so that you will be able to judge for yourself their potential as investment vehicles. Included are family homes, residential complexes, shopping centers, and office buildings, as well as types of land.

  Chapter 4, "Understanding Economic Cycles and Their Effect on Real Estate." This chapter examines business cycles, both in general and specifically, as related to real estate investments.

  Chapter 5, "Calculating the Long-Term Potential Profits from Real Estate." This chapter takes a numbers-crunching view of the long-term value of investing in real estate.

- *Part II: Investing in Real Estate*

  Chapter 6, "Getting Started as a Small Investor in Commercial Real Estate." Using the recommended investment group strategy, in this chapter we begin to explore the actual investment process. It's an easy-to-follow, step-by-step discussion of all you need to know.

Chapter 7, "Finding and Evaluating Properties." Expanding on what you learned in Chapter 3, here you'll learn where to look and how to look at properties so you can make informed decisions that improve the chances of your investment increasing in value.

Chapter 8, "Negotiating, Financing, and Closing Real Estate Transactions." Once you've found a suitable income-producing property in which to invest, how do you negotiate the transaction? And how do you finance the undertaking? This chapter explains all of that, including the importance of understanding why the seller is selling, dealing with tough negotiators, getting bank financing and mortgages, understanding interest and liens, and more. You'll also be guided step-by-step through the all-important closing process.

Chapter 9, "Managing Your Real Estate Investment." Okay, you've made it through the closing and now own a piece of real estate. You can't just sit in your armchair and watch the profits add up. You've got to manage that property. This chapter tells you how.

Throughout the book I have included real transactions I have done or participated in.

The book concludes with three appendixes: Appendix A discusses additional real estate transactions I have conducted. Appendix B offers a primer on taxes and real estate. Appendix C provides you with samples of forms and documents inherent in the real estate business.

BEFORE YOU BEGIN

As I've said, this book is designed for the first-time commercial real estate investor. But let me clarify exactly who falls into that category. If you can agree with the following two statements, you are ready to embark on the exciting and rewarding experience of investing in real estate.

1. I have a well-established and secure career that generates enough income to cover home ownership costs, insurance, and pension maximization.

2. I have enough savings to cover at least 12 months of living expenses.

If you're one of the lucky ones, join me as we explore this fascinating investment realm. But keep in mind at all times that real estate should be regarded as a secondary, albeit lucrative, investment. Why do I say "secondary" when real estate is the primary focus of this book? The answer lies in one simple phrase: *lack of liquidity* (the speed at which an asset can be converted into cash). Real estate is not considered a liquid investment. To clarify this point, consider the order of liquidity—again, convertibility into cash—of various other asset categories, listed here in declining order:

- Cash on hand; that is, actual money in your possession.
- Checking accounts, which can be drawn upon by writing a check or by conducting an automatic teller machine (ATM) withdrawal.
- Savings accounts, which can be withdrawn upon presentation of a passbook.
- Insured certificates of deposit, which can be cashed in, albeit incurring a possible penalty for premature withdrawal.
- Marketable securities, which includes stocks and bonds that can be rapidly sold in the stock and bond markets. Usually, the settlement of the buy or sale takes five business days. These are considered investments, and, like any other investment, may be sold at a profit or loss.
- Real estate, which is the topic of this book. (Note its position in this list.)
- Art, antiques, and other collectibles, which usually have to be sold through dealers on consignment or through auction houses.
- Privately held businesses.

Real estate, as this book elaborates, is a time-consuming, relatively complex investment to make. The process involves looking for and finding a suitable property, inspecting and researching it, negotiating for it, financing it, and finally, completing the acquisition process (or *closing*). Selling the property later is also an involved process and can take as much time as buying it—if not more.

Ironically, the lack of liquidity of real estate is both its advantage and its disadvantage. First, though it takes time and patience to find the ideal property to invest in, this forces you, the investor, to act slowly and methodically, which usually means you'll make a wise decision. Second, the difficulty of later selling your investment encourages you to hold on for the long term, which usually means you won't make hasty, and potentially costly decisions. In real estate, there is no liquid market like that for securities, which report daily price fluctuations in all forms of the media. The psychological impact of these daily price fluctuations and the related "explanation" or "analysis" of the market's actions is difficult to ignore and can cause investors to sell prematurely. All serious investment professionals agree that the best way to invest is for the long term. Real estate, because of its lack of liquidity, is ideal for this.

To summarize: In real estate investing, the lack of liquidity, or relative difficulty of "cashing in," can be a problem should you need quick cash in an emergency situation. That is why real estate investing should not be part of your primary liquid investment strategy.

Anyone preparing to embark on a program of real estate investing should first have some basic financial planning structures in place. At the very least, consider the following:

Career Preparation

By *career preparation*, I mean that you should maximize your professional or vocational training and education, preferably in combination with work experience. The advantage of laying an academic foundation prior to entering the workforce is that it broadens your perspective and imparts a professional flexibility, two capabilities essential to enhancing career performance.

Once you have your training, it is very important to engage in frequent career analysis. Review on a regular basis other opportunities that may present themselves.

Insurance

Upon expanding your commitments, whether it be through marriage and children or through individual home ownership or other financial involvements, you should make provisions for adequate insurance to cover life (preferably a term policy), disability, and medical costs. If these things are not covered where you work, or are covered inadequately, find a good insurance broker. You will need him or her eventually to insure your real estate and other assets as your investments grow.

Pension Planning

Don't wait to plan for retirement. In addition to plans offered through your company, invest in pension plans on your own. Well-managed pension plans are the best investment. Contributions are tax deductible and profits are not taxed until withdrawal. The new tax law liberates the amount of deductible contributions an individual can make. This is in addition to employer contributions to employer-sponsored plans. Here, too, develop a close working relationship with a professional pension advisor. Maximize your pension plan contributions.

Employer contributions are not included in the employer's total income. Individual contributions are tax deductible. The income (dividends, interest, capital gains, etc.) is not taxed until taken out (withdrawn).

Pension plans are not taxed to the participant until he or she takes out the money. The minimum retirement age for withdrawal, per the Internal Revenue Code, is 59.5 years; the maximum age is 70. If any money is withdrawn from the plan before age 59.5, it is subject not only to regular income tax but to a 10 percent excise tax for premature withdrawals, with certain exceptions: The new pension law allows withdrawals for first home ownership down payments, college tuition, and medical expenses.

Home Ownership

The best real estate investment is a home. The advantages of home ownership include, first—obviously—shelter. In addition, you benefit from deductions of interest and real estate taxes. There's also appreciation in value. Furthermore, getting term mortgage insurance can provide some measure of security to you and your family. That said, it is recommended that no more than 20 percent of your pretax income go toward home ownership mortgage payments and other carrying costs. Obviously, the interest portion of the mortgage and real estate taxes is tax deductible.

Let's plug some actual numbers into this discussion to illustrate the benefits of home ownership:

Purchase price of home	$105,000
Mortgage (first-time home buyer)	$100,000
Down payment, if any	$ 5,000

	Annual	Monthly
Mortgage payment (8%, 25-year, self-liquidating)	$10,000	$833
Real estate taxes (say, 1.5% of value)	$ 1,500	$125
Total	$11,500	$958

Tax deductions	
Interest (8% of $100,000)	$ 8,000
Real estate taxes	$ 1,500
	$ 9,500
Tax bracket (for example)	28%
Tax savings	$ 2,260

The out-of-pocket cost of home ownership is:

Mortgage and real estate payment	$11,500
Less tax savings (see the following)	($ 2,260)
After-tax cost	$ 9,240

If you assume that home values double every 10 years (7.5 percent per year compounded), your annual appreciation would approximate:

$$(\$105,000 \times 7.5\%) = \$7,875$$

Thus, your net cost of home ownership is: $1,365 (net after-tax cost of $9,240 minus annual appreciation of $7,875).

Net after-tax cost	$9,240
Minus appreciation	($7,875)
Net cost of home ownership	$1,365

Of course, there are other costs, like insurance, repairs, occasional remodeling, and appliance replacement. But when all of these factors are taken into account, home ownership is still cheaper than renting.

Let's see what would happen after 10 years. Say the value of the home has doubled:

$$($105,000 \times 2) = $210,000$$

Let's also say the mortgage has decreased by approximately $2,000 per annum, or $20,000. The mortgage balance would then approximate $80,000.

House value	$210,000
Less mortgage	($ 80,000)
Equity (value – mortgage payment)	$130,000
Cash invested (down payment)	$ 5,000

As you can see, not only have you earned shelter and other benefits of home ownership over the years at a lower cost than if you had rented, you also have had the benefit of appreciation. In this case:

Net value	$130,000
Less cash invested	($ 5,000)
Net appreciation	$125,000

Your equity is now $130,000 on a $5,000 investment, or 26 times greater!

The tax benefits of the interest and real estate tax deductions, plus the appreciation in value (even at 5 percent per annum), reduce your net shelter cost substantially and make home owner-ship a very good means of building up equity.

Savings

From the beginning of your career, institute a savings program. Your goal should be a minimum of 20 percent of your after-tax income, beyond basic necessities (shelter, food, clothing, and transportation). And before you even consider investing, you should have a minimum savings reserve of 12 months' living expenses. Excess savings above that 12-month reserve should be applied to pension plans first, before you consider other investments like real estate. Let's look at some actual numbers here, too, to demonstrate (plug in your own actual expenses to make this more meaningful):

Monthly income before taxes	$3,000	
Less taxes	$ (800)	
After-tax income		$2,200
Basic expenses:		
Rent or mortgage	$ 700	
Groceries	$ 400	
Auto expenses	$ 400	
Miscellaneous	$ 400	
Total expenses		$1,900
Available for savings		$ 300

CONCLUSION

For the purposes of the rest of this book, I'm going to assume you have taken the admonitions for proper investment preparations to heart and that you are ready to proceed to the next phase of your investment strategy—commercial real estate. Along the way, I'll share with you some deals from my own investment career in real estate, including how those deals got done and pitfalls along the way. Now let's get started!

2

Comparing Real Estate to Other Investments

Before we can begin to compare real estate to other types of investments, it's important to understand the life cycle of land development—in particular in the last 50-plus years—and how that gave rise to real estate as a growing territory on the investment frontier.

With the advent of the industrial revolution came the onset of worldwide migration from rural areas to cities. As cities strategically located along waterfronts, on plateaus, or as crossroads developed into major trading centers, they also became the destination for those seeking employment or hoping to build their own businesses. Not surprisingly, as the focal points of economic strength, these urban centers also became centers of government. Soon it became desirable to reside near these sources of power and wealth. The upper classes built their homes near their offices and factories; to have the labor and household help they required readily available, they built tenements to house these people.

As these city infrastructures continued to expand, access to them also had to grow and improve. This had the converse effect of generating outward expansion as well. At the same time, a segment of the migrant population began to establish itself financially by working hard, saving money, and educating its children. This *middle class* began to seek bigger and better housing, while the upper classes began to move away from business areas to what became known as the *suburbs* (from the Latin *sub-*, meaning near, and *urbs*, meaning city). The city buildings abandoned by these two groups (and by now deteriorating) usually became housing for the newly arriving urban poor, who still had little choice but to live in and around the city centers.

Perhaps the classic American example of suburban growth is that surrounding New York City, which in a very short time became the world's major international business and financial center. To accommodate the rapidly expanding housing needs of a population multiplying exponentially, the subway and elevated train ("el") systems were built. At first, public transportation extended into the still undeveloped land in northern Manhattan. Later, it reached out via tunnel and bridge to link the boroughs of the Bronx, Queens, Brooklyn, and Staten Island. Within walking distance of the various subway stations, land was divided into 20 or 25 × 100-foot lots for home construction. Every half mile or so, a street was designated as commercial office and retail space to service the neighborhood residents.

Like the original city centers, these areas soon filled in and aged as well, and many residents moved still further out, to Long Island, New Jersey, Connecticut, and upstate New York, in search of better, cheaper housing—and the dream of staying in touch with nature. A major factor in this continuing growth was the expanding availability of public transportation, which had commenced during President Eisenhower's administration in the 1950s with the construction of parkways and the interstate highway system.

It didn't take long, however, for the new suburbs to become urbanized themselves through the construction of roads, housing developments, and the commercial and government buildings and schools and hospitals necessary to service them. Then, in a reversal of fortune, as the suburbs stretched ever farther away from the cities, the time and out-of-pocket costs of commuting to the more vibrant original inner city became prohibitive to many. Coming full circle, the new generation of children who had grown up in the suburbs started relocating back to the inner cities—especially young upwardly mobile professionals, dubbed *yuppies*. The original yuppies, or urban pioneers, began to buy—cheaply—old buildings in the inner cities, rehabilitate them, and reside there or rent the space for additional income. This process came to be called *gentrification*.

As you can see, real estate is an integral part of a long-term cycle of the growth and movement of humanity, with its ever changing needs and desires and definitions of success. And real estate values reflect both short- and long-term factors. In the long run, however, due to these factors—especially inflation and the increased replacement cost of suitable land, buildings, or location—values go up.

In this chapter we begin to compare real estate to other investment categories—specifically cash, savings, debt instruments (bonds and notes), stocks, collectibles (art, antiques, etc.), and precious metals—so that you can better determine the role real estate investments should play in your long-term investment strategy. Each of these other types of investments is briefly defined; then its advantages and disadvantages relative to the others, based on liquidity, are highlighted so that you can see at a glance how to compare each option to real estate as part of your long-term investment program.

DEFINITION

Liquidity is the speed with which an asset (something you own) can be converted into cash. For example, a savings account (which is really a receivable from a bank) can be withdrawn (cashed) by standing in line during business hours at a bank. A car, in comparison, takes time to sell; thus it is less liquid than a savings account.

You are probably already familiar with most of these other investment categories, at least in terms of media exposure. There is seemingly no end to the availability of books, magazines, and Web sites offering help in investing in these other categories. In contrast, as I mentioned, other than misleading infomercial-type get-rich-quick schemes, or resources geared strictly to the established professional, there is a dearth of real estate investment information for someone like you—the small investor who is interested in the enormous potential of real estate as an investment but who has no idea how or where to begin.

Of course, the primary criterion for evaluating any investment is to weigh the potential profit (reward) versus the risk involved for you personally. For example, though it is obvious that savings accounts insured by the Federal Deposit Insurance Corporation

(FDIC) are arguably the safest investment, their returns are also the lowest. Again, that is the purpose of this chapter: to help you evaluate your investment options. We begin with cash.

<blockquote>

NOTE

The descriptions and definitions in this chapter are not meant to be comprehensive. The goal is to "put you on the playing field," so to speak, so that you can more easily understand the investment potential of real estate.

</blockquote>

CASH

Even today, as greater numbers of people conduct their business electronically and never see or talk to another human being, cash remains our basic medium of exchange. By *cash* I mean cash on hand, available to be spent. Its advantage is liquidity—it can easily be converted into something else. Cash is the criterion by which all assets are measured. To exchange one person's or company's goods and services for another person's or company's goods and services is to *barter*. For centuries now, we have accepted printed paper currency or coin as the medium of exchange in lieu of bartering.

The value of paper money—that is, cash—is solely a function of the general public's confidence in it, and the public's willingness to accept it in payment for goods and services. For example, from 1929 until the end of World War II, there was a period of general price decreases due to a shortage of cash and price controls. These price controls were imposed by the U.S. Government Office of Price Administration (OPA) to overcome wartime shortages. In a period of severe *inflation*—that is, price increases—the general public can lose complete confidence in the government's ability to control the quantity of paper money in circulation, and the acceptance of paper money for goods and services can reach very low levels. The current goal of our Federal Reserve system under Chairman Alan Greenspan is to try to control the cost of money and money supply through monetary policy, thus keeping inflation in check.

DEFINITION

Inflation can be defined simply as the amount by which the asking price of goods and services, in exchange for a certain quantity of cash, rises. This usually happens when there is an oversupply of cash. That is the significance of the term *money supply.*

A historic example of inflation occurred when, prior to World War II, the government in Nazi Germany issued enormous sums of paper money to finance its war preparations. The value of the German mark became so grossly inflated that citizens rushed with armloads of money to pay for groceries before prices went up later in the day.

Advantages

- Cash is easily portable; thus it can be used to purchase goods and services in lieu of bartering.
- Cash is the standard of value used in our society.
- Cash is readily accepted for goods and services.

Disadvantages

- Cash itself does not earn any interest, and in a period of high inflation, cash can rapidly lose its value and its capability to be exchanged for goods and services.
- Cash is subject to theft, fire, and other hazards. Large quantities of cash are also cumbersome to handle.
- Large quantities of cash are difficult and risky to carry; thus most major transactions today are done by check or by electronic transfer.

SAVINGS ACCOUNTS

Insured savings accounts are the most liquid of all investments, meaning they can be most easily converted to cash, which in turn can be used to purchase goods and services. Savings accounts are receivables from a bank. As opposed to cash on hand, FDIC-insured savings accounts earn interest and are insured by the

FDIC. For the purposes of this discussion, the term *savings* will also include money market accounts and certificates of deposit (CDs). The legal order of liquidity for these types of savings is as follows:

- Money market funds are immediately available.
- Savings accounts are "time deposits"; legally, the bank could ask you to wait for your money if it is short of cash.
- CDs are long-term savings accounts in which depositors agree to let the bank hold their money for certain periods of time in return for higher interest.

> **NOTE**
>
> There are also uninsured bank accounts, but I don't recommend that anyone put cash reserves in anything other than an FDIC-insured account.

Advantages

- The principle is safe. Savings accounts are the safest interest-bearing investment. Your principle is usually protected by the FDIC and bank regulations.
- Savings accounts earn interest.
- Thanks to the advent of electronic banking, money in savings accounts is readily accessible.

Disadvantages

- There is potential loss of purchasing power (or value) due to inflation.
- The maximum FDIC insurance is $100,000 per account. If the bank fails, it might take a while to get your money while the FDIC auditors verify balances.
- There is a penalty for premature cashing in of certificates of deposit.

Debt Instruments

Debt instruments (bonds or notes) are obligations of an individual, a business (a corporation), a government, or others. Notes have an original life (*maturity*) of fewer than 10 years; bonds have a maturity of more than 10 years; Treasury bills (short-term IOUs of the federal government) and commercial paper (short-term debt of major corporations) have a maturity of less than 1 year.

Bonds and Notes

The safety of a bond or note is a function of the financial strength of the issuer. In the United States, the safest debt instruments are United States government bonds and notes, followed by state and local (*municipal*), corporate, and individual bonds and notes. The riskier the bond, the higher the interest rate.

Safety ratings of bonds and notes may overlap; for example, a $50,000 note represented by a first mortgage on a home worth $150,000 may be safer than a corporate bond or note, because the $50,000 first mortgage is secured by the $150,000 value of the home, or three times ($150,000 ÷ $50,000 is three times). The house has to drop in value from $150,000 to less than the $50,000 mortgage before there is any risk to the mortgage holder or lender. A corporation's bond or note may not have any collateral at all, other than simply "faith and credit," that is, promise to pay. If the business begins to fail, the corporation may not be able to pay its debts.

Usually, government bonds, which are considered to be the safest investment, pay 3.0 percent basic interest plus the rate of inflation. The federal government is especially interested in encouraging more small investors to buy government bills, notes, and bonds. (For more on this, contact the U.S. Treasury Department or visit any stockholder-related Web site.) Keep in mind that interest rates are a function of inflation.

Advantages

- Bonds and notes pay higher interest than savings accounts. To the extent that there is a trillion-dollar trading market in government and corporate bonds, there is a measure of liquidity.
- There is safety of principle at the maturity of the bond; you know you will receive the face, or *par*, value of the bond.
- You can use bonds and notes as collateral for loans if you don't want to sell them.

Disadvantages
- Bonds and notes are less liquid than savings accounts.
- Their safety depends on the strength of the issuer or borrower.
- If interest rates go up, lower-paying bonds may temporarily drop in value until their *maturity,* when the bond or note comes due.
- Like savings accounts, bonds and notes are subject to inflation risk.
- In a period of inflation, the face value of the bond will be worth less than when you first bought it.

Stocks

Because of their liquidity (again, the speed at which they can be converted to cash), stocks are subject to daily and short-term price fluctuations in the stock markets in which they are bought and sold.

DEFINITION

For the purposes of this discussion, the word *stock* is used to represent equity investments, including mutual funds.

Short-term stock price fluctuations may be due to international, national, industrial, and corporate events—for example, wars, new products, corporate restructuring, and so on. Such events may cause a stock to go up or down dramatically—usually temporarily. These price swings may be outside the long-term potential price range for the stock. The long-term return on stocks for the past 100 years has been 9 percent compounded annually, or doubling on the average every 8 years. The risk of stock ownership is that temporary price fluctuations, especially on a daily basis, can psychologically impact the investor, who may be watching nervously on a daily basis as his or her stocks fluctuate up or down. The temptation in such a circumstance is either to sell to make a fast profit or to cut losses when the stocks drop. This is the difficulty small investors have in holding stocks for the long term.

NOTE

Over the past century, the average rate of return for the stock market has been a little less than 9 percent per annum. For the purpose of this book, we will use 9 percent as a normal rate of expected return, allowing for upward (bull) and downward (bear) price movements over time.

Advantages

- As a shareholder in a corporation, an investor "owns" a piece (albeit a small one) of a business, enabling him or her to benefit from the distribution of profits (dividends) without incurring personal liability for losses.

- In an inflationary period, the prices of the products or services the corporation sells go up and the corporation's profits rise, followed by a corresponding rise in value of the shares.

- Stocks can easily be sold and converted into cash. Thus, they provide a high measure of liquidity.

Disadvantages

- An important factor in stock prices is the ability of management to run the company. If managers are effective—meaning aggressive—ideally the company will grow, earnings will increase, and the stock price will go up. Conversely, poor managers will hinder growth potential by making poor decisions. For example, early in Microsoft's history, Bill Gates offered to merge with IBM and was turned down. Of course, today IBM has different managers.

- Stock prices are subject to general stock market conditions. If there is a temporary downswing in the value of your shares at a time when you need the money for something else, you may have to sell at a loss or for less than the stock's real or potential value.

- Other people are handling your money for you.

COLLECTIBLES

In this category I place objects that are difficult or impossible to duplicate and that have cultural, historical, or social value. Collectibles include, but are not limited to, the following:

Art, including paintings and sculpture

Relics

Antiques

Stamps

Coins

Books

Other collections, such as dolls, sports trading cards, and so on

Advantages

- By definition, rare collectibles, especially art, cannot be replaced, and so are more highly valued.
- Collectibles provide intangible benefits such as the enjoyment of accumulating and caring for such a collection and the pride and pleasure of ownership.
- Recognized, appraisable collections can be used as collateral for loans. Thus, if you need money temporarily and don't want to sell your collectibles, you still have some measure of liquidity.

Disadvantages

- Collectibles suffer from a general lack of liquidity; there is no liquid market. To sell, you have to find a private buyer, a dealer, or use an auction house. In some cases, however, you may be able to borrow against authenticated original rare masterpieces. That said, the art itself will not generate the income necessary to pay either the interest or the principal of the loan.
- The costs of preservation to prevent further aging and deterioration can be high.
- The cost of insurance against fire, theft, and other risks can also be high. You must also deal with the difficulties of determining the insurance value as the value of the collectible changes.

PRECIOUS METALS

By *precious metals,* I'm referring to gold, silver, and platinum. Since ancient times, gold and other precious metals have been accepted as a means of exchange worldwide. Theoretically, precious metals are a hedge against massive inflation. In countries with weak economies, in the midst of war, or devastated by natural catastrophes, paper money may lose its value due to the economic weakness of the issuer—that is, the government. In such a situation, citizens may not accept currency as a means of exchange for tangible goods and services, but usually will accept gold or silver, or barter.

Mining Stocks

If you would like to include precious metals as part of your investment portfolio, a good way to do so is to purchase stocks in mines that produce these metals. Obviously, as the prices of precious metals go up, so do the stocks. As a matter of fact, the stocks would probably go up more than the metals themselves, as illustrated in the following example. Assume the following:

Current price of gold	$320 per ounce
Production (mining) cost	$200 per ounce
Current profit	$120 per ounce
Estimated future price (50% increase)	$480 per ounce
Production cost (same)	$200 per ounce
Future profit	$280 per ounce

$$\text{Increase in profit per ounce } \frac{\$280}{\$120} = 133\%$$

The profit per ounce for a mining company with a 50 percent price increase would be up 133 percent. The reason? Production costs of $200 per ounce will tend to stay constant in the short run, and the increase in price will flow directly to the bottom line (net income). Precious metal stock prices should increase accordingly. (Of course, this is also true on the downside.)

If you had bought the gold directly for $320, and it rose to $480, or up $160, your increase would be:

$$\frac{\text{Price increase } \$160}{\text{Cash invested } \$320} = 50\%$$

In general, precious metal stocks have the same advantages and disadvantages as other stocks.

Advantages
- Precious metal stocks, like any other stocks, can be easily bought and sold on major stock exchanges, and thus have a high degree of liquidity.
- Owning shares in a precious metal company is an easy way to invest in precious metals without having to physically buy and hold the metals. Management of the company will try to maximize profit and shareholder value.
- Precious metals are an excellent hedge against inflation. Historically, platinum, gold, and silver have been accepted as standards of value. In periods of hyperinflation, their prices go up accordingly to keep pace. They are another type of diversification.

Disadvantages
- Precious metals don't earn interest.
- If inflation is brought under control, the attractiveness of precious metals as hedges against inflation diminishes.
- In 2004, the European Common Market, and countries such as Switzerland, were making noises about selling off excess gold bullion to fund domestic projects. A small increase in supply could have a significant downward effect on metal prices and related stocks. (Conversely, an increase in demand would cause the opposite effect.) Precious metal prices are greatly influenced today by the actions of governments. For example, currently, the major producer of platinum is Russia. If Russia were to decide to start dumping its stockpiles of the metal to raise cash, obviously, the price of platinum would go down.

REAL ESTATE

To review and expand on Chapter 1, real estate can be regarded as a superior long-term investment for these reasons:

- It is not subject to daily price fluctuations as are stocks; thus there is less temptation to sell prematurely.

- Making a real estate investment requires patience and a commitment to the study of the real estate market. Once a piece of real estate has been purchased, it takes time to sell— again, meaning it is less liquid. This encourages the investor to hold on for the long run.

- The normal cash flow of an investment in real estate, other than land, approximates 6 to 10 percent per year. You also get amortization (paydown) of loans and some tax benefits.

- As real estate appreciates and/or an equity buildup is achieved by paying down outstanding mortgages, there is the possibility of refinancing the property. Refinancing of an appreciated property for more than the mortgage would pay off the existing debt and provide cash to the owner. This provides some measure of liquidity.

- Real estate is an excellent hedge against inflation. Real estate values tend to rise more than inflation.

In summary, even though real estate requires greater effort than other investments, it more than makes up for this with higher returns, as explained in the following section.

Leverage

An important point to note about real estate investing is that most real estate acquisitions can be financed with other people's money (OPM), a form of leverage. Typically, commercial financing is about 80 percent of the purchase price, keeping in mind that the property should generate more than enough income to cover the financing costs, including interest and amortization (payoff) of the loan.

Leverage will be discussed in more depth later in the book, but a simplified explanation is in order here. For this example, assume the following:

Purchase price of property	$10,000
Less financing (loan)	($ 8,000)
Equity or cash investment	$ 2,000

The leverage here is:

$$\frac{\text{Price}}{\text{Cash}} = \frac{\$10,000}{\$ 2,000}, \text{ or 5 times}$$

The future value of property doubles in 15 years, assuming 5 percent annual appreciation. (See the discussion of compound interest next.)

Future value	$20,000
Less original loan	$ 8,000
Future equity	$12,000

The future equity of $12,000 is *six times* the initial equity of $2,000! In addition, the original loan of $8,000 may have been paid down by the income of the property. This would provide additional equity, making your return even greater. And, if the property generates a positive cash flow after debt, it would also provide cash income while you own it. Thus, you received the benefits of a $10,000 investment with a $2,000 cash payment.

The Miracle of Compound Interest

Compound interest is the earning of interest on previously earned interest. This means that as your money increases every year with interest, the new interest portion also earns interest. I know this sounds a bit circuitous, so let's look at an example to clarify this process. Assume you deposit $1,000 in the bank and the interest rate paid by the bank is 8 percent. After nine years the results would be as follows:

DEFINITION

Compound interest is the earning of interest on previously earned interest.

Original deposit	$1,000
Year 1: interest ($1,000 @ 8%)	$ 80
Balance at end of year 1	$1,080
Year 2: interest ($1,080 @ 8%)	$ 86.40
Balance at end of year 2	$1,166.40
Year 3: interest ($1,166.40 @ 8%)	$ 93.31
Balance at end of year 3	$1,259.71

Year 4: interest ($1,259.71 @ 8%)	$ 100.78
Balance at end of year 4	$1,360.49
Year 5: interest ($1,360.49 @ 8%)	$ 108.84
Balance at end of year 5	$1,469.33
Year 6: interest ($1,469.33 @ 8%)	$ 117.55
Balance at end of year 6	$1,586.88
Year 7: interest ($1,586.88 @ 8%)	$ 126.95
Balance at end of year 7	$1,713.83
Year 8: interest ($1,713.83 @ 8%)	$ 137.11
Balance at end of year 8	$1,850.94
Year 9: interest ($1,850.94 @ 8%)	$ 148.08
Balance at end of year 9	$1,999.02

Thus, by the end of year 9, the $1,000 originally deposited would have grown to $1,999, practically double the original amount. The increase or growth in the money (capital) you invested is called *capital growth*.

In contrast to compound interest is *simple interest* (also called *straight interest*), the interest earned on an investment without compounding. To determine how many years it would take to double your capital using simple interest, you would take 100 percent and divide by the annual interest rate. So, with 8 percent annual simple interest:

$$\frac{100\%}{8\%} = 12\frac{1}{2} \text{ years}$$

DEFINITION

Simple (or *straight*) *interest* refers to interest earned on an investment without compounding.

As shown in the yearly breakdown here, it would take 12½ years to double your money, as opposed to 9 years with compounding. Again, assume the amount deposited is $1,000.

Amount invested	$1,000
Year 1: interest on $1,000 @8%	$80
Year 2: interest on $1,000 @8%	$80
Year 3: interest on $1,000 @8%	$80
Year 4: interest on $1,000 @8%	$80
Year 5: interest on $1,000 @8%	$80
Year 6: interest on $1,000 @8%	$80
Year 7: interest on $1,000 @8%	$80
Year 8: interest on $1,000 @8%	$80
Year 9: interest on $1,000 @8%	$80
Year 10: interest on $1,000 @8%	$80
Year 11: interest on $1,000 @8%	$80
Year 12: interest on $1,000 @8%	$80
Subtotal	$1,960
Amount needed to double	$ 40
	$2,000

As you can see, 40 is half of 80 (annual interest) or another half-year's interest. Thus, it takes 12½ years to double at 8 percent simple interest, as opposed to 9 years with compounding at 8 percent.

Real Estate Investment Trusts

Real estate investment trusts (REITs) are actually a type of stock, but it is more appropriate to include the topic here under real estate, as opposed to in the section on stocks, because the sole investment of REITs is real estate. REITs are publicly traded corporations that invest in income-producing real estate and mortgages. The Internal Revenue Code stipulates that if 90 percent of the operating income of the REIT is paid out in dividends, the REIT does not have to pay any corporate tax. Dividends tend to range about 8 percent of the price.

REITs tend to buy real estate for cash. This means they do not have the benefit of leverage (debt). The possible average long-term return of a REIT is an 8 percent dividend, plus 5 percent annual appreciation, less 1.5 percent fees, or about 11.5 percent per annum. Like the other investment categories already addressed, REITs have advantages and disadvantages that are important to consider.

Advantages

- As stocks publicly traded on major exchanges, REITs are relatively liquid.
- REIT management assumes all of the decision-making and management responsibilities.
- As real estate in general appreciates, so will the dividend income paid to stockholders and the related stock price.

Disadvantages

- Because REITs are stocks, and thus easily saleable, investors may be tempted to sell prematurely, thereby relinquishing the benefit of long-term profits.
- REITs have two layers of management: the corporate officers, who get paid salaries, bonuses, and benefits; and property managers, who get paid to manage the property.
- Because REITs tend to buy for cash, appreciation is limited. Most direct real estate investors buy with 20 percent down, or 80 percent financing, thus getting the benefits of other people's money (OPM).

CONCLUSION

One of my goals for this book is to demonstrate that direct investment in real estate offers more substantial returns than other types of investments. But I would be remiss if I didn't point out the risks associated with its obvious benefits. No one can make a wise investment decision without seeing both sides of the picture, so to close this chapter, as for the other investment categories discussed, I highlight the advantages and disadvantages of investing in real estate.

Advantages of direct ownership of real estate

- There is immediate income from the net cash flow of the property after operating costs and debt service. This should be at least 8 to 10 percent *cash on cash return* on down payment. Cash on cash return is the profit (return) received (in cash) on the amount of cash invested (down payment).
- There is amortization or reduction of the loan balance included as part of the mortgage payments. Remember,

the mortgage payment should be paid by the property's income; it is not out-of-pocket to the investor.

- There is appreciation in the value of property, as discussed previously in the section on leverage.

- You can deduct the "depreciation" of the property for tax purposes. Depreciation represents the effects of aging and obsolescence. This is deductible against property income, providing a tax benefit.

- As long as replacement costs or inflation, or a combination of both, exceed the rate of depreciation, the property will continue to appreciate in spite of depreciation. For example:

Inflation	8%
Less depreciation	(3%)
Net increase in value	5%

Land does not become obsolete the way buildings and equipment do. Therefore, only the depreciation of buildings and equipment can be deducted on your tax return. In every real estate investment, you have to allocate the purchase price between land and buildings in order to know what and how much is depreciable for tax purposes.

Disadvantages of direct ownership of real estate

- Real estate values, like stocks, are subject to the ups and downs of the economy as well as interim value fluctuations. In both cases, if you can hold out long enough, long-term growth in value will occur.

- As I've stated repeatedly, real estate is not a liquid investment, which is the reason real estate investing should be done only with surplus funds and should be designated for long-term investment programs.

- Real estate requires more hands-on management than stocks. This can entail overseeing the outside manager's work and guiding him or her in decision making, or eventually taking over management yourself. (But the advantage to this risk is that you know firsthand what is going on with your property, unlike with stocks, for which you tend to receive only thirdhand data and reports.)

From Stocks to Real Estate: My First Deal

Originally, like many adults beginning to plan for their financial future, I intended to invest in the stock market. That is why I got an MBA in finance to complement my CPA. Unfortunately, my timing was atrocious. When I graduated, in 1968, the stock market was taking a tumble. The main influences on the stock market during the seventies were the Watergate scandal and the Vietnam War, the latter causing superinflation, which in turn caused interest paid on deposits to reach over 16 percent. I didn't have to be a rocket scientist to realize that if I could earn a guaranteed 16 percent rate of return on CDs, why bother with stocks? The high interest rates had also decreased the value of real estate, because a 16 percent insured savings account was very attractive. I realized that real estate could be bought cheaply at less than replacement cost, give positive cash flow and tax benefits, and be an excellent long-term investment without the interim extreme price fluctuations I had experienced in the stock market.

I won't pretend I wasn't trepidatious about becoming involved in a field of investing I knew little about. Luckily, I had the support of my family, which through much hard work and frugality had accumulated savings (as I recommend throughout this book that you do). To learn about real estate, I read several books on real estate investing and management to get a theoretical background. Next I began looking at and answering newspaper ads for small commercial properties, some for sale by their owners, but most through commercial brokers. After answering a few ads, speaking to sellers and brokers, and reviewing their presentations (*setups*), I determined that any real estate investment should meet the following criteria:

- Good location
- Good condition
- Cash return of at least 10 percent on down payment after long-term, fixed-rate, self-liquidating mortgage

After looking at several buildings, we finally decided on a nice three-story corner apartment building in a good neighborhood in Brooklyn (where I grew up). The asking price was

From Stocks to Real Estate: My First Deal
(Continued)

$65,000, but the building had been on the market a long time, so we were hoping to get it for less—we were aiming for $50,000.

Here, in brief, are the steps we took to secure the deal:

1. We verified income and expenses. At the time, gross rents were $9,500 and expenses $4,000, leaving a cash flow of $5,500. (More on this process in Chapter 7.)

2. We offered $45,000 and explained to the seller how we had derived the price. (More on this process in Chapter 8.)

3. After negotiating with the seller, we agreed on a price of $50,500.

4. A contract to purchase was prepared by the seller's attorney, with the price listed at $50,500, subject to financing.

5. We got a mortgage loan from a local bank (where we were long-time depositors) for $33,000 at 6 percent interest with a 20-year payoff.

6. My father did the repairs and painting on the building, while I took over the leasing and accounting responsibilities. After a couple of months of adjustment, everything was operating smoothly. The rents were coming in, expenses were as anticipated, and, of course, we were having positive cash flow of about $230 per month, which in those days was a substantial second income.

(Note: The details of the steps involved here will be explained as we go along in the book.)

The economics of the deal were as follows:

Cost of building, including closing costs	$52,500
Mortgage @ 6% for 20 years	$33,000
Down payment	$19,500

From Stocks to Real Estate: My First Deal
(Continued)

Rental income	$9,500
Operating costs (including taxes)	($4,000)
Cash flow before mortgage payments	$5,500
Less mortgage payments	($2,800)
Net cash flow after mortgages	$2,700

Cash return investment was $2,700 ÷ $19,500, or 13.85 percent.

Total profit included:

Net cash flow after all expenses	$2,700
Payoff of mortgage ($2,800 – $1,980)	$ 820
Total profit	$3,520

(The mortgage payments totaled $2,800. Of that, $1,980 was interest, and the balance of $820 was reduction in the mortgage.)

On a down payment of $19,500, the $3,520 resulted in a return of $3,520, or 18 percent.

We were making 18 percent—plus, of course, appreciation in the value of the property. By 1988, we had paid off the 20-year mortgage and sold the building for $450,000. Remember, our initial cash investment was $19,500!

3

Evaluating Types of Real Estate

We've all heard real estate professionals say that the three most important criteria for making a wise real estate investment are "location, location, location." What goes unsaid is that a valuable location—a strategically situated piece of land or building—is at the mercy of a number of factors, including the ups and downs of the economy, the whims of public attitudes, changes in zoning laws, and many others. These factors all serve to reiterate an important point I've been making so far in the book and will continue to stress: Making a sound real estate investment takes more work and time than other investment categories. Of course, as I've also emphasized, I believe the rewards can be much greater.

This chapter defines and examines the following types of real estate, and the all-important role that location plays in each of them:

- Personal homes and other small residences
- Other residential properties
- Land
- Net leases

- Build-to-suits
- Shopping centers
- Office buildings
- Industrial or office warehouses

> **NOTE**
>
> Our focus is on building a real estate portfolio through direct investment; therefore, we will not discuss real estate securities, such as REITS (defined in Chapter 2), or shares in real estate development corporations.

Being in the right place at the right time is the sum and substance of location. Even when a neighborhood seems to be deteriorating, in the long run there is always value in a good location. We have all witnessed or read about neighborhoods falling in and out of favor, and heard about those "lucky" few who take advantage of such reversals of fortune. We wonder: How did they know that neighborhood would rebound? How did they know that land would be developed? One objective of this book is to prove that it is not luck, but *knowledge,* that enables people to take advantage of potentially lucrative real estate opportunities.

We begin this chapter with the category of real estate that I stated at the beginning of this book is the most sound first investment a novice investor can make: a personal home.

PERSONAL HOMES AND OTHER SMALL RESIDENCES

Almost without exception, I recommend that your first real estate investment should be your own home, whether it be a house, a condominium, or an apartment. It bears repeating that this is a sound and wise first real estate investment, especially because first-time home buyers can get up to 97 percent financing on homes up to $200,000. For homes priced above $200,000, the amount of conventional bank financing can go as high as 95 percent, depending on the appraised value of the home and the income (and stability thereof) of the buyer(s).

It is important, however, to point out that it is equally wise not to go overboard in making this first purchase. By this I mean that a newly married couple, for example, should resist the urge to buy a larger, more expensive home than they really need or can easily afford just for the theoretical advantage of providing tax benefits and a relatively very high rate of appreciation vis-à-vis the original cash invested. Doing so can put you at undue risk that a disproportionate amount of your income may go to carrying the home, leaving you with very little money for contingencies and savings and thus overextending you financially.

DEFINITION

Carrying a home refers to the out-of-pocket cash costs of ownership. These include, but are not limited to, mortgage payments, insurance, heating and air conditioning, repairs, utilities, real estate taxes, and water and sewer fees.

Starter Homes

A smart approach to launching a home ownership program is to buy what is called a *starter home* first. This type of residence can be used as a stepping stone to a better home in the future as your career and financial position improve. The money you save by not carrying a more expensive home can be applied toward other savings and, later, real estate investments.

DEFINITION

A *starter home* is usually relatively small and/or may need work, and thus is reasonably priced (which is, of course, a relative term depending upon the financial capabilities of the buyer).

Changes to the 1997 Internal Revenue Service tax laws made buying starter homes and trading up even more attractive than previously. Provided you live in a home for a minimum of two years, as much as $500,000 profit on the sale for a married couple or $250,000 for a single person is tax exempt. This $500,000 or $250,000 tax-free profit can be used every two years to trade up, or buy something bigger and more expensive. Consider the following example:

	Year 1
Cost of starter home	$ 80,000
Mortgage	$(75,000)
Down payment	$ 5,000

	Year 4
Selling price	$100,000
Less mortgage balance (reduced)	$(70,000)
Cash received (proceeds)	$ 30,000
New home cost	$150,000
Down payment	$ 15,000
Mortgage	$135,000

	Cash available for investment
Cash proceeds from starter home	$ 30,000
Less down payment on second home	($ 15,000)
Cash left over	$ 15,000

The profit on the starter residence is not taxed when you have lived in the home for at least two years and is under $500,000 for a couple or $250,000 for a single person. If you live in the second home for at least two years, that potential subsequent profit would not be taxed either (if it is less than $500,000 or $250,000). Under current tax law, this process can be repeated every two years.

Small Apartment Complexes

Another approach for someone just starting to invest in real estate is to consider relatively inexpensive housing with profit potential, such as a two-family (*duplex*), a three-family (*triplex*), a four-family (*quadruplex*), or up to a six-family dwelling. You, the owner, could live in one unit and use the rent(s) from the other unit(s) to cover most if not all of the total costs of operating the property, as well as possibly most if not all of the building mortgage. This would enable you to save more and subsequently to buy another multifamily unit, or sell the first and invest in a bigger or more expensive one; or you might decide to invest in another type of real estate all together. Either way, you will be well on your way to creating a real estate portfolio.

Let's do some numbers crunching to illustrate the investment potential of small apartment complexes. For our example, let's assume we're talking about a complex comprising four units, each renting (for ease of this discussion) at the same amount, $500 per month.

Annual rental income	$24,000
Less operating expenses	($14,000)
Operating cash flow	$10,000

The price is usually 10 times the operating cash flow—in this case, $100,000. Let's further assume that 80 percent, or $80,000, in financing is available, so the down payment will be $20,000. Mortgage payments on $80,000 at 8½ percent over 15 years will be $788 per month, or $9,456 per annum.

DEFINITION

Debt service is the amount of money needed to pay off a loan or debt—in effect, the monthly payments. It includes interest first, then paydown of principle.

The property in our example will then generate:

Operating cash flow (see the previous figures)	$10,000
Less debt service	$ 9,456
Net cash flow	$ 546

Mortgage payoff initially will be about $2,656 per year, or a total return of:

Net cash flow	$ 546
Paydown of mortgage	$2,656
Total return	$3,202

Thus, $3,202 on $20,000 equals 16 percent return on the $20,000 invested, plus appreciation.

If you reside in one of the four units, the annual rental income will be reduced accordingly:

	Per annum
Rental income (without owner unit) $6,000 × 3	$18,000
Less operating expenses	($14,000)
Operating cash flow	$ 4,000
Less debt service	($ 9,456)
Out-of-pocket costs	($ 5,456)

For $5,456 per annum, or $455 per month, you, the investor, get housing plus the benefits of long-term real estate ownership, which are as follows:

- The $5,456 out-of-pocket cost of ownership is less than the $500 per month, or $6,000 per year, that the same unit would rent for.

- The amortization of the loan initially approximates another $2,656 per annum based on a 15-year amortization schedule.

- The appreciation at a conservative 5 percent per annum represents another $5,000 per annum (5% of $100,000 = $5,000).

- Tax benefits include:

  Seventy-five percent (the rental portion) of operating costs, interest, and depreciation is deductible on a pro rata basis against rental income of $18,000 for 75 percent of the building (that is, three of the four apartments, because one is owner-occupied).

  Only three of the four apartments (or 75 percent) represent rental income and related expenses; the other 25 percent is residential. An owner of a personal residence is allowed to deduct real estate and mortgage interest on his or her tax return. Thus, the 25 percent of the total real estate taxes and mortgage interest not included in the 75 percent rental expenses is personally tax deductible.

Note that depreciation for tax purposes cannot be deducted for a home residence, but it can be deducted on the business portion of the property—in this case, 75 percent. For a $20,000 cash investment, then, you earn:

	Per annum
(a) Rent savings	$ 544
(b) Amortization or loan reduction	$2,656
(c) Appreciation	$5,000
(d) Tax benefits or income sheltering	???
Minimum projected return (a + b + c)	$8,200 + tax benefits

Thus, you would have:

$$\frac{\$\ 8,200\ \text{return}}{\$20,000\ \text{amount invested}} = \begin{array}{c} 41\%\ \text{return per annum plus} \\ \text{tax benefits} \end{array}$$

The tax effects of selling our fictional property would be broken down as follows:

- *Home portion.* In this case, one-fourth is subject to $500,000 (couple) or $250,000 (single person) home ownership capital gains tax exemption after two years.
- *Commercial portion.* This is subject to normal tax rates (see Appendix A).

Advantages
- You have the opportunity to live in one of the units, thereby saving on rent/mortgage payments.
- Often, owner financing is available, either on a primary (first mortgage) or secondary basis, decreasing the amount of the down payment necessary.
- The price of multiple-family dwellings, regardless of size, is a function of income. The selling price of a multiple dwelling is based on the net cash flow after operating

expenses are paid. After mortgage payments are sub-tracted, if the property does not leave an 8 percent return on down payment, it is overpriced.

- A small multifamily dwelling provides a way to learn how to manage property; essentially, it offers on-the-job training.

- If you, as the owner, accumulate enough capital to "buy up," the starter property can either be fully rented and kept for income or sold with the net proceeds applied toward the down payment on the new home and/or possibly another commercial property.

Disadvantages

- If you live in one of the rental units in your multiple-unit dwelling, you are responsible for handling tenant complaints virtually 24 hours a day.

- As owner, you will be responsible for collecting rents, filling vacancies, and doing repairs and maintenance. Even if you hire someone to take care of these jobs for you, the responsibility for ensuring they are done is still yours. This will be explored further in Chapter 9.

Investment Potential for the Novice

Small multiple dwellings, as first residences, tend to sell more cheaply than single-family homes on a relative basis because, as mentioned, multiple dwellings sell for a price that is related to income. Single-family homes have no income, and sell for aesthetic or other intangible reasons. Before making your first residential purchase, whether a single-family home or multiple dwelling, you should have in savings at least six months' expenses, including housing costs, and the down payment.

The novice investor should consider such a property as a starter commercial property investment with both personal residential and commercial benefits:

- Rental income
- Appreciation
- Tax benefits
- Lower net carrying costs

Investing Small to Profit Big: A Small Apartment Complex Deal

This deal was presented to me by a broker in 1974. (I explain how to work with real estate brokers in Chapter 7.) The building he recommended was a four-story walk-up apartment building with six stores on the ground floor and 15 apartments above. The economics were:

Rental income (*rent roll*)	$25,000
Operating expenses	($12,000)
Net cash flow	$13,000

The asking price was $115,000 including the broker's commission of $5,000. I offered to pay $90,000 to the seller plus the broker's commission, for a total offer of $95,000. We eventually agreed to pay the seller $100,000 with $5,000 to the broker, for a total of $105,000.

The issue now was financing. In those days, the capital gains tax was very high, and to minimize the impact of the taxes, sellers were agreeing to an installment sale whereby they took back (or gave us) an $80,000 first mortgage on the property. (More on installment sales in Chapter 8.) This had the following advantages to sellers:

- The mortgage payment would consist of principle and interest spread over a number of years. The selling price proceeds would be spread out and would only be taxed as they were received by the seller.
- The seller would earn mortgage rates of interest on the untaxed portion of the sale.

In this case, the property sold for $105,000. The sellers took a $15,000 down payment, paid the broker $5,000, and netted $10,000 cash plus the mortgage of $90,000. Only the $10,000 was taxed that year to the sellers.

Investing Small to Profit Big: A Small Apartment Complex Deal *(Continued)*

Our deal called for an 8 percent interest payment of $7,200, plus another $10,000 against the mortgage one year later. At that point the $7,200 was taxed as interest income; the $10,000 was taxed as long-term capital gains.

The remaining $80,000 ($105,000 – $15,000, down payment – $10,000 one year later) was a 15-year self-liquidating mortgage that was paying 8 percent interest. Monthly payments were $765 per month, or $9,178 per year.

Let's look at where the payments one year later came from (no payments were made in between):

Payment-principal	$10,000
Interest	$ 7,200
Total payment 1 year later	$17,200
Property net cash flow after expenses	($13,000)
Net amount due from buyer's savings	$ 4,200

Thus, for a total cost of investment of $15,000 initially and $4,200 one year later, or $19,200, I controlled a property worth $105,000.

Let's look at the economics of the deal:

Rental income	$25,000
Less operating expenses	$12,000
Net cash flow after expenses	$13,000
Less mortgage payments	($ 9,178)
($80,000 @8%, 15 years)	
Net cash flow	$ 3,822
Investment	$19,200
Cash return on investment	$ 3,822
	or 20%

Investing Small to Profit Big: A Small Apartment Complex Deal *(Continued)*

Total return was:

Net cash flow	$3,822
Mortgage payoff [$9,178 – $6,400 (8% of $80,000)]	$2,778
Total return	$6,600

$6,600 divided by $19,200 invested equals 34.4 percent—plus appreciation on the $105,000!

Fifteen years later the rent roll was $75,000 and expenses were $30,000. The final mortgage payment had been made, so I was netting $45,000 ($75,000 – $30,000) per year on my investment of $19,200. I later sold this property for $450,000. Thus, ultimately, my $19,200 brought back $450,000 15 years later, plus positive cash flow in between.

OTHER RESIDENTIAL PROPERTIES

Once you are ready to move up from the starter home category, residential property investments come in a wide variety of sizes (from duplexes to major apartment complexes with up to hundreds of units) and price ranges. Equally diverse is the tenant population of these properties; you'll find singles, newlyweds (possibly with their first child), retirees, or empty-nesters. The one thing these people have in common is that, though for different reasons, they don't want the headaches and responsibility of home ownership and prefer to rent for the lifestyle flexibility it gives them. Of course, this means that residential complexes tend to have a high degree of turnover (depending on economic conditions and location; for example, an apartment complex near a university will probably see a regular turnover as students come and go). Usually, however, the demand is greater than the supply, with a clear potential for investment growth.

In general, apartment complexes are divided into these categories: apartment complexes, attached rows of townhouses, low- and high-rise apartment buildings, and boarding and rooming houses. The value of investing in one over the other is relative. If a garden apartment complex reflects a higher rate of return on cash than a high-rise apartment building, you may decide to go with the former. A more conservative, risk-averse investor may prefer a high-rise building. The more management and attention a property needs, the higher the rate of return it should provide the investor.

Methodical Long-Term Investing

Soon, we found that personally managing a small building was not only easy but profitable. (see page 31)

A year later my father told me that the other corner building was available. The two-story building had four stores on the first level and two apartments above, one of which was occupied by the owner, whose husband had just died. The widow decided to sell the building and its related headaches. Her asking price was $50,000.00; rental income was $8,000.00 per year.

We were able to get the price down to $42,000.00, and we secured a bank mortgage of $30,000.00 at 6 percent fixed interest for twenty years, self-liquidating. Thus, for about $14,000 cash we were the owners of a second commercial property. After sorting out some problems, including city regulations, within two months the building was generating a net cash flow of $200.00 per month, a sizable second income at the time. Between the two buildings, on a $35,000 cash investment, we were positioned as follows:

- We controlled real estate worth more than $100,000.
- We owned two buildings that could pay off their mortgages of $33,000.00 and $30,000 on their own, a $2,000 per year payoff.
- We had a positive cash flow of $400 to $500 per month, or about $6,000 per year.
- We looked forward to a conservative 5 percent annual increase in value, or $5,000 per year.

Methodical Long-Term Investing *(Continued)*

Thus, the conservative initial returns were:

Mortgage payoff (amortization)	$ 2,000
Positive cash flow	$ 6,000
Appreciation (5% of 100,000)	$ 5,000
Total initial return	$13,000

Our total rate of return was income investment of $13,000 ÷ $35,000, or 37 percent.

An initial return of 35 to 40 percent on cash invested is not unusual in real estate, based on the following assumptions:

- There's a down payment of about 25 percent.
- The mortgage interest cost is less than the rate of return, or profit, that the property makes.
- There's a positive cash flow after mortgage payments, and so on, of at least 10 percent.
- On a long-term basis, the property appreciates in value 5 percent per year.

The income of the building rose with inflation. Our biggest expense, however, the mortgage payment, stayed consistent. Other operating costs, went up as well, but not as much as the rents. Thus, over time, here's what happened:

- Net cash flow of the building increased.
- Amortization of the mortgage went up every month, and the related interest portion of the mortgage went down.
- The buildings were increasing in value.

Twenty years later, the two buildings were paid off. The gross rents were more than $120,000 per annum as opposed

Methodical Long-Term Investing *(Continued)*

to $15,000 in 1967. Net cash flow, without the mortgage, was $75,000 per year. We sold the two buildings that year for $800,000 cash. We sold for the following reasons:

- We believed the economic cycle was at its peak. In October 1987, the stock market took a tumble; spring of 1988 saw the beginning of a seven-year real estate recession, as business cycles often do.
- We decided to move on to bigger real estate investments.
- We were able to get high prices because of the easy availability of good financing (which is always easiest to get in prosperous times).

On an initial investment of $35,000 cash in 1967, we received positive cash flow averaging about $6,000 per year at the beginning, $75,000 after 20 years, and $800,000 cash on sale. Thus, the total return on the $35,000 cash invested was $1.4 million or *40* times the original investment in 20 years!

Similar results can be achieved with methodical, long-term real estate investments.

Garden Apartment Complexes

Garden apartment complexes usually consist of groups of two- to three-story walk-ups with up to 12 apartments per building, or rows of apartments similar to townhouses. A garden apartment complex may, however, have as large a number of units as a high-rise building, though typically sprawled throughout various buildings on acres of land.

Advantages

- Because they are usually small and more management intensive, garden apartment complexes usually sell for lower relative prices, giving a higher rate of return in comparison to other properties that are easier to manage.

- Usually, garden apartment complexes are spread over larger areas of land, and often the location goes up in value over the years.
- For the same reasons as in the first advantage, you can usually buy garden apartment complexes with a lower down payment. Thus, you are getting additional profits through the use of OPM.

Disadvantages

- Typically, maintenance and management are bigger factors. An offshoot of this is that usually you will have to hire and manage staff to do the landscaping and repairs.
- Insurance costs tend to be higher because garden complexes are made up of many small buildings spread over larger areas of land. This raises the risk of fires and property damage, as well as liability.
- In some areas, garden apartments may have higher security risks and hence guard requirements.
- Residential complexes are subject to shifting local economic conditions and local rent laws.

Investment Potential for the Novice

A small garden apartment complex that can be bought cheaply with a relatively low down payment can be an excellent way for a small group of novice investors to get started in real estate.

After the rent rolls are analyzed, the location, land, and buildings are inspected, and expenses are verified, usually a good deal can be negotiated.

High-Rise Buildings

A high-rise can be defined as an *elevator building* comprising many floors, with many apartments per building. Usually, high-rise buildings are constructed in strategic locations where land is very scarce and therefore expensive. Thus, higher land costs are divided by many units, providing an economically viable cost per unit. Of course, the rents and net income are commensurate with the high land and construction costs.

Advantages

- High-rise apartments offer economy of scale, meaning that because everything is in one building—including electrical and plumbing systems—maintenance, repairs, and management are easier to track.

- High-rise apartments are frequently easier and cheaper to operate on a per-unit basis than sprawling residential complexes.

- Because of the difficulty of duplicating the sites and increasing building costs, high-rise complexes offer excellent long-term appreciation.

- Financing is often easy to get, as lenders recognize that the owner-borrower won't be overly dependent on a limited number of tenants for income.

Disadvantages

- Obviously, high-rise apartment buildings will sell for commensurately higher prices, and so are not suitable for small investors.

- The location may change. It is far easier to demolish a garden apartment complex and use the land for other purposes.

- In some localities with tenant voters (such as in New York), high-profile apartment buildings may be subject to rent control and/or other tenant protection regulations.

Investment Potential for the Novice
High-rise complexes usually sell for large amounts of money due to the large number of apartments and related income. This is not a recommended investment for a single novice or a small group of novice investors. Investors new to real estate should focus on small deals that require more personal attention and provide learning experience as well as income.

LAND

The profitability of land investments is a function of population ebb and flow and location growth and change. Again, the most important criterion is location.

DEFINITION

Land here is used to refer to raw, unimproved acreage, such as farmland or vacant city lots.

Types of Land

Though land can be categorized and subcategorized probably infinitely, for the purposes of this discussion, I divide land into the *rural, exurban,* and *suburban* types.

Rural

In the rural land category, I include farmland, ranchland, tree farms, timberlands, and the like. As population and industrial centers proliferate worldwide, and the developing areas encroach on nearby rural acreage, that land obviously becomes more valuable, making this a potentially high-return investment.

Obviously, land that is part of an income-producing property helps generate more income (and value) than farmland. Although rural unimproved land produces some income, the return is minuscule relative to the farmland's value. For example, in the Midwest, you could probably buy farmland for $1,500 to $2,000 per acre. Renting it to a local farmer, you could probably ask rent of $50 to $60 per acre, based on the type of crop intended for it. The price of the land takes into account its long-term irreplaceability and future appreciation in both crop prices and land value.

Rural land carries with it both short- and long-term value:

- *Short term.* Values fluctuate in relationship to what the land can produce and the value of the production. For example, if the price of wheat goes up, the value of wheat-producing farmland also rises.

- *Long term.* In general, the same factors influencing other long-term investments affect land values in the long run: irreplaceability, population growth, inflation, and the related demand for food and other goods.

Advantages

- Usually, rural land investments enjoy long-term appreciation due to inflation and nearby population center expansion.

- Rural land investments offer intangible benefits such as the pride and satisfaction of owning a farm—"love of the land."

- Rural land is irreplaceable.

Disadvantages

- Relatively large amounts of money have to be tied up for long periods of time.

- Farms usually have limited annual cash return on the amounts invested (less than 2 percent).

- Short-term income and land values are subject to the quantity of, and demand for, the crops produced.

Investment Potential for the Novice
This type of investment is not for the novice investor with limited funds, because immediate cash flow return is relatively low; and if the land lays idle, there may be out-of-pocket costs such as real estate taxes, insurance, and some upkeep.

ExUrban Land
As the suburbs mature and grow, and themselves become urban, the *exurbs*—that is, land just beyond the outskirts of the suburbs— become the new suburbs. Before this takes place, however, exurban land is usually considered rural, as described in the previous section. Rural land becomes exurban land when it is considered to be within a "reasonable" commuting distance from the inner city, usually approximately 50 to 100 miles away.

Advantages

- Owners usually report intangible pleasures of living and managing (if only part-time) "country places," especially when they are raising families.

- The profit potential from future development of exurban land, especially in these times of ever widening city circumferences, is enticing.

- You can buy a mini-estate of 5 to 10 acres at a commutable distance from an urban center, which will provide an excellent place to raise children while waiting for appreciation by retirement age.

Disadvantages

- You tie up capital in a non-income-producing investment.
- You have to pay out-of-pocket costs yourself.
- Exurban residents often face long commutes to work, and sometimes must accept a dearth of city advantages, such as easy access to cultural events, high-quality hospitals, schools, and professional services.

Investment Potential for the Novice
Exurban land is generally not recommended for the novice investor with limited funds, because the money will be tied up for long periods without generating any cash flow. In addition, the owners will have to pay real estate taxes, liability insurance, and other expenses without the benefit of offsetting income. To repeat, it is recommended that initial real estate investments be in affordable income-producing properties.

Suburban Land
We talked about the cyclical nature of city and suburban growth in Chapter 2. Tracking this movement and growth can enable you to make wise suburban land investments. And, in a rapidly growing urban area, along with its bedroom communities, fast profits can be made.

Advantages

- Purchasing strategically placed land for a reasonable price can be an excellent long-term investment.
- Undeveloped land does not require extensive management and therefore can be easily taken care of.
- If there is a home on the land, you get the benefits of home ownership as well.

Disadvantages

- The converse of the first advantage is that out-of-pocket carrying costs—real estate taxes, insurance, and the like—

must be paid by the investor because the land does not produce income.

- You lose interest on the cash invested—though hopefully you will make it up when the value of the land appreciates.
- If you insist on leveraging (borrowing) land investments, you will also have to make the loan payments, as no off-setting income is produced.

Investment Potential for the Novice

Buying a home with, say, a 5-acre tract of land in a rapidly growing area can provide the benefits of owning semirural land and a residence while waiting for appreciation. But I do not recommend that new, small investors with limited funds speculate in ownership of exurban land, as it ties up too much money that could be invested for more immediate returns.

Working the Land

Once you become a real estate investor and get the word out not only to brokers, but to relatives, friends, neighbors—anyone who might provide a lead on a deal—people present opportunities to you.

We found one such deal, a 10-acre piece of land with an old house on it, on a major country road in a fast-growing community. The deal was presented to us in 1967 by a relative living in the area who was not only an active real estate investor, but a politician as well, giving him access to proposed future plans for the town, including road widening and commercialization of certain areas. Rural areas often allow a change of zoning for commercial use because (1) it provides employment for residents, and (2) commercial and industrial properties pay much higher real estate taxes than farms, both of which enhance the town budget. Buying farm or rural land in the path of growth is obviously a lucrative investment. The disadvantages may be lack of return or loss of interest on your money and out-of-pocket carrying costs like real estate taxes, liability insurance, and miscellaneous costs.

We purchased the property in 1967 for $65,000. We told the local bank that we were going to use the old house as a second home, and we secured a mortgage for $50,000 for 20

Working the Land *(Continued)*

years, at 7 percent self-liquidating. We then repaired and spruced up the house to render it suitable as a rental property. The rental income was just about enough to make the mortgage payment, which included taxes. The property was zoned AAA residential, which means that one may build only one home per acre of land. Today, one-acre sites there go for $100,000 to $150,000.

To maximize its value, the zoning has to be changed to some commercial use. Types of commercial uses might be retail (shopping centers); freestanding or single-building uses like fast foods, gas stations, or large pharmacies; single- or multilevel office buildings; parking lots; and industrial uses, such as manufacturing (the least desirable, but necessary from the community's perspective); and purchasing and distribution centers.

We had tried to rezone the property once, but were turned down for political reasons. However, we knew that over time, as the community grew and most readily available space became filled, the pressure would increase to permit change of zoning. Due to the increase in the age of the American population, there is a large demand for senior citizens' housing, including government-subsidized senior-citizen apartment complexes, assisted-care living facilities, and nursing homes. It is usually easier to get a change of zoning for community facilities, including those for medical uses.

We have been approached by such a senior citizens housing developer who already had discussions with the town board and are in the process of selling them the property either as a joint venture or for $300,000 per acre.

NET LEASES

A *net lease* is essentially another form of land ownership, but in this case, a landowner of a strategically placed property (for example, on a busy intersection) leases rather than sells it to a "user." Typical deals in the net lease category are those involving fast food restaurants, gas stations, and office buildings.

Typically, the renter (the lessee) plans to do his or her own construction, and so will insist on a long-term lease (anywhere from 20 years and up) so as to be able to "tie up" the land to recover building costs and earn a return on his or her investment.

A well-known example of a net lease situation is the Empire State Building in New York City. It was constructed on a long term land or *ground lease* that has approximately 60 years left. Technically, the owners of the building are tenants of the land and pay ground rent.

Most long-term net leases provide for the following:

- Rent adjustments based upon cost-of-living adjustment (COLA)
- Fixed increases in rent over time
- A percentage of sales above a certain "strike point"; that is, the tenant's sales level at which percentage rent increases kick in
- Any combination of these factors

A net lease is one in which the tenant of the land agrees to:

- Pay all costs, including real estate taxes
- Carry insurance for the benefit of the land owner
- Make all repairs and replacements to any construction he or she builds and operates
- Keep the property in good condition

In summary, an owner who offers a net lease takes no responsibility for maintenance or management, other than collecting his or her rent and making sure that the real estate taxes and insurance are paid on time. Insurance policies must name the landlord as an additional insured. Of course, if the landowner has mortgaged his or her land, he or she will pay the mortgage out of the net lease collections.

At the end of the lease term, most leases provide for the return of the property to the landlord in its original condition. At that point, one of three things happens:

1. The lease is renewed.
2. The landlord insists on demolition and removal of any construction on the land done by the expired tenant during the

term of the lease, thereby readying the land for other uses and/or tenants.

3. The landlord agrees to accept the return of the leased land *as is*, meaning with any construction that was done during the lease term. As mentioned, because most net leases require that the land be returned to its original condition, an as-is deal is frequently made. This saves the tenant the costs of demolition and subsequent restoration, and enables the landlord to rent the building or convert it to another use.

Net leases come on the market for two primary reasons: Speculators want to take their profits from the development of previously raw land, or owners have personal financial motivations such as estate taxes, financial difficulties, or portfolio diversification.

Net leases are easy to manage. You, the landowner, or *lessor*, simply collect the rent. You have no responsibility to the building and/or business that is renting your land. Furthermore, net leases can be highly leveraged, especially if you have a quality (triple-A) tenant. And over time, usually these locations become more valuable. But even if the value doesn't go up, the long-term lease from the tenant will provide income over its life and pay off the mortgage; and at the end of the lease, the building and all of the improvements belong to you, the landowner. The lease can be renewed or you can rent the land with improvements to another tenant. The income from net long-term leases enables an investor to take advantage of the benefits of real property ownership and leverage with very little management responsibility.

DEFINITION

A *triple-A tenant* is one whose credit rating has been verified as excellent—that is, AAA—by credit rating agencies such as Standard & Poor's. This rating is usually given to major corporations, successful fast-food chains, major oil companies, drug chains, and the like.

An example of a long-term lease that went through the stages of popularity, decline, and, eventually, higher profitability is the Horn & Hardart chain in New York City. During the 1940s and

1950s, this chain of "automats," which sold freshly made food from constantly restocked vending machines, became popular as a precursor to today's fast-food chains. Busy city workers on short lunch breaks counted on the cafeteria-style automats for reasonably priced, freshly prepared hot plates, sandwiches, salads, desserts, and beverages. Customers selected items and deposited the necessary change to release the glass door to their selection. But as other restaurant chains proliferated, the automats' popularity diminished. Horn & Hardart would have gone bankrupt had it not been for one very valuable asset: long-term leases on prime locations in Manhattan. Eventually, the company became one of the biggest franchisees of fast-food restaurants by subleasing and agreeing to convert the automats to their successors in this area of food service.

Rate of Return

Most long-term net leases sell at a *capitalization rate* (the desired rate of return of any investment) of 8 to 10 percent (*capitalization* is another word for *return on investment* or ROI). Thus, if there is a net lease with rent of $30,000 per annum for 20 years, the selling price is related to the rate of return prevalent in the interest rate market on long-term debt, plus a premium to allow for the lack of liquidity of real estate as opposed to savings accounts, bonds, and other marketable (easily salable) securities.

Net rent	$ 30,000	$ 30,000	$ 30,000
Capitalization rate	8%	9%	10%
Selling price	$375,000	$333,333	$300,000

The market capitalization rate, and the related price of a net leased property, fluctuate with changes in market rates or interest and inflationary expectations. In this example, note that the land with a $30,000 net rental income can have different values depending on the expected rate of return (capitalization rate) in different periods.

The interest rate charged by major banks to their prime borrowers for short-term loans is called the *prime rate*. The safest borrower in the world is considered to be the U.S. government, which is constantly borrowing money either to repay old bonds coming due as they mature or to get new financing to cover government budget deficits or to fund new projects. (There is a very active auction market—like the stock market—in U.S. government bonds. To learn the current interest rate, look in the business section of newspapers such as *The Wall Street Journal* or go online to one of the many financial sites proliferating on the Web.)

DEFINITION

Capitalization rate is the desired rate of return of any investment. The *prime rate* is the interest rate charged by major banks to their prime borrowers or short-term loans.

Capitalization rate is a function of:

- Alternative returns on other safe investments like savings accounts and bonds based generally on market conditions
- Quality of the tenant
- Value of the location

In the previous example, the selling price of the net-leased property might range from $300,000 to $375,000 depending on the rate of return (capitalization rate) the investor is willing to accept and at which the seller is willing to sell.

If the acquisition is to be financed, the capitalization rate should be more than the interest cost of financing. This will ensure that the net rental income will exceed the payoff of the mortgage.

Advantages

- Net leases offer a cash on cash invested return, which, as explained earlier, is the rate of return in cash on your down payment—the amount left over after mortgages and so on.
- Net leases offer the benefit of leverage by having the property pay off the loan.
- The land being net leased appreciates.
- If you buy a net-based property with a depreciable building and equipment already on it, you reap tax benefits.
- Management requirements are limited.

Disadvantages

- You take the risk of failure or bankruptcy of the tenant. Although the property may be easily rentable to someone else, it could be tied up in litigation for a while.
- You could take a hit during temporary deterioration of the area.
- There is limited upside income potential during the life of the lease. Because of some upside limits, if there are no provisions for cost-of-living (COLA) increases or a percentage of sales, and so on, the property value may not keep up with inflation for the duration of the lease. This could be a long time.

Investment Potential for the Novice
Owning land with a net lease to a major (triple-A) tenant is the best real estate investment, for the following reasons:

- There is little management responsibility.
- It provides a safe, steady rental income.
- You have the ability to borrow a high percentage of value due to the secure income this type of investment provides.
- It pays a good return on cash invested; plus, the mortgage gets paid off.

One caveat to the novice or small investor: Because the down payment on net leases usually is relatively large, I recommend a group investment approach (as described in Chapter 6.)

Commercially Zoned Land, or Net Leases

Another interesting deal was a 1.25-acre commercially zoned piece of land in a good location. The only small pieces of land to buy are either strategic corner sites, no matter how small, as you control the corner, and a minimum of 1.25 acres, or about 55,000-usable-square-foot sites. This is how much land is desired by most single tenants like fast-food franchises, gas stations, pharmacies, and so on. Usually you can use only up to

Commercially Zoned Land, or Net Leases
(Continued)

one-sixth of the actual land area. In this case, one-sixth equals approximately 9,000 square feet. You must allow for streets, parking, drive-in windows, buffer zones between you and adjacent properties, and so on.

We bought the land in the path of development. Buying well-placed rural or suburban land is an excellent long-term investment, but one that carries the disadvantage of out-of-pocket costs like real estate taxes and insurance. If there is a mortgage as well, it becomes extremely costly to keep land. However, if you can manage to get it rezoned for commercial use soon after you purchase, land can be a very lucrative source of profit.

We found a diner operator planning to build a new, larger diner on his old site, and we convinced him to move the smaller diner to our lot. Diners are prefabricated, modular buildings that are placed on a foundation in sections, joined, and hooked up to utilities. After final decorating and equipment, they are ready for business.

The land had cost us $30,000. The land lease for the diner was for twenty years, paying us $600 per month net, with the diner's owner paying all expenses, including real estate taxes and insurance.

Thus, we were earning $600 per month over twelve months, equaling $7,200 ÷ $30,000, or 24 percent!

A year after the successful opening and profitable operation of the diner, its owner offered us $70,000 for the site, and we sold. In about two years, we made a total of:

Selling price	–	Cost	=	Profit
$70,000	–	$30,000		$40,000
One year's rent				7,200
Total profit				$47,200

To reiterate, we invested $30,000 and got back $77,200 in two years. My partner insisted on selling and I couldn't afford to buy him out. This was a mistake!

Commercially Zoned Land, or Net Leases
(Continued)

Today, commercially zoned property in that area is worth $10,000 per foot, or $550,000 to $600,000. We might have been collecting rents for 25 years.

Again, the best way to make money in investments is to hold on for the long run. Buy and hold and ignore fast short-term profits or interim, recessionary drops in value. If we had held onto the property we would now have equity of $600,000 on a $30,000 investment, or 20 times our initial investment.

After the lease expired in 1996, we could have renewed it for $60,000 per year net. Thus, the income today would have been $60,000 per year net on an original investment of $30,000!

BUILD-TO-SUIT

A *build-to-suit* is just what the name implies: A land or property owner offers to build or convert his or her property to meet the unique requirements of a particular tenant. This is done in one of two ways. One is for the tenant to supply his or her plans and specifications to the landlord, who in turn has his or her contractor give a detailed estimate of the cost of the construction. The landlord then sets the rent at original land or building cost, plus cost of construction, times a percentage (cap rate) on a net basis. For example:

Land value	$100,000
Construction	$300,000
Total	$400,000 × 10% = $40,000 per year rent

If the lease is a gross lease, as opposed to a net lease, the landlord adds projected operating costs to the rent. (More on leases in Chapter 9.)

The alternative, safer way is to let the tenant build to his or her specifications while the landlord finances the cost of construction. In the lease agreement, the tenant would agree to pay a certain cap rate (or percentage rate of return) to the landlord, in addition to a base rent for the property before construction. For example:

Land value	$100,000
Actual construction cost paid by landlord to reimburse tenant	$335,000
Total	$435,000

A 10 percent cap rate or return on investment (ROI) would equal rent of $43,500 per year. In addition to the 10 percent return, a provision would also have to be made for annual depreciation of the construction costs over the life of the lease; this is then added to the rent.

Advantages
- Build-to-suits add to the value of property. The improvements can be financed based upon: (1) the rental income of the lease and quality of the tenant (the loan that the landowner takes out to build can be paid out of rents over the life of the lease); and (2) the tenant's financial strength.
- The loan can be paid out of rents over the life of the lease, or sooner. At the end of the mortgage term, all future net rents go to the owner, as there are no more mortgage payments.

Disadvantages
- If the construction is too specialized, it may be subject to early obsolescence. Some build-to-suits are designed and built for very specific occupancy and use. If the tenant goes bankrupt before the financing is paid off, expensive retrofitting may be required before you can rent to another tenant.
- Manufacturing and other industrial facilities introduce the risk of having to conform to government (federal and local) regulations regarding environmental protections.

Investment Potential for the Novice
Build-to-suits are a form of leased land ownership, meaning the landowner agrees to finance the construction of the building in return for a higher rent. Because of the complexity of putting such deals together, they should be avoided by novice investors.

SHOPPING CENTERS

The term *shopping center* refers to a wide variety of commercial spaces, ranging from a small group of stores on the perimeter of a parking area to a megamall in the center of a sea of parking or featuring its own built-in customer garage. This discussion focuses primarily on two types of shopping centers in the order of size and affordability: anchored and unanchored strip centers. We'll also take a brief look at what have come to be called *condominium stores*.

Anchored Shopping Centers

The *anchor* in a shopping center is a major tenant, such as a "name" supermarket or major department store, that occupies the largest portion and/or heart of the shopping center. An anchor is the main draw, and as such indirectly generates business for other tenants of the shopping complex.

The anchor types in the following list are given in best-to-last order of investment potential, along with a brief explanation:

- *Supermarkets.* Simply put, people have to buy groceries, no matter what the economic conditions are.
- *Drug chains.* Like supermarkets, drugstores sell necessities, which means frequent return traffic, especially in retirement locations.
- *Department stores.* Though these stores supply necessities— clothing and household supplies, and so on—when times are tough and money is tight, customers can forgo shopping in department stores for extended periods of time.
- *Movie theaters.* Though some would say movie theaters repre- sent purely discretionary spending, theaters are proven mon- eymakers. In addition, shopping center theaters generate business for restaurants and other businesses in the center.

Advantages

- Anchored shopping centers are relatively easy to manage, in contrast to residential properties. The responsibilities of the shopping center landlord are limited to grounds and structural upkeep, management, insurance, and real

My First Shopping Center Deal

My first shopping center deal was a 60,000-square-foot "anchor" retail center with 210 parking spaces on 4½ acres of land. The seller was going bankrupt and needed cash. Because of the amount of cash required—$250,000, including down payment ($200,000), closing costs, and operating reserves ($50,000)—I did this deal with nine partners, for an investment of $25,000 each.

The center was composed of:

Store	Square footage	Annual rent
Pharmacy (anchor)	9,000	$ 45,000
Supermarket (anchor)	30,000	$ 90,000
Liquor store	2,000	$ 12,000
Pizzeria	1,500	$ 12,000
Stationery	1,500	$ 12,000
Beauty parlor	2,000	$ 12,000
Restaurant	6,000	$ 30,000
Four miscellaneous stores	8,000 (2,000 each)	$ 40,000
Total	62,000	$253,000

Operating expenses	Amount
Parking lot electricity	$ 12,000
Insurance	$ 4,000
Miscellaneous repairs	$ 6,000
Management (5%)	$ 12,000
Real estate taxes	$ 80,000
Total	$114,000
Cash flow before mortgage payments (253,000 − 114,000)	$139,000

We bought the center in 1981 for $1.2 million (or $20 a foot), with $200,000 cash down, and took over a $1 million

My First Shopping Center Deal *(Continued)*

first mortgage with 20 years left at 8 percent interest. The economics of the deal were as follows:

Rental income	$253,000
Operating expenses	($114,000)
Cash flow before debt service	$139,000
Mortgage payments: $1 million @ 8%, with a 20-year payout = $8,360 per month, or	($103,200)
Net cash flow after mortgage	$ 36,800
Cash investment	$200,000

Cash return on the $250,000 invested was:

Net cash flow $\dfrac{\$ 36,8\ \ ),}{\$250,\ \ 0}$ or 14.45%!

Plus payoff of mortgage total annual payments—interest portion: $103,200 (8,360 × 2 months) − $80,000 (8% of $1 million mortgage):

Total mortgage paymer	$103,000	($8,630 × 12 months)
Less interest portion	$ 80,000	(8% of $1 million loan)
Mortgage paydown	$ 23,200	
Net cash flow	$ 36,800	
Total return	$ 60,000	

Thus, our total initi return was $60,000 on a cash investment or $250,000, r 24%! Plus of course the potential increase in value of t property.

Although the sur market anchor had a low base rent, it also was subject to ying 3 percent above annual sales over $3 million. At the t e of the purchase, reported sales for the

My First Shopping Center Deal *(Continued)*

supermarket were $2.5 million per year and growing. Once sales reached $3 million, the supermarket would pay additional rent of 3 percent of the sales over $3 million.

Six years later, in 1987, the rent roll had risen by about $60,000, with a concomitant $20,000 increase in expenses. Thus, the new cash flow looked like this:

Gross rental income	$315,000
Less operating costs	$135,000
Cash flow before mortgage payments	$180,000
Less mortgage payments	$103,200
Net cash flow	$ 77,000

That's $77,000 per year on a $250,000 original investment. When we decided to sell to take advantage of other opportunities, the property's cash flow was $180,000 before mortgage payments. We sold it at 10 times cash flow, or $1.8 million. The results of this transaction were:

Selling price	$1.8 million
Less outstanding mortgage (paid down over the 6-year period by about $150,000, leaving a balance of $850,000)	$(850,000)
Net proceeds (cash)	$ 950,000

On a $250,000 cash down payment six years earlier, we made an average net cash flow of $37,000 in year 1 and $77,000 in year 6, or $37,000 + 77,000 = $57,000 average cash flow for six years, or (57,000 × 6 years) $342,000 total cash flow for six years. Proceeds from the sale were $950,000; thus the total return was $1,292,000 (342,000 + 950,000). That's right, $1,292,000 on a $250,000 cash investment in six years, or over 5 times.

estate taxes. The tenants themselves are responsible for interior construction, upkeep, and repairs.

- Anchored shopping centers are usually located in heavily trafficked areas on large lots. Eventually, as communities grow, the use of the land may be upgraded—and increase in value—after the expiration of the lease.

- The presence of an anchor store usually makes it easier to get financing, and offers better investment security.

Disadvantages

- Anchor tenants are tough negotiators with original builder-developers. Although they preapprove the site after market studies, demographic analysis, traffic counts, and so on, they are aware that the developer needs their lease for financing and to attract other tenants. An investor should carefully review all long-term lease clauses before acquiring anchored shopping centers.

- Most of the income comes from the dominant tenant—the anchor. If the anchor fails or moves out at the end of its lease, the center as a whole may require retrofitting or, at a minimum, some downtime until a new anchor tenant is found.

- Unless there is some provision for COLA and/or other escalations, a long-term fixed lease can inhibit the increase in the value of a property.

I used to visit my shopping center at least once a week. I met the tenants and the anchor store managers and beame friendly with all of them. You hear a lot talking to the tenants: what problems there are at the property, gossip about the other tenants, neighborhood stories, and so on. Sometimes, this information proved useful.

Investment Potential for the Novice

Anchored shopping centers are an excellent investment for novice investors, in particular as part of a group. Anchored shopping centers are usually built in well-studied locations, and long-term financing may be available to buyers. But, as with net leases, because these investments require relatively large down payments, novice or small investors should buy as a group. Remember, the best anchor is a supermarket.

Strip Centers

Strip centers, or *strip malls,* usually have a series of retail stores whose average size is 20 × 50 feet, or 1,000 square feet each; in total, most strip centers are under 20,000 square feet in size. They typically have good visibility, as they are usually located on the perimeter of a densely populated neighborhood, on a heavily trafficked commercial street with easy access, or on or near a corner.

Advantages

- Strip centers are an income-producing approach to buying and financing strategic locations. As communities grow and develop, the location of a shopping center may be in demand for upgraded and, hence, more valuable uses.
- Strip malls represent a smaller investment than larger anchored shopping centers.
- There is no risk of losing a major draw tenant.
- Leases tend to be shorter term; thus, the renewals have the advantage of inflationary increases and supply-and-demand factors brought about by improvement to surrounding areas.
- Strip centers are relatively easy to manage, in part because of their smaller size.

Disadvantages

- If a strip center is poorly located and/or built without regard to market factors, tenants will be difficult to come by. Without a well-defined, tangible game plan, an investor should not expect to perform miraculous turn-arounds.
- Unestablished smaller tenants tend to have short life spans, and so may cause a higher vacancy factor. A vacancy means lost rent, possible legal fees, retrofitting, and disruption to the traffic stream of the center when that previous store's clientele goes elsewhere. It is important to evaluate the mix of stores in both anchored and unanchored centers to see that they complement, not compete with, each other.

Investment Potential for the Novice

Strip centers are a way to invest in commercial real estate with a relatively low down payment. They usually sell for less than replacement costs by other small real estate owners, and terms can be easily negotiated.

Condominium Stores

In large cities like New York, the ground or street level of most apartment dwellings is used for retail or office spaces. Consequently, developers of condominium buildings not only sell apartments but also the commercial ground-floor space to users or investors.

> **NOTE**
>
> A variety of condominium store ownership is the acquisition of retail master leases from cooperative apartment buildings. This, however, is beyond the scope of this book.

Advantages

- Such space can represent good investments, as it is usually in heavily populated areas with plenty of street traffic; and the building tenants can be regarded as captive customers.
- Condominium leases, like most store leases, limit the landlord's responsibility. Internal store expenses, repairs, and liabilities are the responsibility of the tenants.

Disadvantages

- The intermediate-term growth in value is limited to rent increases.
- The property is already fully developed, which limits growth.

Investment Potential for the Novice

Condominium stores are similar to net-leased land in that the landlord's responsibility is limited and management is less intensive. The total return to the investor should be at least 8 percent cash, plus mortgage payoff, plus appreciation as future rents increase.

OFFICE BUILDINGS

Office buildings can be regarded as similar to apartment buildings for the purposes of investment, but office buildings are more service intensive. The owner not only pays for building electricity, but also usually supplies heating, ventilation, and air conditioning (HVAC), and cleaning services and makes internal repairs.

The lease on a new office usually stipulates that the landlord renovate the space involved to the tenant's specifications, the cost of which is typically added to the base rent and amortized over the life of the lease.

The rental income and related value of office buildings fluctuates with general economic conditions. In good times, there is increased demand for office space, which results in low vacancy, high rents, and higher net income. But in economic downtimes, there are more lease cancellations or nonrenewals, which leads to more vacancies, which results in lower rents and therefore lower rent income. And because the value of real estate is related to its income, prices of office buildings fluctuate widely in relation to economic conditions.

Advantages
- Office buildings are usually in strategic locations.
- Their replacement cost keeps going up.
- A patient investor can buy an office building cheaply during an economic bust and hold until the subsequent economic boom. (You'll learn about the effects of economic cycles on real estate in Chapter 4.)
- Frequently, existing mortgages can be taken over, reducing the required cash investment.

Disadvantages
- Office buildings usually require a large cash investment.
- They are management and labor intensive.
- Occupancy/vacancy factors and related net income and value fluctuate widely with general economic conditions.

Investment Potential for the Novice
In general, office buildings represent too large an investment for a novice individual investor or even a novice investor group.

Managing these properties involves dealing with (typically) demanding tenants who are paying for services as part of their rent. Novices just learning about the inner workings of managing properties will probably find office properties beyond their capabilities, and so should steer clear of them until they are more knowledgeable and experienced.

WAREHOUSES AND PUBLIC STORAGE FACILITIES

Provided they earn a decent return on investment (about 10 percent before debt service) and are in decent locations with growth potential, warehouses and public storage facilities are another potentially profitable real estate investment.

Warehouses are buildings used as storage facilities and distribution centers, generally ranging in size from 5,000 to as much as 1 million square feet. These large blocks of space are rented in as-is condition to business users for storage and distribution. Warehouses can be either one large building or a number of smaller, freestanding structures, and they may contain a small office area. A warehouse is typically rented on a net basis, whereby the landlord pays only for real estate taxes and property comprehensive insurance. All utilities, internal repairs, and other operating costs are the responsibility of the tenant. The landlord's responsibilities are limited to the structure and roof; he or she should also carry insurance.

Public storage facilities are small storage units in a large building, generally ranging in size from 10,000 square feet and up. They are designed for temporary storage of excess personal property, such as furniture, files, and the like. Some business and government entities use them for archival storage. Public storage facilities are more management intensive than warehouses; the tenant billings and collections are more difficult because, frequently, the owner must deal with small users, some of whom may have fallen on hard times. There can be as many as 100 users, occupying space of less than 500 square feet, paying $100 to $200 per month rent, and the landlord is responsible for all common areas. Furthermore, the laws regarding the landlord's repossession of a rented storage location due to rent default, are complex, especially in regard to storage area contents.

Advantages

- Relatively low down payments are required.

- Usually, investing in this type of real estate is a good temporary way to buy and finance a piece of land. Most leases, especially for public storage facilities, are relatively short term. This enables you to sell or upgrade the site as the location improves.

- Other than having to collect rent from many small tenants and leasing vacant units, management responsibilities for public storage facilities are limited. And the rental income and value of the property will help you to get financing.

Disadvantages

- Real estate in this category is usually located in industrial areas, which tend to be less desirable in the long run, especially as facilities age.

- With many small tenants, public storage facilities have the related problems of collections, heavy turnover, vacancies, and the like. Thus they require some hands-on management—showing empty spaces and preparing new leases after repossession (removal) of nonpaying tenants.

Investment Potential for the Novice

Warehouses and public storage facilities should be looked upon like other commercial income-producing real estate investments, with the same inherent advantages and disadvantages.

CONCLUSION

We've covered a lot of territory in this chapter. As a handy review, Table 3.1 summarizes the various types of direct real estate investments ranked in the order of the amount of cash down payment required.

In summary, then, the investment potential of real estate overall is fivefold:

- Cash return on down payment of, say, 8 percent after mortgage payments and other costs.
- Payoff of loans from rental income.

- Appreciation.
- Leverage, or other people's money (OPM). Remember, loan payments stay constant, while rents and related property values have the potential to rise.
- Tax benefits.

TABLE 3.1   Direct Real Estate Investments

Type of Real Estate	Price Range	Down Payment	Level of Management
Owner-occupied small multifamily dwellings (apartment buildings)	$100,000	$ 20,000	Intensive; owner lives in building and must make repairs and handle tenant complaints personally.
Small warehouse or public storage facilities	$200,000	$ 40,000	No responsibility for repairs, but must collect rent from many tenants.
Large multifamily properties	$500,000+	20%	Intensive.
Strip shopping centers	$1 million	20%	Hands-on, but limited.
Anchor shopping centers	$3 million+	20%	Hands-on, but limited.
Net leases	$1–5 million+	20%	Easy.
Larger warehouses leased to triple-A tenants	$1–2 million+	$200,000	Similar to net lease.
Land, not income-producing	Varies	Varies	Easy management but no income.

Later on, when we discuss how to find, evaluate, negotiate for, buy, and subsequently manage property, you may want to refer back to this at-a-glance review. But now let's continue to Chapter 4, where we discuss the next step in ensuring that you have a well-rounded introduction to the exciting world of real estate investing.

4

Understanding Economic Cycles and Their Effect on Real Estate

Economic cycles have been with us since the dawn of recorded history. In ancient agrarian times, they were represented by periods of bumper crops followed by periods of drought and/or pestilence. One of the earliest written examples of the effects of economic cycles is the Old Testament story of Joseph and his brothers. Joseph advised Pharaoh that during the seven years of feast (good crops), he should store surplus grain against future periods of famine. When the seven years of famine came, Pharaoh was able to use the stored grain to alleviate the effects of the down times.

Today, we track economic cycles by the relative strength or weakness of money, our medium of exchange. In a time of economic boom—a period of usually four to eight years—people often become lulled into believing the good times will last forever. Jobs are abundant. Plenty of money is changing hands. Workers demand—and get—higher wages. More money is available for goods and services. More people invest in the stock market, and it goes up, a direct reflection of these rising expectations.

Investor purchases create demand, which pushes prices higher. Every investor believes he or she will be able to sell at a profit to someone else later (the *greater fool theory*). Investors ignore the intrinsic value of what they are buying. They think they are buying future profits. Then, when rising expectations are no longer being met, prices start dropping. Investors who are unsure of themselves panic and start "dumping." This pushes prices down even further. After a while, the economy runs out of steam and goes into a slump.

DEFINITION

A short-term (two or three years) economic slump is called a *recession;* a severe, long-term economic slump is called a *depression*. The Great Depression lasted 12 years, from 1929 to 1941, and was broken by the onset of World War II.

There may be many reasons for this to happen:

- Labor shortages and demands for increased wages.
- Material shortages.
- External factors, such as the oil embargoes of 1974 and 1981.
- War.
- Acts of Congress that affect the economy, such as tax increases.
- Actions of the Federal Reserve that make money tighter and more expensive. The Federal Reserve controls both the money supply and interest rates. The Fed uses its control of the money supply to curb inflation in good times and to supply money to the economy in bad times, in an effort to smooth out economic cycles.

Since the end of World War II, recessions have lasted on average less than three years. During a recession, the greater and more widespread the pessimism, the lower prices sink. When the prices drop to near the bottom, most investors find either that they have no money, because they have lost it, or, if they do have money, they are too pessimistic or scared to buy. Only after the market has made a recovery and prices run up does the general public come back. Then the cycle begins again.

It is important to note that, historically, each subsequent boom has reached a higher level than the previous boom. That is why a careful, long-term investor:

1. Maintains a long-run perspective.
2. Avoids getting caught in speculative fervor in good times, and acts more conservatively.
3. Views bad times as providing investment opportunities for the long run.

By doing this, such an investor would avoid getting hurt during temporary downsizings in the economy. In fact, he or she may even be in a position to take advantage of them. Over the long haul, his or her assets will grow in value along with the overall net growth in the economy. That is precisely the reason financial advisors emphasize long-term investment.

Keep in mind also that it is very difficult to tell when we are at the top or the bottom. If you do your homework and valuations, you should be able to avoid overpaying during booms—and likewise getting scared and selling prematurely in busts.

ECONOMIC CYCLES AND REAL ESTATE

Now let's get to the point of this discussion: what the ups and downs of the economy have to do with real estate, the topic of this book. As with stock prices, when people see real estate prices going up, they start speculating in real estate, helping to fuel further price increases. Real estate prices may reach temporarily high levels.

Though it may seem to be putting the cart before the horse, since we haven't yet covered how to find, evaluate, and ultimately invest in properties, it's important to this discussion to consider how a real estate investor (that is, someone who already has property or properties) should respond during economic booms. The alternatives are to (1) do nothing or (2) sell a property. Let's examine each of these options.

- *Do nothing.* If the investor has a good property that pays a decent income or is paying off its mortgage, the best advice is to stand pat. In the long term, the value of such a property will continue to rise.
- *Sell a property.* If the investor has two or more properties, he or she might sell part of his or her holdings and use the cash proceeds to pay off the mortgages on the properties he or she wants to keep. Or the investor might choose to save the

money from the sale as available funds to enable him or her to take advantage of possible future economic slumps.

Simply put, property prices are also affected by changes in economic and speculative conditions. In periods of economic boom, the goal is to save, not only to protect yourself from economic downturns, but—just as important—to be able to take advantage of them instead of being one of those financially hurt by them.

For example, when the economy is on a downward trend, real estate properties may be:

- Available at distressed prices from panicked holders
- Abandoned by speculators
- Temporarily vacant as a result of the economic slowdown, and, thus, selling cheaply
- Foreclosed by lenders anxious to dispose of them, even at a loss

SPECULATION

I've mentioned speculation a number of times in this discussion. It's important that you understand the role speculation plays in the economy in general and in real estate in particular. The actions of speculators influence prices in all areas of the economy. When there is a lot of speculative buying, prices go up due to the increased demand. Conversely, when there is a lot of speculative selling, prices drop.

SPECULATING: A THING OF THE PAST

The actions of speculators have been felt for hundreds of years. In the early nineteenth century, in London, an interesting book on this economic practice was published. Written by Charles Mackay, *Extraordinary Popular Delusions and the Madness of Crowds* reveals how the lure of easy money can entice the masses to start speculating. Sample chapter titles from the book say it all: "The Mississippi Scheme," "The South-Sea Bubble," and "The Tulipomania."

Throughout history, speculators have been *trading*, that is, buying and selling goods and services for the short term (less than one year). In ancient times, if a trader (a.k.a. speculator) knew that, say, grain was going to be in short supply, he would buy as much as he could afford and store it to sell it later, hopefully at a higher price. If, as he hoped, the price went up, he made a profit; if the price dropped, he lost money. That seems clear enough. But consider this: Even if the price stayed the same, our ancient speculator lost money. Why? He had to take into account:

- The interest lost during the holding period; that is, what's known as the *time value of money*
- Costs of shipping, warehousing, insurance, and so on
- Commissions, if any

It seems obvious, then, that investors should speculate only when they are relatively confident that the net profit after costs will yield a higher rate of return than simply holding onto the money and earning interest. Let me give you an example.

In the early 1980s, we had economic conditions that today seem extraordinary: Interest rates, including those paid on savings accounts and CDs, reached 18 percent. The conventional wisdom was that interest rates would continue to rise. But I realized that the newly rewritten tight money policies (that is, reduction in the money supply) of Paul Volcker, chairman of the Federal Reserve, would reduce the demand for loans, and that the lower availability of money would eventually decrease the inflation and related rate increases. Interest rates usually are a real 3 percent (net of inflation). Thus, if inflation is 10 percent, interest should be 3 percent (real) plus 10 percent (for inflation) or 13 percent. (*Real interest rates* are the net interest paid after subtracting inflation.) This was an excellent time to make investments.

Meanwhile, the oil crisis of 1981, during which the price of oil reached $35 per barrel, created a boom atmosphere in cities with a heavy presence in the oil industry—Houston, Dallas, Denver, Oklahoma City, and others. The result was rampant expansion and overbuilding. At the same time, the northern oil-dependent states were hit by the double whammy of high fuel costs and high interest rates.

In hindsight, it's easy to say that the proper real investment strategy would have been to sell in the oil states for high prices and invest in the Northeast at cheap prices. When oil prices and inflation subsided in the mid-1980s, the massive overbuilding caught up with the oil patch, particularly in cities such as Houston.

First Houston Deal—Distressed Property

I formed a partnership with a couple of wealthy clients to buy distressed properties. Then I called every bank in Houston asking to speak to their real estate owned (REO) or foreclosed property department. I soon learned that most Houston banks were still in limbo; they hadn't completed their foreclosures and were playing a waiting game. But by November 1988, I was able to get two appointments, one with NCNB (which later became Nations Bank and even later Bank of America). Management there had hired a real estate consultant to help the bank move its portfolio. After talking to the consultant and looking over what he had to sell, I came to the conclusion that asking prices were too high. I was anticipating a seven-year turnaround, and was subsequently vindicated.

Over the next few months I looked at more than 70 buildings with various real estate brokers. (The best way to get to know a community is by driving around with a local broker looking at properties.) In August 1989, 10 months after I started looking, I received a phone call from a broker about a six-story, 145,000-square-foot office building; it was 10 years old and was priced at $3.5 million, or $24 per foot. (Most buildings I had seen prior to it had been selling for $40 per foot and up.)

The next morning I was on the plane to Houston, was met at the airport by the broker, and went to see the property. Although I knew the seller was only paying $3 million for it ($20 per foot), I felt that if it hit the market, it would go for $30-plus per foot, or $4.5 million to $5 million. I reached this conclusion as a result of knowledge of comparable values, which I had gained during my 10-month search.

After seeing the building and examining the rent roll and expense statements, I made an offer of $3.45 million, or $23 per foot. I derived this number as follows:

Seller's (contract holder's) cost	$3 million
Broker's commission	$150,000
Contract holder's profit (10%)	$300,000
Total offer	$3.45 million

First Houston Deal—Distressed Property
(Continued)

I told the seller that if I didn't get a written agreement that day, I would not pursue the deal. Seeing a fast profit, he agreed. We put together a Letter Of Intent outlining all of the terms of the deal:

- Price: $3.45 million.
- Terms: cash, subject to lease confirmations, environmental and engineering, inspections, and, obviously, marketable title.
- Inspection period: 30 days.
- Good-faith deposit: $100,000.
- Closing: time of the essence, 45 days. (*Time of the essence* means that the closing must take place by the assigned date or the contract will be automatically canceled and the deposit forfeited to the seller.)

All inspections and verifications were satisfactory, and we were prepared to close. Thus, the one-page letter of intent stated all of the terms of the deal. I sent a copy of this, with pictures and financial and building information, to my clients and received the go-ahead. They wired $100,000 to the title company as a good faith deposit. I then proceeded to perform the due diligence, or verification procedure. Two weeks after this, the seller phoned, asking for more "consideration, or something." Apparently, he had another buyer at a higher price. When I called my attorney, I was told that, without a signed contract, I had nothing. I pointed out that I had a signed letter of intent. I faxed him a copy. Because the letter of intent contained all the significant clauses, it was enough to tie up the property.

All inspections and verifications were satisfactory, and we were prepared to close. My client decided to finance the $3.45 million as follows:

A note guaranteed by a letter of credit from a major Swiss bank	$3,000,000
Cash down payment to title company	$ 450,000
Working capital to building corporation	$ 150,000
Total cash invested	$ 600,000

First Houston Deal—Distressed Property
(Continued)

First Interstate Bank of Houston agreed to accept the letter of credit and my signature as collateral for a note from the buying corporation for $3 million. They agreed to lend the $3 million upon verification of the letter of credit from the Swiss bank.

The closing had been planned as follows: I would have a tentative closing in the morning, with the $3.45 million in certified funds and all documents to be held in escrow by the title company. The contract seller would close with the actual owner seller in the afternoon and would pay them $3 million of the $3.45 million. This would be done by the title company in return for the signed recorded deeds. The title company would then issue my corporation—the buyers—a deed, title policy, and so on. After deductions of title fees, and so on, the net $450,000 ($3.45 million minus $3 million paid to the original seller) was distributed by the title company as follows:

Contract seller profit	$300,000
Commission to me	$ 75,000
Commission to other broker	$ 75,000
Total	$450,000

This transaction, however, like many others, had its own quirks. In order for First Interstate to wire $3 million to the title company in return for one note, it wanted verification from the Swiss bank.

This usually comes by SWIFT, a coded, confidential telex. The day before the closing, on October 17, 1989, the San Francisco earthquake occurred. First Interstate Bank was headquartered in San Francisco. All communication lines were down and it was impossible to get SWIFT verification. With a time-of-the-essence closing, we were on the verge of panic. However, the banker was astute enough to contact his international department colleagues in New York City, who were, in turn, able to contact the Swiss bank and get SWIFT verification of the existence of the letter of credit for $3 million in favor of

First Houston Deal—Distressed Property
(Continued)

First Interstate Bank. Upon receipt of this, First Interstate wired $3 million to the title company, and the closing proceeded the next day.

The deal at that time shaped up as follows:

Rental income (three floors; 50% of the building was vacant) 75,000 sq. ft. @ $8 =	$ 600,000
Operating expenses ($5 per sq. ft.) or 5 × 150,000 sq. ft.	$ 750,000
Annual cash flow shortage	$ (150,000)

We had reserves for initial anticipated cash flow shortages, and that is why we were able to buy the building for $23 per square foot!

After six months, a major tenant that had previously occupied one floor of the building needed 75,000 square feet of temporary space while constructing its own building. I agreed to a three-year lease at an average of $9 per square foot, or $675,000 per year. And because this was a short-term lease, the tenant agreed to do its own improvements. Usually, in office leases, the landlord pays for the tenant improvements (called *build-outs*) and charges rent accordingly.

With the additional $675,000 in rental income, the cash flow of the building shaped up as follows:

Rental income at time of purchase	$ 600,000
Additional rent from new tenant	$ 675,000
Net operating income	$1,275,000
Less operating expenses	($ 750,000)
Net operating income	$ 525,000

Using a 10 percent return, the building was now worth $5,250,000 ($525,000 ÷ 10%):

First Houston Deal—Distressed Property
(Continued)

New value of building	$5,250,000
Less mortgage	($3,000,000)
Net worth or equity	$2,250,000

So within a year, we had a net equity of $2,250,000 on a cash investment of $600,000, a profit of $1,650,000! The building had cost $14 million to build 10 years earlier, and I had paid $3.45 million for it!

About three years later, the real estate market had turned in Houston. The oversupply of space had been gradually filled up and the impact of the improving national economy was also felt. Today, the original cash investment of $600,000 ten years ago would be generating:

Rental income (74,500 sq. ft. × 22)	$ 3,200
Operating expenses (145,000 × 8)	$1,200,000
Operating cash flow	$2,000,000

At a 10 percent return:

The building is worth	$20 million
Less mortgage	$ 3 million
Equity	$17 million

Our $600,000 has grown to $17 million (or 28 times) in 12 years!

Who Is a Speculator?

There are basically two types of traders: *users* and *speculators* (really, gamblers). Users, as the term implies, buy for their own use; for example, a home builder who buys vacant lots to build on. Speculators, in contrast, buy or sell with the goal of making a profit— preferably fast. They prefer *not* to take possession of the property or goods they speculate in. Speculators, instead, want to deal in paper to represent their ownership, such as:

- Publicly listed shares of corporations.
- Bonds.
- Real estate contracts (not deeds). Remember, a contract is an agreement to buy and sell, not the deed to the property. Some contracts permit transference, although most do not.
- Commodity futures or options. Both are agreements for future delivery, not actual goods.

A speculator will "go into contract," meaning he or she will agree on a price with a seller, sign a contract of sale permitting "assignment," or transfer, and, finally, try to sell the contract at a profit. Take a look at the following example:

Property A

Selling price	$ 70,000
Speculator thinks value is	$100,000
Speculator signs contract at	$ 70,000
Down payment on contract (10%)	$ 7,000
Speculator has potential profit of	$ 30,000
[Value ($100,000) – purchase price ($70,000)]	

Based on these numbers, the speculator can either:

1. Close the transaction at $70,000 and then sell the property for $100,000.
2. Try to sell the contract for, say, $27,000. This includes a $20,000 profit, plus reimbursement of the speculator's $7,000 down payment.

Now let's look at what this means to the new buyer.

Cost to new buyer

Contract price	$ 70,000
Purchase price of buying contract	$ 20,000
Total cost to new buyer	$ 90,000
Value	$100,000

New buyer cash* requirements

Cash contract price	$70,000
Less down payment on contract	($ 7,000)
Balance due at closing	$63,000
Price of purchasing contract from speculator	$27,000
Total cash	$90,000

The point to keep in mind as you set out on your real estate investment journey is that prices keep rising as speculation grows, and as more people believe the price increases will continue. Eventually, though, prices reach such a high level that the smallest failure in expectations can cause a panic. Speculators then rush to sell en masse, pushing prices further down. This scenario is essentially what caused the stock market crash of 1929. It also reiterates the most important point of this book: *Real estate is a long-term investment.*

An example of a successful but difficult speculation appears in "Tribeca, A Manhattan Assemblage."

ECONOMIC CYCLES AND LENDERS

Like speculators, lenders affect and are affected by economic cycles. They are under pressure to lend to cover their costs, which include interest paid to depositors and operating expenses. So in a boom period, when the good times seem to keep rolling, and values keep rising, lenders, too, get caught up in the excitement. The result? They begin to make more daring loans. They:

- Accept the borrower's future projections of income and value, as opposed to today's results. Theoretically, this would justify a higher purchase price and a related higher loan.

- Aggressively pursue loan business.

- Lend to weaker borrowers.

Of course, the *spread,* or profit, on these loans would theoretically be higher than normal, but so is the risk of default.

---

*The cash could be either from personal funds or borrowed. (See Chapter 8.)

Types of Lenders

Before we go any further, let's define what we mean by *lender.* Traditionally, there have been two major types of lenders in the United States that deal with the general public: *commercial banks* and *savings banks* or *savings and loan associations* (SLAs). Two other common types are *pension plans* and *insurance companies.*

Banks and SLAs

Banks lend depositors' money and make interest payments to their depositors. They try to match the length of deposits and the cost thereof (interest on deposits) to the length of the loan. The interest on loans is a function of the bank's cost of funds (interest paid for deposits), plus administrative costs, plus loss reserves and net profits.

Historically, banks were generally not permitted to do anything other than lend money. Their profits came from the spread between interest paid and interest charged. Remember, this is all money belonging to other people, and indirectly to the Federal Deposit Insurance Corporation (FDIC).

Commercial banks usually offer short-term accounts such as checking accounts, money markets, and some certificates of deposit. Likewise, they specialize in making short-term loans to businesses against short-term assets such as accounts receivable, inventory, contracts, and so on.

Originally, savings banks and savings and loan associations were intended to accumulate the funds of small savers for long periods of time and reloan those funds to small home buyers. But between 1979 and 1982, when interest rates went up to 16 percent on certificates of deposit and money market accounts, savings banks were stuck with many low-interest-paying loans from prior years. This resulted in massive losses to the banks. To help offset these losses, Congress liberalized the banking laws, leading to widespread abuse and, ultimately, to the banking crisis in the late 1980s. The federal government had to subsidize the FDIC and the Federal Savings and Loan Insurance Corporation (FSLIC) for approximately $250 billion to protect the insured small depositors of these banks. Today, the distinction between commercial banks and savings banks has blurred, and the liberalized banking laws allow them to go into other financially related businesses such as stock brokerage, insurance, and so on. Because their deposits are subject to withdrawal, banks today would prefer to make short-term loans. However, many also act as intermediaries (brokers). They put together long-term loans for long-term lenders, such as pension plans, that don't have short-term liquidity (withdrawal) risk. For this, banks earn a *spread* or commission on the loan, plus *servicing* (collection) fees.

Pension Plans and Insurance Companies
Pension plans and insurance companies are responsible for covering projections for future payouts, sales and administrative costs, reserves (usually government mandated), and profit. They invest policyholder premiums or pensioners' money for this. Most of the money is long-term retirement funds and is not subject to short-term withdrawal risk. If anything, more money keeps coming in and has to be invested. The goal of these plans is to make conservative long-term investments to cover their responsibilities to policyholders and/or pensioners and to enable them to pay sales and administrative costs, reserves, and net profit. Long-term real estate mortgages are ideal for this, and thus they are the primary long-term lenders. (We discuss mortgages in greater detail in Chapter 8.)

How Lenders Profit

Banks, insurance companies, pension plans, credit companies, and other institutional lenders generally look to make profits as follows:

- They pay their depositors, policyholders, future pensioners, or other lenders interest or a "guaranteed"—but low—rate of return on their money.
- They lend or reinvest the money at a higher rate.

Their goal is for the difference to be enough to pay the lenders' operating and administrative costs and leave a profit. Of course, these lenders have diversified loan portfolios comprising, for example, government bonds, AAA corporate bonds, business loans, mortgages, personal loans, and credit card loans.

Part of the aforementioned administrative costs include *loss reserves*. Lenders know in advance that a certain percentage of loans they make will go bad. What they don't know is which ones. Ideally, of course, the profit on the good loans will more than offset the occasional losses. For those loans that the lender determines to be higher risk, a higher interest is demanded, and received, by the lender.

The availability of loans consequently fuels speculative growth in prices, because people are buying primarily with borrowed money, or OPM (other people's money). Theoretically, if you make a down payment of 10 percent on a property, and the property goes up another 10 percent, you have doubled your money!

To summarize, during the upward slope of a business cycle, especially toward the peak, lenders tend to be more aggressive—and easier. But then, as always, the downturn begins:

- Business slows, profits drop, and borrowers have difficulty making loan payments.
- Rents start dropping as more vacancies occur. Some real estate owners have difficulty meeting loan obligations.
- Lenders start foreclosures.
- Weak owners start panic selling, or *dumping*, properties, pushing prices down.

As buyers who have purchased properties with low down payments see the prices drop and their equity wiped out, they try to:

1. Renegotiate the loan with the lender
2. Abandon the property
3. Offer the property to the lender in lieu of foreclosure and release from a possible deficiency judgment, which occurs when the property value drops below the mortgage. The difference is the responsibility of the borrower

Look at the following example:

Purchase price of property during boom	$100,000
Bank mortgage	($ 90,000)
Equity of investor (down payment)	$ 10,000
During boom property goes up to	$115,000
Bank mortgage stays constant	($ 90,000)

New equity	$ 25,000
Original equity (down payment)	($ 10,000)
Profit	$ 15,000

$$\text{Rate of return} \quad \frac{\text{Profit}}{\text{Equity}} = \frac{\$15,000}{\$10,000} = 1.5\times, \text{ or } 150\%$$

During a slump or recession

Property drops to	$82,000
Bank mortgage stays constant	($90,000)
Negative or minus equity	($ 8,000)

This $8,000 negative is called a *deficiency* if the borrower does not pay it—remember, he or she owes $90,000, and $82,000 would come from a sale. The bank can sue the borrower and get a deficiency judgment from the court for the $8,000.

$$\text{Loss is} \quad \frac{\text{Cost}}{\$100,000} - \frac{\text{Value}}{\$82,000} = \frac{\text{Total}}{\$ 18,000}$$

This is made up of:

Original equity or down payment	$10,000
Negative equity	$ 8,000
Total	$18,000

As you can see, not only have you lost your down payment of $10,000, but you owe the bank an additional $8,000. Your total loss is $18,000 ($100,000 − $82,000).

Subsequently, lenders face possible liquidity—that is, cash—crises because of:

- Reductions in cash flow due to defaulting loans; at the same time, interest and administrative expenses remain relatively constant.

- Decreases in savings accounts as depositors either withdraw funds to cover personal expenses due to unemployment or investment losses or reduce their savings activity as their incomes drop.

■ Costs of foreclosures, which include legal and other out-of-pocket costs; taking possession; management fees; repairs and maintenance; and marketing of property, including advertising and brokers' commissions.

The last item—costs of foreclosures—is why banks do not like to foreclose. We talk more about foreclosures in Chapter 7.

During such slowdowns, banks start setting up large loss reserves on their books. Loss reserves are tax deductible; these are not cash outlays, they are simply book entries based on estimates. Remember that losses can be carried forward for tax purposes. Near the bottom of the bust period, sophisticated investors start buying at what they feel are very reasonable prices. Gradually, the economy begins the climb upward again, as businesspeople start taking advantage of bargain opportunities. Bank deposits start increasing, and bank cash profits are sheltered from taxes by the carried-forward tax losses from loan losses and loss reserves. The bank starts accumulating large cash balances and again starts looking to lend as the economy strengthens.

CONCLUSION

Lending generally follows a 10-year cycle of aggressive lending, recession losses, and eventual recovery, when the process begins all over again. All segments of the economic cycle affect each other and act in concert. What you as a novice real estate investor need to take away from this chapter is a basic understanding of business cycles. Your perspective should always be long range to avoid getting caught up in intermittent periods of boom and bust, which will enable you to make investment decisions accordingly.

5

Calculating the Long-Term Potential Profits from Real Estate

Since 1926, the average long-run return of the stock market through good years and bad has been 9 percent per year compounded. Real estate has had similar returns. As I've emphasized throughout the book so far, a proven way to make long-term profits is to buy assets when they are out of favor (and cheap), and *hold them*. Ideally, of course, we would always buy in "bad" years and sell at peak in "good" years. But let's face it: No one can be sure when we are at a peak or at the bottom of any economic cycle. That is why there is always a risk of selling prematurely.

In real estate, two good guidelines are (1) to buy property in a good area that has been overbuilt, as I described in the previous chapter in the Houston deal, and (2) to buy in deteriorated, but well-located, areas on the brink of so-called gentrification. (Chapter 7 is devoted to finding and evaluating properties.)

As described in the introduction to this book, this chapter takes a numbers-crunching view of the potential of real estate investments. To begin, though, keep this rule of thumb in mind: If a commercial real estate investment does not have a positive cash flow after payment of operating costs and mortgages, don't buy it! (Evaluating properties is discussed in Chapter 7.)

REAL ESTATE PROFIT SOURCES

Real estate profits come from three sources: positive cash flow, appreciation, and leverage.

- *Positive cash flow.* Commercial properties generate approximately 8 to 10 percent cash flow after operating expenses and loan payments on a cash investment.
- *Appreciation.* Properties approximately double in value every 10 years.
- *Leverage.* Properties appreciate while the debt stays constant. (Remember, leverage is the use of debt to increase the buying power of your cash down payment.)

The examples in this chapter expand on each of these profit sources. Here are the parameters we'll use for all the examples: We'll assume you have purchased a property for $200,000 with a down payment of $50,000. The mortgage is $150,000 at 8 percent interest only; there is no amortization (or payoff) of the mortgage. At time of purchase, cash flow from the property was 10 percent of the $200,000 selling price, or $20,000.

Positive Cash Flow

The first calculation we'll make is to determine cash flow return on the $50,000 investment (down payment):

Profit before debt service	$20,000
Interest on $150,000 at 8% (no mortgage payoff)	$12,000
Net cash flow after debt service*	$ 8,000

$$\frac{\$8,000 \text{ cash flow}}{\$50,000 \text{ investment}} = 16\% \text{ cash return on investment}$$

Why the disparity? Remember the property earns 10 percent, and the loan costs 8 percent; the difference goes to the owner-borrower.

---

*Recall from Chapter 3 that *debt service* is the amount of money you need to pay off a loan or debt; in effect, the monthly payments, including interest then pay-down of principal.

Now, using the same set of facts, instead of an *interest-only mortgage*, let's calculate the effects of a *self-liquidating mortgage* on $150,000 at 8 percent, payable over 15 years:

DEFINITION

An *interest-only mortgage* is one on which only interest payments are made, with no paydown or amortization. At the end of the mortgage life (or term) the entire mortgage must be paid, since only interest was paid in between.

A *self-liquidating mortgage* is one that has a level series of payments over its life, which includes interest and paydown. The payments are structured so that at the end of the mortgage, the paydown (amortization) portion of the monthly payments has paid off the mortgage.

Profit before debt service	$20,000
Debt service on $150,000 mortgage at 8% self-liquidating	$16,500
Net cash flow	$ 3,500

Thus in this example your cash return of $3,500 is:

$$\frac{\$3,500 \text{ cash flow}}{\$50,000 \text{ investment}} = 7\% \text{ cash flow}$$

To the cash flow of $3,500, we must add the mortgage payment, or $4,500; your total return then is:

Cash flow	$3,500	
Amortization of loan	$4,500	(16,500 payments –
Total	$8,000	12,000 interest @ 8%)

Or:

$$\frac{\text{Total return}}{\text{Cash investment}} \quad \frac{\$8,000}{\$50,000} = 16 \text{ percent}$$

This includes mortgage payoff. (Mortgages are discussed further in Chapter 8.)

Positive cash flow from real estate investments takes on even greater significance when you take into account that, today, the average dividend on stocks is less than 3 percent, as opposed to 8 percent on real estate. And, of course, this cash flow can be reinvested or saved. Some so-called growth companies don't pay any dividends at all—mangement reinvests the cash that the business generates in expansion or reserves. Some academic stock market evaluators believe that the value of a stock is a function of current and projected dividends. Isn't that what we said about real estate values being a function of cash flow?

Appreciation

What doesn't the preceding example include? The second source of real estate profit: *appreciation.* As discussed earlier, the long-term increase in value (appreciation) of real estate results from its irreplaceability, general economic improvements, and inflation, among other factors. For a first example, assume you have bought a property for cash, that you have held it for 10 years, and that it has doubled in value.

Initially

Original purchase price	$200,000
Original cash flow	$ 20,000 per annum

10 years later

Value	$400,000
Cash flow	$ 40,000 per annum

The profit is twofold: from appreciation and cash flow income, that is, increase and value.

Appreciation (increase in value)

Future value	$400,000
Less original purchase price	($200,000)
Net appreciation	$200,000

Income

Original annual income	$ 20,000
Final annual income	$ 40,000
(10 years later)	

Income goes up as the value of the property rises, and property values rise as the income goes up.

Average income over the 10-year period is the original income, plus final income, divided by 2. In this case, average income per year computes as follows: Initial income of $20,000, plus income 10 years later of $40,000, equals an average of $30,000 per year. Over the 10-year period, the total income was the $30,000 average annual income times 10 years, or:

$$\$30,000 \times 10 \text{ years} = \$300,000$$

At the end of 10 years you will have:

Property worth	$400,000
Accumulated income	$300,000
Total return	$700,000
Original investment	$200,000

Or 3½ times your original investment!

$$\frac{\$700,000}{\$200,000} = 3\frac{1}{2} \text{ times}$$

Remember, this example assumes an all-cash purchase; furthermore, it ignores the additional interest earned by the annual cash flow of $20,000 to $40,000 per annum. If we take into account the interest or other return generated by the annual cash flow, the profit will be even higher.

Leverage

Our second example of appreciation will include the third source of real estate profit: effects of leverage, or borrowed funds. We'll again assume the purchase of a property for $200,000 with $150,000 loan at 8 percent interest, and for simplification, we will ignore the effects of amortization of the loan.

NOTE

The net cash on cash return after debt service should be 8 percent after the debt service has been paid by the property. If you do take on debt, make sure it is self-liquidating and at a fixed rate. This will be discussed further in Chapter 8.

Now let's go back to our example. Here, too, you've held the property for 10 years:

Price of property (initially)	$200,000
Mortgage	$150,000
Down payment	$ 50,000

Original cash flow		$ 20,000 per year
Future cash flow		$ 40,000 per year
Average cash flow	$\left(\dfrac{\$20,000 + \$40,000}{2}\right)$	$ 30,000 per year

Less interest on $150,000 at 8%	($ 12,000)
Average net cash flow after interest	$ 18,000

After 10 years

Value of property	$400,000
Mortgage (assuming no amortization)	$150,000
Net equity	$250,000

Plus 10-year cash flow

Average annual income	$30,000
Less annual interest	($12,000)
Net annual cash flow	$18,000

Cash flow over 10 years ($18,000 × 10)	$180,000
Total after 10 years	$430,000
Original cash investment	$ 50,000

As you can see, your original investment of $50,000 increased to $430,000, or 8½ times in 10 years! This is a typical example of a well-chosen, conservatively leveraged piece of commercial real estate. The numbers speak for themselves.

Let me also point out that, in addition to the advantages just described, you benefit in another way: You get tax benefits as well. (Real estate and tax issues are explored in detail in Appendix B.)

Let's recap: Assuming a 7½ percent per annum appreciation of a property, on an all-cash purchase with a 10 percent annual cash flow, your initial investment (down payment) would typically increase about 3½ times over the 10 years. This includes cash income and appreciation.

In fact, assuming reasonable leverage (or borrowed money) in the same scenario, usually your investment would increase about 8½ times! That is the effect of leverage—using other people's money (OPM) to augment your own. You pay the lender a fixed amount, plus the lender's money back, and the rest is yours. Both cases—an all-cash purchase and a purchase using debt (leverage)—demonstrate the profitability of real estate over the long term.

You may be wondering why, if the use of leverage can be so beneficial in real estate, it's not applied to the stock market as well. The answer lies in the difference between long- and short-term speculation. In today's stock market, dividend yields are about 2 percent or less on blue chip stocks—even zero on high-technology issues. The cost of borrowed money, or *margin,* is above the prime rate, which is say 6 percent. The most you can borrow using stocks and bonds as collateral (which is in the possession of the lender during the life of the loan) is:

- Stocks: 50 percent of value
- Government bonds: 90 percent of value

Let's set up an example using one share. You can multiply to compute other scenarios.

Price of share	$100
Dividend	$ 2

Using leverage to buy:

Cost of share	$100
Margin loan (50%)	($ 50)
Equity	$ 50

Dividend income	$ 2
Margin interest (say, 6%) 6% of $50 loan	($ 3)
Out-of-pocket cost	($ 1.00)

Let us say the stock doubles in 10 years:

Future price in 10 years	$200
Less margin loan	($ 50)
Out-of-pocket interest ($1 × 10 years)	($ 10)
Net equity	$140

Thus, on a $50 investment, at an anticipated appreciation rate of doubling in 10 years (7½ percent per annum), you would have a total net equity of $140, or:

$$\frac{\text{Future value}}{\text{Original investment}} \quad \frac{140}{50} = 2.8 \times \text{your original investment}$$

A similar investment in real estate with leverage would produce 8½ times your initial investment. Why?

- *The debt service would be paid by the property.* If the operating cash flow is not enough to cover the debt service in a real estate deal, not only will most bankers refuse to lend, you should not want to do the deal either. Referring to our second example of appreciation, the net income always exceeded debt service, as opposed to being less than the dividend of the stock in the previous example.

- *Not only did the leverage pay totally for the property cash flow, but higher leverage (70 to 80 percent) is available than on stocks (50 percent).* Current margin loans on stocks are 50 percent of the value, whereas real estate deals are generally financed at a minimum of 70 to 80 percent of value, depending on the parameters or quality of the deal and the aggressiveness of the lender.

- *If the stocks dip below a certain point, the broker will ask for more money to cover them (called a* margin *or* cash call). If the investor does not meet the margin call, the broker can simply sell him or her out. And if there is still a shortfall, the investor is responsible. For example:

Original cost of stock	$100
Less original margin	($ 50)
Original equity	$ 50
Drop in price to	$ 40
Margin originally	$ 50
Margin allowed at price of $40 (50%)	$ 20
Margin shortfall	
Original maximum margin	$50
New maximum margin	($20)
Margin call (cash call)	$30

If the investor does not come up with the $30, the broker can sell (liquidate) his or her position, resulting in the following:

New selling price—proceeds of sale	$40
Margin (loan)	($50)
Shortfall	($10)

The investor is responsible for the shortfall of $10.

Remember, stock markets are supposed to be very liquid, meaning your stocks can easily be sold and converted back to cash. That is why an investor can get hurt by a sudden margin call resulting from a temporary decrease in the price of a stock, especially if the stock recovers shortly afterward.

Disadvantages of Leverage

I would be remiss if I didn't tell you that though leverage enhances your purchasing power and related appreciation potential, it also has downside risks, and you need to be aware of these risks if you intend to become successful at investing in real estate.

Here's how leverage can become problematic. If the underlying asset (the property) drops in value, the following will occur:

1. The investor's equity will decrease.
2. If the value drops more than the owner's equity, the property

value may reach a point at which it is less than the mortgage on the property.

A drop in value usually occurs during a general economic downturn. Let's say this downturn impacts rental income: Perhaps tenants become insolvent, forcing them to vacate the premises; or you, the owner, agree to make a temporary rent adjustment to keep the tenants. Either way, your rental income is reduced. And if, ultimately, you can't keep up the mortgage payments, the property may be foreclosed by the lender. (Foreclosures are discussed in Chapters 7 and 8.)

CONCLUSION

The five chapters in Part I have illustrated that real estate can be a very lucrative long-term investment. The profits come from a combination of:

- Net cash flow after mortgage payments of at least 8 percent per year
- The property paying the mortgage—thus the payoff is additional profit
- *Appreciation*, or traditional long-term increases in value

In Part II, I will show you step-by-step how to make potentially lucrative real estate investments of your own.

Part 2

Investing in Real Estate

6

Getting Started as a Small Investor in Commercial Real Estate

This is the chapter that will guide you as you take your first steps in investing in real estate. At this point, I assume that you've carefully read through Part I, that you've taken care of your essential personal financial needs, as discussed in Chapter 1, and that you've accumulated enough savings to live on for 12 months and have additional savings available for investment.

In Chapter 1, where I described the organization and purpose of this book, I mentioned that I recommend a "club" approach for novice investors in the commercial real estate market. The reasons for this are as follows:

- Most novice investors don't have enough money of their own accumulated to enable them to make a down payment on even a small property. The minimum cash available for the first commercial deal should be approximately $150,000. With that amount and proper leverage, a $400,000 deal can be done, using $100,000 as a down payment and the remaining $50,000 for professional fees, closing and financing costs, and startup reserves.

- By definition, novice investors are inexperienced, and therefore find safety in numbers; that is, they benefit from interchange with others who have the same dreams and goals and the same need for knowledge.

- Novice investors can divide up the work it takes to determine which properties to invest in and to share the financial commitment. Numerous small properties are available to novice investors as vehicles to get started investing in real estate, including small apartment complexes, certain net leases, strip stores with small groups of tenants, and others, all of which were defined and assessed for their potential to the novice investor in Chapter 3. (Finding and evaluating these properties is covered in Chapter 7.)

- Even if an individual has the funds available to purchase property on his or her own, becoming involved with a group will limit the amount that a lone investor will have to risk on the first deal, enabling him or her to concentrate more on learning the intricacies of making real estate investments.

SAFETY IN NUMBERS

In 1983, a group of 16 women of a "certain age" in Beardstown, Illinois, formed a club with the goal of helping them individually and collectively to better manage their personal assets and to learn how to invest in the stock market. Their success (though somewhat lessened in 1998, when it was discovered that an input error had resulted in an overstatement of their 10-year annualized return—it was not 23.4 percent but a still respectable and impressive 9.1 percent) brought widespread media attention to what is in fact a century-old practice: the formation of investment clubs. Today there are thousands of such clubs worldwide, though most have been organized for the purposes of investing in the traditional stock market. This chapter will explain how that same concept can be implemented to invest in commercial real estate. But first, an example from my own experience to demonstrate that how you form such a group is as important as investing itself.

Garden Apartment, Complex Partnership

I've said before that I practice what I preach in this book. What I also do is learn—and teach—from my mistakes, so let me share with you one of my early deals I undertook as part of a group, in 1974. It was for a garden apartment complex in the New York City area. (Remember from Chapter 3 that I name small garden apartment complexes that can be bought with a relatively low down payment as an excellent way for a small group of novice investors to get started in real estate.) In this case, a real estate broker offered friends of mine the complex in question for $1.5 million, with $50,000 in cash, subject to existing mortgages (which means that the buyer is buying the property already mortgaged and agrees to make the payments on it). In this case, the existing mortgages were:

- A first mortgage for $1.25 million, *self-liquidating* with 5¾ percent interest payable by 1991.
- A second mortgage for $200,000, which I negotiated, paying 8 percent interest and *self-amortizing* in 10 years.

DEFINITION

Self-liquidating and *self-amortizing* are synonyms for mortgages for which the payments include interest and payoff. By the end of the term, the mortgage will be paid off.

Total rents in the complex at that time were about $600,000 per year, which just about covered operating costs and mortgage payments. My friends and I decided to form a partnership. In addition to the $50,000 cash needed for the seller, we needed approximately $10,000 for closing costs. Thus our total investment was $60,000. For my investment of $20,000, I received a one-third interest. Initially, there was to be no cash return on our $60,000 investment because we were paying off about $75,000 a year in mortgages. The plan was to struggle for a few years, with the annual payoff of the mortgages being our profit.

Garden Apartment, Complex Partnership
(Continued)

To summarize the deal:

Cash return	$ 0
Annual mortgage payoff	$ 75,000
Appreciation @ 5% of $1.5 million	$ 75,000
Total initial annual return	$150,000 + tax savings

$$\frac{\text{Annual return}}{\text{Cash invested}} = \frac{\$150,000}{\$60,000} = 250\% \text{ per annum!}$$

The $150,000 profit was partially tax free, as we were able to deduct depreciation allowances on our partnership tax return (which is discussed further in Appendix B).

As I figured it, in 10 years (1984) we would have paid off the second mortgage, and those payments—$30,000 per year—would belong to us. Seven years later, in 1991, we would also have paid off the first mortgage, meaning that $100,000 would be ours. Thus, I projected a minimum of $150,000 to $200,000 per annum of cash flow to us (ignoring rent increases due to inflation) after the mortgage payoffs. This on an investment of $60,000! In addition, we would own the property free and clear!

That, at least, is how I saw the deal. However, my partners had other motivations that were unexpressed to me at the time. They saw the investment as an opportunity to make a fast profit. In addition, there were a number of other factors we never considered.

First, because we bought the property in the winter, we got hit with high heating bills which resulted in a negative cash flow (though the spring and summer months would make up for this later). In New York City, most apartment buildings have central heating systems and the landlord supplies and pays for the heat. Needless to say, from that point on, I scheduled my purchases of apartment buildings to take place around March, to give me about eight months (April to November) before having to pay

Garden Apartment, Complex Partnership
(Continued)

fuel bills. Second, prior to the purchase, we conducted only a visual inspection of the property's exterior. After the closing we did a more comprehensive inspection and found out that:

- The public areas (hallways, etc.) needed fixing up.
- The roof was of poor quality and close to 15 years old.
- A number of the tenants were in the low income bracket and had subsidized rents. This meant we were collecting rents for many of the apartments either in the form of two-party checks sent by welfare to the tenant (the tenant would sign the check and then give it to us, the landlord, the second payee) or from the federal government's Housing and Urban Development (HUD) Section 8 program, whereby a low-income citizen does not have to pay more than 30 percent of his or her income in rent, and every month HUD sends a check to the landlord for HUD's portion of the rents for all qualified apartments in the building complex. Needless to say, the problem in both cases is collecting the balance of the rent from the tenants.

Thus, our actual collections were less than we had calculated and our cash outlays were more than we had calculated, worsening the initial cash flow problem. We had to sink a lot of money and effort into:

- Landscaping, making repairs, painting, and decorating
- Tightening rent collections, which included taking tenants who short-paid their rent to court, and so on
- Improving the quality of new tenants by interviewing, checking employment, and doing credit and background checks
- Hiring additional on-site porters
- Conducting weekly inspections of the premises

Garden Apartment, Complex Partnership
(Continued)

Within a year, however, all the hard work began to pay off: The property was turning around, and we were able to face the following winter with a positive bank balance to help us get through. My jobs were to handle the books, records, and correspondence; my partners were responsible for handling the day-to-day on-site management, renting vacant apartments, supervising repairs, and so on. But because my partners were looking to make a fast dollar, as opposed to me who was looking for longer-term profit, after four years they decided they wanted to sell. I had to agree because I couldn't handle the property by myself. So in 1978, we sold, as follows:

Price	$1,800,000
Less	
First mortgage balance	($1,000,000)
Second mortgage balance	($ 150,000)
Other closing cost and adjustments	($ 100,000)
Total deductions	$1,250,000
Net proceeds	$ 550,000

You're probably thinking, "Not bad, $550,000 on a $60,000 initial cash investment four years earlier." (My share was $180,000 on a $20,000 investment in four years.) But if we had held on to the property, as I had wanted, it would have been completely paid off by 1991 with gross rents of $1.4 million, generating a net cash flow of about $700,000 per year, and worth $7 million!

What would I have done differently before investing with this group of people? I'd have been a lot more careful to ensure that we were all on the same page. And that's the purpose of this chapter, to give you the guidelines you need to form or become a member of an existing investment club that's right for you and your financial objectives.

INVESTING ON YOUR OWN

If you're are one of the lucky individuals with enough savings or other money from investments available to invest in real estate on your own, all the information in this book still applies; just skip the section on forming an investment club.

FORMING AN INVESTMENT CLUB

It only takes one person—you!—with a dream, a desire, and a goal to start an investment club. Start spreading the word: Talk to your friends and relatives to find out who's interested. Then invite them to meet informally to discuss the possibilities of organizing such a group. It's not a bad idea to try and gather people with diverse, but complementary, skills and experiences that will help ensure the success of your group's investments. For example, if possible, it would be beneficial to invite people from the following professions: accounting, law, finance, engineering, even real estate brokerage. You might even find that experienced investors in other arenas want to expand their interests to include real estate. Their investment experience in the stock market will add to the skills base of your group and will help new investors become more comfortable with the process and terminology of investing.

General Guidelines for Starting an Investment Club

It is beyond the scope of this chapter (indeed, it would take a book in itself) to dissect in great detail the formation of an investment club. The objective here is to delineate the general steps you should take to launch an investment club within the context of the topic of this book. When you have completed the entire book and are ready to begin investing in commercial real estate, I recommend you come back to this chapter, review this background information, and then refer to the sidebar titled "The Club Scene," which directs you to sources dedicated to the topic of investment clubs.

Assuming you have done the preliminaries (talked to a number of people who might be interested in joining to invest in commercial real estate), there are essentially six basic steps to take to form an investment club.

The Club Scene

As mentioned, the concept of an investment club is not a new one; consequently—and fortunately—a great deal of information and many resources are available to anyone who wants to learn how to form or become a member of such a group.

One of the best places to research the ins and outs of investment clubs is through the National Association of Investors Corporation (NAIC). Though geared primarily at traditional investment vehicles—that is, the stock market—the NAIC can provide a wealth of information particularly regarding the formation and maintenance of investment clubs of all sorts.

Founded in 1951 by George A. Nicholson, Fredrick C. Russell, and Thomas O'Hara, the NAIC is a nonprofit, tax-exempt organization composed of investment clubs and individual investors. Its objective is to "provide a program of sound investment information, education, and support that helps create successful, lifetime investors." Its programs, services, and products are "designed to help individuals of all knowledge levels to become sucessful, long-term investors."

The NAIC is headquartered at 711 West 13 Mile Road, Madison Heights, Michigan 48071; telephone (877) 275-6242. And since there are more than 110 regional chapters in or near most major cities across the United States, you should have no trouble contacting someone from this organization. But probably the best and fastest way to learn about the organization and take advantage of its many offerings is simply by logging on to its Web site at www.naic.com.

For still more on investment clubs, go online and search amazon.com or b&n.com using the keyword *investment clubs;* you'll find numerous titles available on this topic. Or just drop in at your local bookstore and cruise the business and finance section.

I also recommend that you join—individually or as a group—some real estate–related trade associations. Here are three good ones to consider:

- *International BOMA (formerly the Building Owners Management Association).* Founded in 1907, BOMA

The Club Scene *(Continued)*

comprises a network of more than 17,000 commercial real estate professionals representing 84 U.S., 10 Canadian, and 9 overseas associations. It offers comprehensive industry research and office building performance data, as well as publications, products, and services. Contact BOMA via the Web at www.boma.org; via phone at (202) 371-0181; or via mail at 1201 New York Avenue NW, Suite 300, Washington, DC 20005.

■ *Small Property Owners Association (SPOA).* Started in Massachusetts, SPOA now has members across the United States. The organization focuses on property rights. For a $35 annual membership, you'll receive a newsletter that will update you on housing laws, strategy, and more. Contact SPOA via the Web at www.spoa.com; via phone at (617) 354-5533; or via mail at P.O. Box 398115, Cambridge, MA 02139.

■ *International Council of Shopping Centers (ICSC).* This global trade association was founded in 1957 to serve the shopping center industry. Composed of some 38,000 members in the United States, Canada, and more than 70 other countries, the ICSC provides services to its members (which include shopping center owners, professionals, academics, and public officials) to help them compete in today's market. Contact the ICSC via the Web at www.icsc.org.

1. *Identify members.* Determine those people willing to commit the time, money, and work it will take not only to invest in commercial real estate, but to keep the investment club running smoothly. There is no ideal number of members; it's more important that they be compatible, share common goals, be willing to participate actively in the group, and have a similar investment philosophy—in the case of real estate, that means being willing to invest for the long term. And to repeat from the introduction to this section, it is

advantageous that the members represent a variety of professional and personal types.

2. *Determine operating parameters.* This includes deciding how often you'll meet and where. More important, at this stage, you should also itemize the individual roles and responsibilities of each of the members, including financial capabilities. You might want to elect officers and assign formal titles.

3. *Formalize the operations in a legal agreement.* The members should agree to hire an attorney (if one is not a member of the group) to draw up a strong, legally binding agreement that includes (but is not limited to) the name of the group, the names of all the members of the group, the purpose and goals of the group, and the financial and other responsibilities of each member. (To save time and money, consider using as a template the NAIC's partnership agreement, available in its Official Guide.) Don't forget to include in the agreement how to deal with a member who decides to withdraw or does not meet his or her financial obligations. Include a provision for a buyout, and allow time to find other financing if you're involved in a new deal, or to appraise the property and give the withdrawing member notes paying interest for his or her share if it is a previous, completed deal.

4. *Decide on the amount of money each member will deposit for the first deal.* At least $150,000 should be raised by the group for the first deal. Each member should agree to deposit his or her share in advance, to be applied toward the down payment and closing costs of the first deal. The ideal situation is when all members can invest an equal amount; this serves as an equalizer, preventing the domination of the funds by one or two large investors. However, if the group agrees to accept varying amounts of investments, it should set up a *system of shares,* or units; for example, $5,000 each or $150,000 divided into 30 units. The group might also then want to consider proportionate voting.

5. *Deposit the initial investments in an interest-bearing money market account.* Major stock brokerage accounts, such as the Merrill Lynch Cash Management Account (CMA), provide higher money market rates than most banks and offer unlimited checking as well. The cash is usually insured up to $100,000 by the SIPC or the FDIC. Before deciding where to put this

money, the group member in charge of accounting should interview the banks to determine which one is most interested in helping your real estate venture grow. Banks have lock box accounts, sweep accounts, credit lines, mortgage money, and other services available to real estate owner-operators. Find out about all of them. The money should be deposited in the name of the group, with the appropriate authorized signatures (preferably three or more). The bank will advise you of the paperwork you need to fill out to open the account. After the first property has been chosen, set aside 5 percent of the gross price of the deal for closing costs and another 5 percent for start-up reserves.

6. *Monitor your progress and establish a process for reporting on it.* Put another way, make sure that a system of checks and balances is in place and functioning smoothly. The last thing you want where your hard-earned money is concerned is surprises. Though you can never foresee all potential pitfalls of any deal, they should never be caused by the failure of your investment group to govern itself professionally.

Perhaps most important is that the members of the group need to hire their team of professionals to navigate them through the legal and financial waters they will be entering as real estate investors. These professionals include an attorney (who will be used immediately to set up the group's membership agreement), a CPA to serve as a tax consultant, and an insurance broker (discussed later).

Once the group is structured properly and functioning smoothly, it's time to begin looking for an initial property to invest in. In succeeding chapters I explain in detail how to find and evaluate properties and how to negotiate the deals, but for the purposes of this discussion I'll just say briefly that most deals are located through real estate brokers, whose function is to bring together buyers and sellers and to help negotiate price and terms. We're going to assume that your group has identified a property that all members agree to invest in. At this point, in addition to deciding whether to do an all-cash deal or involve leverage—that is, borrowing—you have to choose a *form of ownership*. One caveat: Be sure you have collected *all* the cash from *all* the members before looking for your first deal. Some people may lose interest when the time comes to put up their cash.

FORMS OF OWNERSHIP

There are several forms of ownership to consider for a given piece of property, including individual or joint, general partnership, limited partnership, C and S corporations, limited liability companies(LLCs), and others. The type of ownership entity should be decided on by the group with the advice of counsel and a certified public accountant.

The type of ownership selected should be a function of legal and tax ramifications, including:

- Nature of investment
- Estimated length of investment ownership
- Investor requirements of individual or group owner
- Attorney and CPA recommendations

The following sections offer brief descriptions of the various business forms of property ownership.

Individual or Joint Ownership

Individual or joint ownership is primarily undertaken by individuals or married couples respectively or people involved in other similarly committed relationships. The property owned is normally a single-dwelling house or other residence, usually with the *right of survivorship*, which means that if one of the joint owners with the right of subownership dies, the surviving owner (typically a spouse) gets the whole property.

The risk of individual or joint ownership is that each owner is responsible for all bills, including losses. Property ownership may expose an owner to liability risk (negligence lawsuits). That is why real estate owners must carry adequate liability insurance for protection in this litigious society. Real estate investors also need *umbrella policies*. A normal property and casualty insurance policy will cover the value of the property, and is usually issued in conjunction with a liability insurance policy covering anticipated normal risks set by the insurance company for nonproperty damage risks such as lawsuits. In addition, you can also buy a policy to cover excess risks, to kick in after the regular insurance policy coverage is exhausted. The excess risk policy is called an umbrella policy. Here's how this works. Let's say you are insured as follows:

Primary insurance	$1 million
Umbrella (excess) policy	$5 million
Total insurance	$6 million

Now let's say that someone was injured on your property and was awarded $2.5 million. Your primary carrier would pay its $1 million limit and the carrier of the excess policy would pay the $1.5 million balance.

An additional risk of joint ownership is that either party can sell the property without the other's consent. If the parties ever decide to dissolve their relationship, they may be forced to divide up the property or sell under duress.

TIP

Always consult with your attorney and CPA before entering into any ownership relationship.

Joint Ventures

A *joint venture* refers to a group of people who pool their resources to do a deal or venture together under a predetermined investment and profit-sharing arrangement. Anyone or any entity can be part of a joint venture—individuals, partnerships, corporations. It is similar to a general partnership, but theoretically not as formalized, although some joint venture agreements are more comprehensive and complicated than simple partnership agreements. Many very large real estate deals in which the participants must make large investments are structured as joint ventures.

A joint venture agreement has these advantages:

- It is easy to form.
- Fewer formal arrangements are required for smaller deals.
- No partnership tax return is necessary. Each member of the joint venture simply lists his or her net share of profits and losses on his or her individual tax return.
- The members can be individuals, partnerships, or corporations. The individual investor can choose with which entity to make his or her investment.

Partnerships

A general partnership can be regarded as a more formalized joint venture. An agreement is prepared to delineate the purpose of the partnership, along with the rights and obligations of each partner.

The IRS treats partnerships as separate entities; each must have its own identification number and file partnership returns every year. A partnership pays no federal tax, but must provide information to the IRS every year, listing the partners' names, addresses, Social Security numbers, and shares of profits/losses and showing balance sheets and income statements. In real estate, the income would consist mostly of rental income; expenses would include building operating costs, mortgage interest, and depreciation. The IRS compares this information to the individuals' tax returns. In addition, individual forms called K-1s must be prepared, copies of which go to the Internal Revenue Service along with the annual partnership tax return.

The following are some important facts to keep in mind if you are considering entering into a partnership:

Each partner is individually liable for partnership losses. In the event of a lawsuit, these could conceivably be astronomical, which is why all real estate investments should include adequate property liability insurance as well as individual coverage.

Legally, any partner can make agreements on behalf of the partnership, thereby obligating, or *binding,* the partnership.

Upon the death of a partner, the partnership is automatically dissolved. The assets are divided among the partners on a pro rata basis (this distribution includes the estate of the deceased partner). The remaining partners can form a new partnership that includes the heirs of the deceased. Most partnership agreements include *buy-sell clauses* that come into effect upon the death or withdrawal of a partner. Note that many partnerships also carry partnership life term policies on the lives of the partners. If one partner dies, the insurance proceeds are paid to his or her heirs, and the partnership keeps the deceased partner's share.

Limited Partnerships

A limited partnership is a type of general partnership. In a general partnership described previously all partners have equal authority, share profits and losses equally, and are individually liable for the partnership's bills. A limited partnership has both *general partners* and *limited partners.* The general partners have the "run of the partner-ship" and, as just noted, are personally liable for partnership bills; they are entitled to a share of partnership profits per their agree-ment. In contrast, limited partners are simply investors, or *silent part-ners;* they have no operating authority. They get a share of profits, but their risk of losing money is limited to the amount they invested.

Limited partnerships are generally formed by promoters who want to entice investors to invest. The enticements are that the limited partners don't have the responsibilities of general partners but they reap benefits of partners.

The disadvantage of a limited partnership is that the limited part-ners have no say in the partnership's decision-making process. And because of tax abuse in the past by promoters using limited partner-ships to peddle tax shelters, the IRS has limited the deductibility of accounting losses stemming from depreciation. (The tax treatment of a limited partnership is overall the same as for a general partner-ship, as just discussed.)

For the purposes of this book, whose goal is to encourage active participation in real estate investing, limited partnerships do not fit the bill.

Corporations

A corporation is an entity created by the state (law) that can act as a person.* A person who wants to incorporate notifies the secre-tary of state or other designated state officer. The incorporator chooses a name for the corporation, and if the name is not already in use, it is reserved upon payment of a fee to the state and a cer-tificate of incorporation is issued by the state and given to the incorporator. (Note: You do not need an attorney to set up a cor-poration, but it is a good idea to have one examine your corporate records to ensure that they are in order.) A corporation is solely responsible for its actions, bills, debts, and so on.

Once formed, the corporation issues or sells shares to investor-owners called *stockholders.* The stockholders (owners) have no responsibility for the corporation's acts. If the corporation does well, the stockholders will profit from dividends and/or increases in the value of their shares. The stockholders elect the board of directors annually or on some other periodic basis. The board of directors:

---

*The person who forms a corporation is called an "incorporator."

- Sets company policy
- Discusses and ratifies important corporate decisions
- Selects the chief corporate officers: the president, secretary, treasurer, and sometimes the chief financial officers and the senior vice presidents
- Holds meetings on a periodic basis, during which members of the board review periodic management reports, vote on acquisitions or sales, and set general corporate policy

In small corporations, such as small real estate investment groups, most of these functions overlap; the stockholders, directors, and corporate officers tend to be the same people. Meetings of shareholders and directors are held once a year, usually on the same day. The only other shareholder or director meetings are held as necessary to discuss important corporate business.

Because a corporation is legally considered a separate entity from its shareholders, the shareholders are not personally liable for corporate acts or liabilities. The most a shareholder can lose is the amount invested when the shares were purchased. This important benefit is, however, offset by taxation.

A corporation is required to file an annual report to the state in which it is incorporated. Also, an individual must be designated to receive legal notices involving the corporation. This person is called the *registered agent.*

Taxation of Corporations
A regular corporation is called a *C corporation* for tax purposes. A corporation pays corporate taxes on its profits (if any), because, as just noted, it is considered a separate entity from its shareholders. Corporation tax returns must be filed annually, listing:

- Income and expense information and annual profit
- Comparative balance sheets
- Answers to a questionnaire regarding ownership
- Supplemental data and information, if necessary

If the corporation has profits and distributes them (dividends) to its individual shareholders, the shareholders have to include the dividend income on their personal tax returns, which are subject to personal income tax. This paying of corporation tax on profits, and then personal tax on corporate after-tax dividends, is called *double taxation*. It is one of the major disadvantages of corporate ownership of real estate.

Subchapter S Corporations

To provide small businesses with relief from double taxation, the Internal Revenue Service agreed to recognize and tax small business corporations, called *subchapter S* (sub S) corporations, differently. The advantage of sub S corporations is that they provide protection from personal liability for shareholders; but they are taxed like partnerships.

Taxation of S Corporations

S corporations don't pay income tax. Profits and losses are flowed through to the shareholders by listing each shareholder's proportionate share of profit and loss on a K-1. In turn, each shareholder includes the figures from the K-1 on his or her personal tax return and pays tax accordingly. Thus, the tax is only paid once.

Limited Liability Companies

A more recent form of ownership entity is the limited liability company (LLC). LLCs were created to make it even easier for small businesspeople to form businesses and take advantage of the legal protection of a corporation and the tax benefits of a partnership. LLCs provide limited liability, but are taxed like partnerships, thereby avoiding double taxation. In terms of real estate ownership, there is not much difference between an LLC and a subchapter S corporation, unless capital gains taxes on sales of property pass through directly to the LLC owners, as opposed to being taxed by subchapter S corporations.

CONCLUSION

The form of property ownership should be decided upon after consultations with attorneys, accountants, and other professionals.

7

Finding and Evaluating Properties for Investment

At this point in the investment process, you've formed or joined an investment group, collected the initial investment from each member, and deposited it, preferably in a money market interest-bearing account. Your group has been holding regular strategy meetings and you've had member agreements prepared and signed. Now the fun begins: looking for a suitable investment for the group.

FINDING PROPERTIES

There are numerous sources for finding real estate properties. Some are obvious and some will surprise and delight you as you become more involved in this exciting investment arena. This chapter will introduce you to the most common, which include:

- Real estate brokers (in person and online)
- Advertisements in printed periodicals (hard copy and online)
- Word of mouth

- Foreclosures (including online)
- Government surplus (including online)
- Auctions (including online)
- Private sales
- Sale leasebacks

> **NOTE**
>
> Today, most traditional sources of information on any topic you can imagine have online counterparts, and the real estate world is no different; and though it is beyond the scope of this book to report on the innumerable sites focusing on all aspects of real estate, where appropriate in the following sections there are some suggestions to get you started searching the Internet.

Real Estate Brokers

Without question, the major source of properties is real estate brokers. It is, after all, a broker's job to bring together sellers and buyers of real estate—in the profession, called a *meeting of the minds*. Brokers also help to negotiate deals and facilitate closings—for good reason; if a deal does not get done, they do not get paid. Brokers earn their money from sales commission usually set as a percentage of the final price at the closing (this is explained more fully later in this section).

With so much knowledge of properties in hand, it follows that brokers are also useful sources of other information of importance to investors of real estate: neighborhood status, local trends, places to invest for maximum returns, and more. In fact, any competent broker should be willing and able to answer any and all potential investor questions. A broker usually also has contact with other qualified professionals with whom real estate investors will need to become familiar, including appraisers, attorneys, engineers, insurance brokers, and lenders.

Finding a Qualified Real Estate Broker

Unless you or someone in your investment club has a personal relationship with an independent broker, in general I recommend that novice investors contact a long-established local real estate

. . . It's Who You Know

In addition to learning how to find and evaluate properties (the "what" you know), you'll need to find and evaluate a number of people to help you navigate your way through the sometimes rough waters of the real estate business. In addition to a real estate broker, the following are brief descriptions of other professionals with whom you'll be forming (hopefully long-term) relationships.

Attorney. If you or your investment group doesn't already have a lawyer, get one now. He or she will advise you regarding the various forms your group can take, then help you prepare your group's partnership agreement. Your attorney will also represent you at the closing, and review all documents for accuracy. In short, your attorney represents your legal interests.

Banker. No doubt you already have a bank, but do you have a banker? By that I mean a relationship with a person at your bank who is qualified to help you with financing, banking services, and more. If not, make an appointment with a bank representative to explain your plans to become involved in real estate investing.

Accountant. Your CPA will help you set up your account books and records, advise you regarding the tax implications of various real estate transactions, and help you to prepare financial statements and tax returns.

Engineer. You'll hire a professional engineer (licensed by the state) after you've entered into a contract of sale. He or she will conduct a comprehensive property inspection that will include the foundation, the overall structure, electrical and mechanical systems, and so on. The engineer will prepare a report that will explain any physical shortcomings and necessary repairs.

Mortgage broker. For a fee (usually 1 percent), a mortgage broker will help you to get financing. Mortgage brokers have access to lenders nationwide, and will know which might be willing to lend you money for your particular

> ### . . . It's Who You Know *(Continued)*
>
> project. They will help you prepare the loan application and put the loan package together. Because of their far-reaching network of contacts, mortgage brokers can save you a lot of time (and probably money).
>
> *Insurance broker.* Similar to a mortgage broker, an insurance broker specializes in knowing what's available to protect you and your investments. He or she will help you to apply for policies and negotiate prices.

brokerage firm in the locality they wish to invest in. Another safe alternative is to contact the commercial department of a regional or national firm, such as Century 21 or Coldwell Banker.

At the beginning, you may want to interview three or four different brokers to find your level of comfort. Tell them what you are looking for, and see which serve you best based on your criteria. Brokers often represent different properties (listings), so it is a good idea to look at as many properties as you can before deciding to buy one. Doing this will also expand your knowledge base about the real estate business in general and the market in your location.

Broker Specialization
Most independent brokers specialize in one of the following categories of real estate:

- Homes—single-family dwellings, including condominiums
- Commercial, including multifamily residential, retail, offices, and net leases
- Industrial, including warehouses and public storage
- Land, including farm acreage

Similarly, larger national firms such as Century 21 will have departments specializing in these areas.

Real estate brokers serve both sellers and buyers. For the seller, the broker will provide the following services:

- Check comparable sales, then advise the seller as to the value of the property and what price to ask
- Advertise the property
- Contact known buyers of similar properties
- Show the property to prospective buyers
- Represent the seller in negotiations with the buyer, especially if the commission is being paid by the seller

After an agreement has been reached and a formal contract of sale has been signed by both the buyer and the seller, the broker will help close the transaction by coordinating and compiling *due diligence paperwork,* introducing the buyer to sources of financing, and attending the closing.

DEFINITION

Due diligence refers to the process of thoroughly examining a deal after going to contract but before closing. It includes reviewing all documents (leases, service contracts, inspection certificates, etc.), confirming the inspection by a licensed engineer, verifying environmental inspections, confirming rents, surveying the property, and so on.

When serving buyers, the broker will interview them, then compare their requirements and desires to their financial capabilities, desired rate of return, and other criteria. After this preliminary interview, the broker will:

- Examine lists of properties available for sale and appropriate for the buyer
- Contact other brokers for additional appropriate properties for sale. (Usually, brokers prearrange to split commissions, so it behooves them to work together.)
- Arrange property inspections
- Help the buyer through the negotiation process
- Introduce the buyer to lenders or mortgage brokers to help him or her get financing
- Assist in the final closing

From the Broker's Mouth: The Role of a Real Estate Broker

Small and or novice investors need to realize that real estate brokers are their greatest asset, because brokers come in contact with more properties than any individual or group ever could. And once investors establish a good relationship with a broker (which means accepting that he or she will be making money from their transactions), they will form an extended trust. Most wise investors realize that a broker's commissions are usually paid on the seller's end of the transaction, and thus it is not costing the investors any more than if they were dealing directly with the seller. If investors "massage" that relationship, by proving to the broker that they have the knowledge and desire, together with the financial capabilities, to move forth on a deal, that broker is going to put them on his or her "A" list. When the broker comes upon anything that looks really good, he or she will run it by those investors first. Even if an investor cannot move on a given deal, the broker will continue to present deals to his or her "A" clients. Successful brokers recognize that their skills are really that of a third-party negotiator, with the ability to bring people together—as well to advise people walk away from the deal if it's not right for them.

Creative financing is one of the most important aspects of a good real estate broker. [Creative financing is the putting together of a deal using a combination of conventional mortgages and some kind of future payment of the down payment. This facilitates the ability to further leverage limited funds available to a buyer, and may have tax benefits to the seller.] How brokers are trained to use creative financing to structure their deals is extremely important, because more money is made in real estate during bad times than in good times. Ironically, most investors shy away from getting involved in real estate in bad times because they do not know how to deal with the uncertainties of the market. In the long run, however, investors can be far more effective and do better buying property in bad markets than in good markets. In good times, when there is plenty of demand, it is easy to be a successful broker. With the availability of liberal financing, buyers tend to overpay for properties.

From the Broker's Mouth: The Role of a Real Estate Broker *(Continued)*

Conversely, in a bad market, conventional financing is more difficult to get due to the general atmosphere. The rates are at their highest and the banks—stuck with properties that they would like to unload—are reluctant to lend. With outside money not available, brokers have to use creative financing.

Furthermore, though many sellers will wait until a good market to sell their properties, there are those who either want to or have to (because of divorce, illness, retirement, or other reasons) unload property at low prices in bad markets. Such situations create opportunities for properties to be picked up for the assumption of existing debt and seller financing.

In summary, with a broker who knows how to use creative financing, and with some staying power, real estate investors can pick up property that can be "turned around" often in three to five years, with overall profits far greater than if purchased in an exceptionally hot market.

Reprinted with permission from Frederick Arnoul, a successful real estate broker in central New Jersey for more than 35 years.

Broker Compensation

Real estate brokers are paid a commission that is generally computed as a percentage of the final agreed-upon selling price for the property. The commission is paid by the seller. It is not due until the deal closes and the seller has received his or her money from the buyer.

NOTE

If a deal is nearing completion—a final contract has been signed and all the conditions have been met—and the buyer reneges for whatever reason, the broker still may be entitled to a commission because he or she has performed his or her end of the deal.

Often, two brokers are involved in a commercial real estate deal, one to represent the seller and another to represent the buyer. As mentioned, in such a case, the two brokers would split the commission. This is called *co-brokerage*. In commercial transactions, many brokers will agree to reduce their commissions if they see that the buyer and seller are nearing an agreement on price, believing that by doing so they may get the parties to agree more quickly. For example:

Buyer's offer	$ 97,000
Seller's asking price	$100,000
Less commission (6%)	($ 6,000)
Net to seller	$ 94,000

Seller is willing to accept $97,000 net.

If, however, the broker reduced his or her commission to $3,000 from $6,000, the following would result for the seller:

Asking price	$100,000
Less reduced commission	($ 3,000)
Net to seller	$ 97,000

NOTE

Learn to regard all fees—whether brokerage commissions or fees for the service of professionals such as attorneys, certified public accountants, engineers, or other consultants—as negotiable. The worst that can happen if you request a fee reduction is that the the provider may say no. Usually, however, in longstanding relationships, or if they anticipate repeat business, professionals who work on a commission basis will consider—and often agree to—the request. Commercial real estate brokerage commissions are considered negotiable because of the large amounts of money involved: The larger the size of the deal, the lower the commission percentage.

Thus, by virtue of the broker lowering the commission, the new net proceeds to the seller ($97,000) match the offering price of the buyer ($97,000), thereby expediting the deal—a win-win situation for all. As you can see from the previous example, the seller is concerned with his or her net after commissions and other selling costs.

Thus, brokers often have conflicts of interest. Because their income is based on a percentage of the selling price of properties, the lower the selling price, the lower the commission. On the other hand, if the selling price is too high, the deal may not get done and the broker will get nothing. That is why savvy brokers point out to the seller what a reasonable market asking price for a property would be. In large commercial transactions, it's a good idea to negotiate the broker's commission in advance. A buyer may decide to pay the broker's commission and tell the broker to advise the seller accordingly. This accomplishes the following:

■ The seller feels he or she is "saving" the commission, and is then willing to negotiate on a net basis.

■ The broker (having notified the seller) is now working for the buyer.

■ With the broker's compensation (commission) an agreed-upon fixed amount (not a percentage), he or she will not earn less if the deal gets done at a lower price, making it reasonable to try to get the seller to reduce the price to meet the buyer's offer and get the deal done.

Brokers Online

No matter where you live or where you want to look at properties to invest in, you'll find brokers online to help you. It's as easy as logging on and typing in a keyword or two. If you know, for example, that you want to work with a large brokerage firm, such as Coldwell Banker, just type in that name, and in seconds you'll be at the firm's home page, from which you can do a property search of its more than 200,000 listings according to size, price, and type of property. You can search neighborhoods anywhere in the United States and contact the Mortgage Center, where you can calculate how much you'd like to spend, apply for a loan, and more.

If you prefer to work with an independent broker and you have no idea how to find one, especially if you're looking to invest in properties in out-of-the-way places, all you have to do is type in some appropriate keywords. For example, I typed in "real estate brokers" and received hundreds of listings to choose from. You can narrow your search by adding a specific location, say, "real estate brokers AND New Mexico." One good site for commercial properties to begin with is www.realestatejournal.com, *The Wall Street Journal's* guide to residential and commercial property. It includes a number of pertinent, timely articles, as well as a discussion forum.

DEFINITION

Broker, realtor, and *real estate agent* are different terms for the same thing.

Periodical Advertisements

A good source of investment properties, which is often linked to real estate brokers, is newspaper and magazine advertising. Brokers who advertise properties in the real estate classifieds usually have exclusive listings. You'll also find "private" listings in newspapers and magazines; these are offered directly by owners or sellers who are attempting to sell their property themselves without having to pay a broker's commissions.

Almost without exception, newspapers in every community, large or small, run weekly real estate sections; the newspapers with wider circulations, such as *The New York Times, The Wall Street Journal,* and *The Washington Post,* contain ads from all over the country.

Local law journals, such as the *New York Law Journal,* are a good source of foreclosure auction announcements, bankruptcy proceedings, property liens, properties in default on real estate taxes, and the like. And be aware that all foreclosure auctions must be advertised in local newspapers a certain number of days in advance of the auction. This is a legal requirement whose purpose is to try to attract as many potential bidders as possible, to maximize the selling price. This theoretically protects the owner (mortgagor or borrower) from a possible deficiency if the property goes for less than the loan balance.

Periodicals Online

Many newspapers, magazines, and journals have online counterparts; and, especially in the case of newspapers, it's easy to access their classified sections and from there to find the real estate listings. For example, if you type in "San Jose Mercury News AND real estate," you'll be one click away from the paper's Virtual Real Estate Forum, where you can then click your way through buying and/or selling your home, mortgage money, neighborhoods, and much more.

Word of Mouth

Verbally spreading the word that you are looking for a commercial property may seem like a somewhat primitive approach, but you may be surprised at the results you'll get. As in every profession or vocation, the people involved in real estate, whether professionals or novices, tend to communicate and share information. Learn to take advantage of your expanding circle of contacts. As you and your fellow club members become more knowledgeable about the marketplace and establish relationships with real estate professionals, you can ask them to notify you of any interesting deals that come their way. Moreover, once you make your interest in real estate investing known, you'll find that your friends or relatives will pass on tips.

> **TIP**
>
> Give a token of appreciation to a nonbroker who alerts you to a potential property. This could be a gift or money, depending on how valuable the information is to you. If the deal gets done at a good price, this "referral fee" will be worth it, especially as an incentive for future deals.

But beware of stepping on toes. By this I mean that you shouldn't act on a tip that might backfire because you would be taking something away from someone who could be of long-term help. A former colleague of mine once beat a broker out of a commission. Soon afterward, when a very lucrative property came across this broker's desk, the broker offered it to someone else, and my colleague missed out on what turned out to be an extremely profitable transaction worth more than 100 times the commission he had saved.

Spreading the Word Online

The best way to notify others online that you're looking for properties to invest in is to e-mail anyone and everyone that you consider a possible link to real estate information. Take advantage of the cc: function on your e-mail software to type your message once and send copies to everyone on your list.

Foreclosures

It's a fact of life that one person's misfortune is another's good luck, and perhaps nowhere is this more apparent than in real estate. Foreclosed properties would not exist unless their owners were having problems. And, as just mentioned, by law all foreclosed properties have to be advertised and go to auction, so information on them is easy to find. (Read more about auctions later in this chapter.)

When a foreclosed property is sold, the lending institution, or *note holder,* is entitled only to the note or mortgage balance plus accrued interest, attorney's fees, and any out-of-pocket costs such as insurance, property taxes, and possible receivers' fees related to the foreclosed property. Any surplus money raised at an auction goes to the owner or borrower.

NOTE

Recall from Chapter 5 that if not enough cash is generated at the auction to reimburse the lender, the shortfall is called a *deficiency;* and if a personal guarantee was signed by the borrower for the loan, the lender is entitled to collect the deficiency from the borrower. If no personal guarantee was signed, then the borrower is not liable for any deficiency or shortfall; only the property itself is liable for the mortgage. (A *deficiency judgment* is a court-ordered legal judgment obtained by a lender as the result of a successful lawsuit against a foreclosed borrower for a shortfall.)

Sometimes the owner-borrower may agree to waive the foreclosure proess, including the auction, by giving the lender a deed directly. This expedites the bank's taking over the property, thereby saving legal and other costs. In return, the bank may agree to waive any possible deficiency. This is called *giving a deed in lieu of foreclosure.*

Foreclosures comprise a rich source of potentially profitable investments. You can get foreclosure listings from:

- Banks, local and national. Bank foreclosure departments are called by various titles, commonly some version of real estate owned (REO) or owned real estate (ORE). Banks want to sell their foreclosed properties quickly for two major reasons: First, they are required to set aside capital reserves for foreclosed properties they own; this ties up money that could be put to use elsewhere. Second, they do not want the management headaches.

- Insurance companies and pension plans.

- United States government agencies or affiliates, including the Department of Housing and Urban Development (HUD), the Federal Housing Administration (FHA), the Federal National Mortgage Association (Fannie Mae), and the Small Business Administration (SBA).

- Real estate brokers, who are notified of foreclosed properties by owners anxious to sell them quickly.

- Foreclosure newsletters or services. These compile lists of properties under foreclosure from various sources. These sources cost money, so make sure you know what you're getting before you put down your hard-earned cash. (Or consider accessing these lists via the Internet; see the "Foreclosures Online" section later in this chapter.) A disadvantage of these lists is that they usually only post properties available to the general public. As an investor, you'll want to know about foreclosures *before* everyone else. That is why I recommend direct contact with local financial institutions, whose foreclosure properties are rarely advertised.

- The Internet. (See the "Foreclosures Online" section.)

Don't, however, presume that foreclosures are always a good deal just because they represent "trouble" that someone is trying to "unload." Foreclosed properties require time, money, and effort to make profitable; therefore, the purchase price should be a substantial enough discount from the potential market price (especially if you're paying all cash) to justify the risk and effort. You must always keep in mind that foreclosures are problem properties and that when you purchase them you are assuming those problems, which include but are not limited to neglect, vacancies, tax arrears, deferred maintenance, and sometimes necessary capital improvements. For these reasons, I usually don't recommend that novice investors get involved with foreclosure properties unless a deal presents a unique opportunity and the investors have the support of professionals to ensure that all the necessary aspects are dealt with.

One good way to obtain a foreclosed property at a good price is to buy the note (IOU) on the property from the bank or other lender and complete the foreclosure yourself. Here's how it works: A real estate lender gets a mortgage note with the property as collateral from the borrower. The mortgages often are sold from one lender to another. To avoid the time and costs of a lengthy foreclosure process, the lender or holder of a mortgage note on a defaulting property may simply sell the mortgage note to an investor at a discount. The investor can then complete the foreclosure process. This is also profitable for the lender, who saves the following costs:

- Completing the foreclosure
- Taking possession of the property
- Managing the property until it is resold
- Paying operating and any necessary repair costs for the property until it is resold
- Paying the brokerage commission on the resale
- Setting aside necessary legal reserves

The lender may be willing to sell the note (mortgage) at a substantial discount. Since the mortgage itself may be less than the value of the property, the potential profit is magnified. Of course, this entails additional work, including completion of the foreclosure process to gain possession of the property.

In summary, the main drawbacks of buying foreclosures are:

- Usually, you have to pay all cash. Lenders rarely want to take back mortgages on foreclosed properties, as they are afraid they may have to foreclose again.
- Often foreclosed properties have been abandoned by the previous owners and may be in poor condition.
- If the foreclosed property is an apartment building or complex, there may be substantial vacancies. Conversely, there may be nonpaying tenants who have to be dispossessed, which entails legal fees and time.

- Extensive capital improvements and marketing may be required. Therefore, in addition to the cash required for the purchase, you will need to budget for repairs, possible tenant build-outs, and other marketing and carryings costs, including taxes, insurance, management, and so on.

DEFINITION

A *tenant build-out* is an improvement that must be under-taken to ready a property for a new tenant.

Foreclosures Online

Information on foreclosures is abundant on the Internet. All you have to do is type in keywords such as "real estate foreclosures" and you'll be rewarded with choices such as Foreclosure World, which bills itself as "America's only online foreclosure multiple listing service." It contains residential, commercial, and land listings in all 50 states. Another comprehensive site is foreclosure.com, which, among other things, offers "courses" in foreclosure buying, including Foreclosure Investing 101, Avoiding Foreclosure Scams, and Foreclosure Sites to Avoid. A third comprehensive site is called foreclosurelistings.com. This site contains much more than just property listings; it also offers basic information vital to novice investors, answering such questions as "What is a foreclosure?" and explaining how to buy at a foreclosure sale and how to finance foreclosures. If you want to narrow your search, simply add the location name to the previous keywords, for example, "real estate foreclosures AND Sedona, Arizona."

Government Surplus

Federal, state, and local government agencies often have surplus properties they want to unload. They include:

- Properties taken for nonpayment of real estate taxes.
- Surplus property bought for public works as part of condemnation proceedings.
- Old, obsolete government buildings that have been replaced by newer ones.

- National defense bases closed as a result of the downsizing of the military.
- Properties in the possession of the FDIC, SBA, or other agencies that have taken over bad banks with bad loan portfolios.

These properties may be available for cash or terms. To find out about government surplus or foreclosed properties, you can contact various government agencies and ask to be put on their mailing lists for announcements. The primary agencies to contact are the Federal Deposit Insurance Corporation (FDIC), the Small Business Association (SBA), the Department of Housing and Urban Development (HUD), and the General Services Administration (GSA).

Government Surplus Online
There's no shortage of easily accessible information online regarding government surplus properties. It's a simple matter of typing in keywords such as "government surplus AND real estate" or going directly to the Web site of a particular government agency, such as sba.com or fdic.com, then searching on "real estate." For example, at the SBA's site, you'll find the SBA Lender Directory, which is a mortgage lender and real estate loan service. And at talewins.com (found by typing "FDIC AND real estate") you'll find page after page of FDIC properties for sale (updated at least every two weeks) in categories such as Family Attached, Not Owner Occupied; Industrial; Land, Improved; Land, Unimproved; and more, all further divided by location.

Auctions

Auctions are held to attract more buyers in the hope of selling properties faster. Sellers, whether private individuals, government entities, or professional brokers, all use public auctions. They advertise extensively in the media: newspapers, television and radio, brochures, and the Internet. The objective of an auction is to generate excitement and competition among bidders to drive up the price. In the event there is limited interest and the offered price remains low, as protection sellers may set a *reserve*, or minimum, price below which they will not sell. This is usually announced in advance.

In practice, however, widely publicized public auctions frequently don't present much of an opportunity for a buyer to make a good deal, because:

- Too many people know about them.
- Usually reserve prices have been set.

Anyone can bid at an auction. Lenders may bid the amount of the mortgage and related costs to ensure that they get a least that amount. Of course, if no one bids more, the lender gets the property and may consequently sell it for less.

If you want to try to buy at a real estate auction, scan newspapers and the Internet for announcements. Call the number listed to set a time to inspect the property with a representative of the auctioneer. Review the paperwork on the property, and determine the maximum price you are willing to pay. If at the auction you are the top bidder, you will be expected to give a certified bank check for 10 percent of the amount of your bid immediately; otherwise your bid will not be accepted. A closing date is then set, usually 30 days after the auction.

Auctions Online

Increasingly, auctions for everything from collectibles to carriage houses are being publicized on the Internet. To find auctions for real estate, just type in "real estate auctions," and you'll get more information than you know what to do with. For example, using those keywords turned up Agriland Exchange, listing real estate auctions for farms and farmland, hunting and recreational land, and more. The same search turned up private auction companies, such as the American Bureau of Auction Marketing Exchange (ABAMEX), all of which have sections devoted to real estate.

Private Sales

Some owners choose to sell privately—that is, without brokers—in order to avoid presale publicity and to save on brokers' commissions. I prefer private sales (dealing directly with the owner) to auctions, because usually there is less public competition. Buying directly from a motivated owner often enables you to strike a better deal, for the following reasons:

- You may not have to deal with a professional broker who is representing other potential buyers in competition with you.
- The seller may often be compelled by personal difficulties (family illness, divorce, business problems, financial or tax constraints, etc.) to generate cash, and therefore may be willing to deal quickly and, for you, profitably.
- The seller may need to raise cash for such expenses as paying for a child's college education.

Where private sales are concerned, I can't stress strongly enough the importance of information—specifically, finding out why the seller is selling. The more you know, the better positioned you'll be later, during the negotiating process. As with foreclosures, it is an irony—and a sad fact of life—that you may be able to benefit from the misfortune of someone else.

The best places to find out about private sales are newspaper advertisements, the Internet, and word of mouth. Also, estates are a very good source of private sale deals. (Note: For the purposes of this discussion, *estate* refers to the assets of a deceased person.) All estates over a certain size have to be appraised for estate tax purposes, and an estate tax return must be filed. Often, the heirs want quick cash; they may not want to hold onto the property, especially a residence of the deceased, and so may be willing to sell at a discount.

Sale Leasebacks

To free up capital tied up in real estate, some businesses may do what's called a *sale leaseback*. They sell a property to an investor for cash, then lease it back for a long period of time at a rent priced to give the investor 9 to 10 percent return on the purchase price. If the seller-tenant is strong, the investor can get financing for the deal. In addition to freeing up capital, the seller retains use of the property with the long-term lease.

The deal should generate positive cash flow from the rent. The price of the sale leaseback should be set by an independent appraisal of the property and generate a 9 to 10 percent return to the buyer.

Sale leasebacks are similar to net leases, which we discussed in Chapter 3, except that in the sale leaseback, the owner is selling and leasing back (usually on a net lease basis), whereas typically outside investors are involved in net leases.

Though sale leasebacks are potentially profitable, investors considering them should be aware that some sellers agree to pay an artificially high rent for a property they are selling to justify a higher selling price, which is usually higher than the market value. For example, let's say a property is worth $100,000: A normal return on a net lease for a similar property would be 9 percent (the capitalization rate), which is:

$$\$100,000 \times 9\% = \$9,000 \text{ rent per annum}$$

A seller may offer to pay net rent of $18,000 per annum in order to justify the following price:

$$\frac{\$18,000}{9\%} = \$200,000$$

The $18,000 is 9 percent of $200,000. The risk here is that if the seller goes out of business, the property rent will drop to $9,000 and the value will then reflect the actual $100,000 market value. Remember, the value of an asset is a function of income and replacement cost.

If you're interested in sale leasebacks, there are brokers who specialize in them. These brokers advertise over the Internet, in real estate journals, and in major national newspapers, such as *The Wall Street Journal.*

Real Estate Source Roundup

Looking for properties for sale, going to see them, and deciding which ones to pursue can be a very enjoyable and exciting pastime—it's the thrill of the hunt! For the novice investor, the best way to start is to go to three or four brokers, state your criteria, and see if the brokers have any properties listed that meet your requirements. Do not buy the first property you find! You need to look at four or five properties to familiarize yourself with relative values.

Once you've gotten the lay of the land, start scanning local newspapers, bulletin boards, and the Internet for commercial property listings; and remember to spread the word to neighbors, friends, and coworkers that you and your group are looking for commercial properties.

EVALUATING PROPERTIES

Now that you know where to go to find properties, you can begin to look at some and evaluate them as potential investments. To begin this section, I want to stress that evaluating (also called *appraising*) properties is an art, not an exact science. The general steps are:

1. Gathering information—the sellers will provide you with a description of the property, including floor sizes, number of rooms, tenancy, income and expenses, and any other information you ask for.
2. Examining the property and the neighborhood.
3. Determining estimated depreciation and expense amounts (I detail this with examples later).
4. Setting the rate of return.
5. Organizing the values under comparable sales, cost, and income approaches (which I explain shortly), and then averaging them.

I also want to emphasize that you should *always* make a point of seeing the property you are interested in, whether you do the official appraisal yourself (see the next section) or hire a professional; do not expect anyone else's description or appraisal, no matter how qualified the person may be, to determine your decision to invest or not. It's your money and only you can have the last word on whether the purchase suits you and/or your group. You can arrange to look at properties in the evenings or on weekends; this process does not have to interfere with your work. In fact, you may find that looking at properties is enjoyable, especially as you become more experienced. It is, essentially, a form of shopping. Make an appointment for you and your group with the owner or his or her broker to show you the property. You can all go together. Examine all common areas—hallways, entrance, lobby, and so on. View as many units—apartments, stores, offices—as possible

Once you find a property you like and think you might want to invest in, the next step is to contact the seller or the seller's brokers to express your interest. At this time, also request what's called a *setup*, which lists pertinent information, including:

- Street address.
- Formal description of the property.
- Tax lot and block numbers (legal address).
- Assessed valuation of the local property tax authority (this will not necessarily be the same as the appraisal value).
- Detailed schedule of income and expenses and net income. Income should include a detailed rent roll (tenants' names, date of lease signing, amount of rent paid, lease expiration date); expenses should be itemized and backup invoices made available for inspection.
- Asking price.

The next step is to arrange for a more formal inspection of the property with the seller or seller's broker, which you can either do yourself or hire an appraiser to do for you.

Self-Evaluate or Hire an Appraiser: That Is the Question

As mentioned, you can appraise a property yourself or hire a professional appraiser to do it for you. Banks, life insurance companies, and other institutional lenders hire professionals to appraise property for them, to compare the value to the selling price of the property and the amount of loan requested, and to verify the property's income and expenses. As an independent investor, you will want to tag along with appraisers to learn the details of property evaluation before you attempt to self-evaluate and make value projections. Carefully examine all property appraisal reports, in particular the calculations used to derive comparable sales, replacement cost, and income (these will be explained later in this chapter).

You may be wondering why you can't just use the lender's assessment, since the lender is conducting (or has already conducted) an appraisal of the property you're interested in. There are a number of good reasons not to:

- By going through your own appraisal, you will learn about the property being considered. It is not that difficult to go through the various appraisal steps. If you take each part of the appraisal process systematically, usually it's just a matter of filling in blanks. Eventually, you will be able to conduct your own evaluation of deals presented to you.

- A professional appraiser will have a different outlook from you. You will be looking at the property as a long-term investment, and will value it accordingly; you may see future explosive growth potential, whereas a professional appraiser will be interested in an evaluation of the property as it stands today, not what it might be able to become tomorrow. The appraiser must take this approach to protect him- or herself from liability for errors.

- Professional appraisers also make assumptions based on information supplied to them, and their results reflect this input accordingly. (For example, a buyer could supply the appraiser with future income projections that are higher than the current income). If you do your own analysis, you can compare it to the independent appraisal used by the bank. If there are major differences, recheck your figures; if you believe you are correct, point out the discrepancies to the appraiser before he or she makes his or her report.

Hiring a Professional Appraiser

When you hire a professional appraiser, the first and most important step is to make sure he or she is qualified. One good way to determine this is to ask if he or she is a Member of the Appraisal Institute (MAI). The Appraisal Institute, headquartered in Chicago, Illinois, has been educating real estate appraisers for more than 60 years, and has some 19,000 members and 112 chapters across the United States. Its programs are dedicated to educating its members in the ever changing field of real estate valuation, and to encouraging adherence to the Code of Professional Ethics and Standards of Professional Appraisal Practice.

Appraisal Institute members earn one of the following designations: General MAI, Society of Real Property Appraisers (SRPA), or Society of Real Estate Appraisers (SREA).

Lenders and other real estate professionals alike hire Institute appraisers. Appraisal fees, set by Institute appraisers for lenders, are paid by the borrower as part of the loan closing costs. If you want your own Institute appraisal done, you can usually set the guidelines as to why, when, and where you want it done and negotiate the fee.

Professional Appraisals in Dispute Resolutions

Many business agreements contain clauses that address potential internal disputes among partners and/or shareholders. In the case of property ownership, a *dispute resolution clause* usually refers to the disposition of the property. Typically, the owners divide the net proceeds based upon their ownership interest, or one keeps the property and buys the others out.

To ensure an equitable resolution, a formal appraisal may be called for. Commonly, each side will hire its own appraiser. These two appraisers then select a third appraiser acceptable to both of them. The value of the property is determined by each appraiser, and the three evaluations are averaged to obtain a fair and true estimate of value.

New or Used: That Is Another Question

Whether to buy an existing building or construct one new on your property is an easy question to answer. For the novice investor, it is almost always wiser to buy an existing building than to get involved in construction.

The advantages of buying existing buildings are:

- The building produces income from the date of purchase.
- The purchase cost is a set, known figure.
- You may be able to buy at less than replacement cost.

In contrast, new construction entails the following:

- Getting preliminary zoning approvals.
- Working with architects, engineers, contractors, and the like.
- Getting construction and permanent loans. (Financing a construction project entails two loans: first, a short-term construction loan from a bank, and second, after the project is completed, a permanent, long-term mortgage to pay back the short-term construction loan.)

- Handling cost overruns caused by delays and other construction-related problems.

- Getting final approvals by municipality.

- Premarketing to possible tenants from a set of plans.

- Waiting for completion before generating an income stream.

In short, construction is a long and costly process, and not a good idea for small or novice real estate investors.

This is a good place to review some of the material we discussed in Part I. When looking at existing buildings to buy, you should focus on those rented cheaply, that are in good locations, and that can be had for less than replacement cost (which I explain shortly). The major benefit of this approach is that cheap rents produce lower net incomes, which will result in a low valuation for the property; thus it can be bought for less. As lower-rent leases expire, the rent can be raised to increase the return on the original investment and the related value of the property.

The biggest risk in owning commercial property is the loss of a tenant, but if the property has been rented cheaply you should be able to rerent (or re-lease) it at higher rents, eventually more than making up any losses generated from the vacancy. Furthermore, the capitalized value of the higher rent would give the property a higher value. For example, let's assume a 10-year-old lease with 5 years to go on it. The current rent is $24,000 per year, but the building is worth $40,000 per year in rent today. So:

$$\text{Value} = \frac{\text{Current net income}}{\text{Capitalization rate}} = \frac{\$24,000}{10\%} = \$240,000$$

If the tenant leaves and the property is rented at $40,000 per annum net:

$$\frac{\$40,000}{10\%} = \$400,000 \text{ (new value)}$$

The property value is now $400,000

Under the previous lease, it was $240,000

Increase in value $160,000

Rental levels result from supply, demand, and replacement cost of new buildings by the required rate of return. For example:

New building cost (10,000 sq. ft.) $1 million

Capitalization rate   10%

Required net income $100,000

Or

$$\frac{\text{Net rent } \$100,000}{10,000 \text{ feet}} = \$10 \text{ per foot}$$

DEFINITION

Required net income is the net income required to justify a selling price. If, for example, the construction cost is $100 per foot, and the desired rate of return is 10 percent, you would need a rent of $10 per foot (10 percent of 100 feet) *net* of expenses to justify the deal.

If you are getting $6 per foot net, and you want a 10 percent return, you would pay:

$$\frac{\text{Net rent } \$6}{10\%} = \$60 \text{ per sq. ft.}$$

Compare this with $100 per foot to build a new building. Paying $60 per foot for an older building that has been appraised as worthy of investment and is earning $6 per square foot net annual rents is a wiser decision than putting up a new building at $100 per square foot and requiring net rents of $10 per square foot in the same area.

Evaluation Approaches

There are three approaches you can choose from to appraise a property: the comparable sales approach (nicknamed COMPS), the replacement cost approach, and the capitalization of income approach (usually shortened to *income approach*). I'll explain each in turn.

Comparable Sales Approach

Under COMPS, you look for comparable properties that have sold recently in the area. This information can be obtained from county or town records offices. Most of these records are now on computerized databases, so you can look them up yourself or subscribe to real estate services that will sell you this information for a fee. Recently, most of this information has been made available online as well.

Looking at comparable properties and evaluating them on a building price-per-square-foot basis will give you a general idea of what the building you're interested should sell for. If the real estate market has been stable over the past one to two years, these evaluations provide reasonable comparisons.

The risks of using the comparable sales approach are:

- There may be no comparable properties that have been sold recently.

- The real estate market may have changed dramatically (either upward or downward) in the past two years, in which case comparables of previous periods probably do not accurately reflect current conditions.

As an example of using the COMPS approach, we'll say that the building we're interested in buying is 5,000 square feet, 10 years old, and in good condition. We'll compare it to the sales shown in Table 7.1.

TABLE 7.1 Comparison of Sales Data

Date	Size (sq. ft.)	Price	Price per Square Foot
January 1995	10,000	$600,000	$60
September 1995	8,000	$440,000	$55
March 1996	6,000	$300,000	$50
December 1996	7,500	$400,000	$53
January 1997	9,000	$380,000	$42
Average price per square foot (rounded off)			$52

Let's get back to the building we are interested in:

Square footage	5,000
Average price per sq. ft.	$52
Value based on the average price per sq. ft.	$260,000

The last deal done per the table was for $42 per square foot in January 1997.

Building size, sq. ft.	5,000
Last price done per sq. ft.	$42
Value based on last deal done	$210,000

You can see that the building we're interested in is worth somewhere between $210,000 ($42 per square foot) and $260,000 ($52 per square foot). We can average (that is, compare) the two:

$$\frac{\$210,000 + \$260,000}{2} = \$235,000$$

Therefore, using the comparable sales approach, we determine the value to be approximately $235,000.

The comparable sales approach can be used for any type of property. Sales and new deeds to the buyer have to be recorded along with the prices. A recording fee and transfer tax (based on price) are paid to record a new deed from a seller to a buyer.

Replacement Cost Approach

The replacement cost to evaluating property entails:

- Evaluating the land by comparing it to recent sales of similar land in the area.
- Getting estimates from builders or contractors of the cost of constructing a similar building today. The appraiser would allow for depreciation and obsolescence to arrive with a replacement cost "as is."

By checking comparable land sales or asking prices for similar raw land, we come up with a reasonable land value per square foot. This is done using comparables (COMPS), as we did in the previous section.

One major factor inherent in determining land value is zoning. Local zoning laws control your ability to build on a piece of land, and the value of land is a function of what you can do with it (this determines the income it will generate); the potential income, in turn, determines value.

DEFINITION

Zoning is the classification of the permitted usage of land by the local planning board. Zoning is usually part of a municipality's master plan.

For our first example of the replacement cost approach, we'll evaluate some purely agricultural midwestern farmland. The value of farmland is a function of crop yield and price. Let's say that 1 acre in Idaho can produce approximately 40 bushels of potatoes at $5 per bushel:

Gross income per acre	$200
Less cost of production (seed, fertilizer, labor, etc.)	$ 80
Profit per acre	$120

Capitalized at 10 percent, the price per acre equals $1,200. If the capitalization rate is 8 percent, the price per acre is:

$$\frac{120}{8\%} = \$1,500 \text{ per acre}$$

For our second example, we'll evaluate some commercially zoned land, in this case a corner acre, leased as is, to a fast-food chain for $3,000 per month, or $36,000 per year, net.

$$\text{Net rent (10\% cap rate)} = \frac{\$36,000}{10\%} = \$360,000 \text{ per acre}$$

For our third example, we'll consider a vacant lot in Manhattan whose size is is 40,000 square feet. Let's say that local zoning regulations allow you to build 10 times your land area. So in this case, 10 times 40,000 equals 400,000 square feet, which means you can build a 400,000 square foot building on that site. Let's also say that you can erect an office building in Manhattan for $150 per square foot.

Construction cost of Manhattan office building	<u>$150</u> per foot
Income of a new Manhattan office building	$ 40 per foot
Operating cost of a new Manhattan office building	$ 15 per foot
Operating profit of a new Manhattan office building	<u><u>$ 25</u></u> per foot

The capitalized value of operating profit of $25 per foot at 10 percent, then, is $250 per building foot.

If a value per new building foot is	$250
Less construction cost per foot	($150)
Difference	<u>$100</u>
Developer's profit (100 ÷ 2)	$ 50
Land would be half of the $100 or $50 per foot	$ 50
Total difference	<u><u>$100</u></u>

At $50 times the size of the building—400,000 buildable feet—the land is worth $50 times 400,000 square feet, or $20 million! The calculation for a 40,000-square-foot vacant lot zoned for an office building is:

$$\frac{\text{Land value } \$20 \text{ million}}{40,000 \text{ feet}} = \$500 \text{ per land foot!}$$

or $500 × 43560 sq. ft. (one acre) = $21,780,000 per acre!

If we take into account the fact that you can build 10 times your land area, each land square foot equals 10 buildable square feet. Thus, in Manhattan, the price of land is quoted at price per buildable foot.

Building Replacement Cost   As explained earlier, an appraiser will estimate the current replacement cost of the building in question. If you are buying a new building, you must ask builders or engineers in your area a couple of questions to determine estimates of what it would cost to erect such a building today. Probably you will be given a range of cost estimates, but they still should be in the same range, and so can be averaged. Our example here will be a 5,000-square-foot new office building. You would ask three local builders who do work in the area. Based on those interviews, let's say you get the following construction cost estimates:

Builder	Estimate
A	$250,000
B	$270,000
C	$240,000
Total bids	$760,000

So, in this case, $760,000 ÷ 3 bids = $253,333, the average cost of new building construction in that location.

If, on the other hand, you are buying an old building, you must have it inspected by an engineer or an experienced builder, who should tell you not only its general condition, but also the status of its component parts [heating, ventilation, and air conditioning (HVAC) system, plumbing, electrical system, elevators, roof, etc.]. For example, again using a 5,000-square-foot building, but this time one that is not new, values are shown in Table 7.2.

TABLE 7.2   Sample Values of Components of an Old Building

Property	New	Less 30 Years' Depreciation	Current Value
Building Shell (30 years old)*	$250,000	($187,500)	$ 62,500
Components (various lives) (as is)	$150,000	—	$150,000
Land (Based on COMPS)	$ 20,000	—	$ 20,000
Total	$420,000	($187,500)	$232,500

*Although the IRS says a building depreciates in 39.5 years, builders use 40 years.

The $187,500 depreciation of the building shell is determined as follows:

$$\frac{\text{Cost of building}}{40 \text{ years}} = \frac{\$250,000}{40 \text{ years}} = \$6,250 \text{ depreciation per year}$$

The building is 30 years old; thus 30 times $6,250 equal $187,500. (You can find out more in Appendix B.)

Of course, we would take the various estimates of costs and equipment and average them, then add the cost of the land plus the cost of the building to arrive at the replacement cost of the property. *In this example, the replacement cost of the land and the building is $232,500.*

Capitalization of Income Approach

With the capitalization of income (or simply *income*) approach, you take the property's net operating income and use that as a basis for value. You begin by analyzing the property's profit and loss (or operating income) as follows:

1. *Determine income.* Do this by reading and analyzing all leases. If the property is vacant and you have a potential tenant, you can use the new tenant's potential rent.

2. *Itemize expenses.* Analyze and check each of the following: real estate taxes (check local property tax records); insurance (ask your insurance broker); repairs (check your responsibility per leases and your building inspector); electricity (ask a local power supplier); fuel (check with a supplier); and management (ask your real estate broker or prospective manager; Chapter 9 covers property management).

3. *Replacement reserves.* Get the information from your engineer for the replacement reserves of component parts. After the building and its component parts have been inspected, the engineer will give a schedule of the remaining useful life of each part, along with how much money you should reserve annually for replacements.

Let's go through this process using the following hypothetical amounts:

Gross rental income (leases)	$42,000
Less operating costs:	
Real estate taxes	$ 5,000
Insurance	$ 2,000
Repairs	$ 2,500
Electricity	$ 1,000

Fuel	$ 4,000
Miscellaneous	$ 2,500
Total operating costs	$18,000
Net operating income	$24,000

Net operating income divided by our capitalization rate (or desired rate of return) equals the capitalized value, or value of the property based on income or $240,000. Table 7.3 shows how things work out for our example.

To summarize, the income approach is composed of the following parts:

- An income analysis, to determine actual projected net income. In our example, we did not provide (subtract) reserves for replacement, but this should be done in real life.

- Rate of return (capitalization rate) that you want from that type of investment.

NOTE

The capitalization rate is a function of the quality of the investment, determined by comparing it to similar investments elsewhere.

- The value based on income, which you get by taking the net income after reserves, then dividing by the capitalization rate desired.

TABLE 7.3   Calculating Capitalized Value

Net income is $24,000	Different Capitalization Rates				
	12%	11%	10%	9%	8%
Value is:					
	$24,000	$24,000	$24,000	$24,000	$24,000
	12%	11%	10%	9%	8%
Value based on income can be	$200,000	$218,182	$240,000	$266,667	$300,000

If a property has a short-term lease with low rents, and you are confident that you will be able to rerent at higher amounts upon expiration of the current lease, you should account for that as well. To do so, take the present value of the future income and discount it at your desired rate of return. Table 7.4 shows an example.

TABLE 7.4   Calculating Rerent Increases

	1	2	3	4	5	6	7	8	9
Year	1997	1998	1999	2000	2001	2002	2003	2004	2005
Net rent	$24,000	$24,000	$24,000	$24,000	$40,000	$42,000	$44,000	$46,000	$46,000

We would take the 10-year net income and apply our rate of return percentage discounted for time to get the present value of that current and future income. This can be done using financial calculators, computer programs, or present value tables.

> **NOTE**
>
> You can buy computer programs to make these calculations for you, or you can ask a consultant to compute them for you.

For the next example, we'll use a desired rate of return, or capitalization rate, of 10 percent, assume that the net operating income is $24,000 per annum, and say the value is $240,000, which is the net operating income ($24,000) divided by the capitalization rate (10 percent). Now let's look at the three approaches to value based on our 5,000-square-foot building with a net income of $24,000 per annum. Our calculations have resulted in the following:

	Page	
Comparable sales approach	146	$235,000
Replacement cost approach	150	$232,500
Income approach	151	$240,000
Average of the three		$235,833

The average was achieved simply by adding the three— *$707,500—then dividing by 3, which comes to $235,833, which rounds off* *to $236,000.* Thus the appraised value of the property would be $236,000.

CONCLUSION

In this chapter you have learned how to find properties and evaluate them. Once you have identified a property you like, have conducted your preliminary inspections, and have evaluated the property, you should know the price you are willing to pay. Then it's time to negotiate the purchase of the property with the seller.

CHAPTER

8

Negotiating, Financing, and Closing
Real Estate Transactions

Believe it or not, the most important part of the negotiation process is already behind you: gathering as much information as you can about the property you want to invest in and the circumstances leading to its being placed on the market. That's what the evaluation/appraisal process is for: to determine the value of the property and the price you are willing to pay for it. That price is the basis of your negotiations.

> **NOTE**
>
> Engage a competent real estate lawyer to represent and protect you in all real estate transactions. An attorney can also be a source of introductions to bankers, other deal makers, and real estate professionals. After negotiating with the seller and reaching a mutually acceptable price and terms, the contract of sale is prepared, usually by the seller's attorney or broker. The buyer's attorney reviews it before the buyer signs it.

By this stage of the real estate investment process, you have selected a property or properties you would like to buy, and you have done all your homework:

1. Conducted a preliminary inspection
2. Reviewed the income and expense statements
3. Compared the property with similar real estate in the area
4. Questioned the broker in detail about the property
5. Determined the price you are willing to pay

TIP

I recommend that you identify two or three properties as potential investments, in case your first deal doesn't come to fruition.

The next step is to verify that you have been given complete documentation about the property, which includes but is not limited to:

- Copies of leases
- Lot number and area of land
- Survey or detailed diagram of the property, showing actual borders and structures on the property
- Building size and age
- Zoning regulations for the area
- Real estate tax, insurance, and other expense data

After doing your preliminary reviews and information gathering, you take the income and expense projection and make allowances for reserves to determine an approximate value, as explained in Chapter 7. This amount should be the maximum price you are willing to pay for this particular property, called the *target price*. Now it's time to negotiate.

TIP

I caution novice investers not to get carried away with the "thrill of the chase" and agree to pay more for a property so as not to lose the deal. Trust me, there will always be numerous new opportunities in your price range as long as you are patient.

NEGOTIATING

Webster's defines *negotiate* as "to confer with another so as to arrive at the settlement of some matter." Another definition given is "to convert into cash or the equivalent value." In real estate, we function under both definitions. What we're negotiating is *market value,* which I defined as "the price agreed to by a willing buyer and a willing seller in an *arm's-length transaction,* without undue pressure on either side to agree."

DEFINITION

An *arm's-length transaction* is one involving unrelated parties, where neither exerts undue pressure on the other to agree. The proverbial "offer you cannot refuse" obviously is not an arm's-length transaction.

Assuming that the target price is realistic, based on location of property, condition of property, income and expense analysis, and capitalization of net income at a *reasonable market rate of return,* the negotiation process will follow these steps:

NOTE

Depending on the nature of the property, your return can range from 8 percent for very safe AAA net leases to 12 percent for secondary properties with high rental turnovers and so on. I usually use a 10 percent rate of return.

1. Compare your target price to the asking price of the seller.
2. Offer 10 percent less than your target price.
3. If the seller counteroffers with a reduction in his or her asking price, raise your offer closer to your target price.

DEFINITION

A *counteroffer* is both a rejection of an offer and the issuance of a new offer by the other side.

As a negotiator, you have to be at least outwardly tough, especially when you are a novice, so that you come across as someone who knows what you want and how to get it. Make it clear that you have spent time and effort researching the property in question, that you know the value of what you are negotiating, and that you have set a maximum price you are willing to pay (which should be interpreted to mean that you are willing to "walk" if you can't conclude the transaction at that price).

In any transaction, if you do decide to "walk," don't slam the door shut, because the other side may come back in the future and may be more willing to either meet your terms or to negotiate closer to them. Or you may have occasion to deal with this party in the future, so stay focused on the long term, even if you're disappointed with the current deal. Ultimately, the best negotiation is one in which both sides feel that "maybe we could have done a little better, but. . . ."

To demonstrate how this process bears out, let's put some numbers in as examples. For our first scenario, we'll say that the asking price of the seller is $240,000 and the target price of the buyer is $200,000. During the first round of negotiating, the following takes place:

1. Buyer offers 10 percent less than $200,000, or $180,000.

2. Seller counteroffers with $220,000.

They could split the difference (average), which would result in this calculation:

$$\frac{\$180,000 + \$220,000}{2} = \$200,000$$

Since $200,000 is our target price, we agree to go ahead with the deal.

For our second scenario, we'll assume the asking price of the seller is $250,000 and the target price of the buyer is $200,000. In this case, the following "opening" moves are:

1. Buyer offers 10 percent less than target price of $200,000, which is $180,000.

2. Seller refuses to counteroffer with a lower amount.

3. Buyer offers $190,000. If the seller refuses to budge from his or her $250,000 asking price, the buyer will courteously back out of the negotiations to "buy something else."

In our third scenario, let's say the asking price of the seller is $190,000 and the target price of the buyer is $200,000—that is correct: the seller is asking for less than we are willing to pay. In this case, I would offer $180,000, and then if the seller remained firm or made a small counteroffer (like $185,000), I would agree. We would then proceed to have the seller's attorney prepare a formal contract of sale, and eventually finalize or close the deal.

Using Brokers or Other Intermediaries

Many experienced buyers prefer to negotiate through a broker or other intermediary, such as an attorney. A broker who can, on an ongoing basis, find good properties for a buyer, and who is willing to work hard to get both sides to agree during the negotiation process, is worth every penny of his or her commission.

During the negotiation process, the broker or other intermediary will:

- Make an offer on his or her principal's behalf.
- Relay the seller's counteroffer to the principal.
- Allow the principal time to consider.
- Play the "good guy-bad guy" routine; that is, engage in repartee such as, "I agree, but my principal (i.e., boss) is pretty tough. But, he does have the money; he is for real."

Negotiating Leases

A common component of the overall negotiation process of purchasing commercial real estate is the negotiation or renegotiation of leases (we cover leases in more detail in Chapter 9). Here, too, the most important factor is information. All parties involved—tenants, landlord, seller, and buyer—should do their market research, specifically to determine what similar space is renting for. Armed with this information, they should be able to come to terms.

DEFINITION

Renegotiation is an attempt to negotiate a change in the terms of an existing agreement—in this case, a lease.

In addition to negotiating (or renegotiating) the amount of the rent, lease clauses usually have to be negotiated as well. Lease clauses are explained in Chapter 9.

Negotiating these clauses is where being tough will stand you in good stead. As an example, let us assume that a new lease is being negotiated, and that the landlord, Mr. Dealmaker, sees that his tenant is doing good business and apparently making a lot of money, so he asks for a higher-than-market increase in rent. The tenant, Ms. Shopkeeper, must then calculate how much it would cost to move her business before agreeing or disagreeing.

Ms. Shopkeeper must factor in these costs of moving her business: notifying customers, paying moving expenses, and incurring the losses during the downtime. But if the capitalized value (rate the return) of the cost of moving is significantly less than the additional rent, she may decide to move. For example:

Old rent (lease expired) per year	$ 30,000
Proposed new rent	$ 90,000
Difference is increase of $60,000 per year	
Rent at alternative location (10-year base)	$ 20,000
Cost of move including construction, delays, and lost business	$150,000
Desired capitalization rate or rate of return	15%
Capitalized cost of moving ($150,000 × 15%)	$ 22,500
Plus rent	$ 20,000
Total cost of moving per year over 10 years	$ 42,500

Thus, instead of paying $90,000 per year rent, moving to a new location would cost $42,500 per year, so Ms. Shopkeeper would save $47,500 ($90,000 minus $42,500).

The art (and it is an art) of business negotiation is predicated on the perceived costs and benefits *of* the parties involved *by* the parties involved. To become a good negotiator, it's very important that you try to find out what the other side's problems are (where he or she "hurts") in relationship to this deal. Then you work to help him or her solve those problems, which should result in a satisfactory deal that meets both your needs.

One common example of this problem-solution aspect of negotiation arises regarding certain tax effects of a transaction, which both parties may benefit from if they cooperate. You could work together to formulate the terminology and manner to present the closing to the Internal Revenue Service (legally, of course). The tax benefits of investing in real estate are addressed in Appendix B, but I'll mention two examples here for the purpose of this discussion:

- *IRC paragraph 1031.* This is an exchange for another property that would allow the seller defer taxes to the new property.

- *Installment sale of property.* The seller takes back a Purchase Money Mortgage (PMM) to spread the profit over time. Under this method, the seller reports profit only as he or she receives it (over the life of the mortgage), to, hopefully, put him or her in a lower tax bracket. (I explain more about installment sales later in the chapter.)

Contracts of Sale

The end of the negotiation process is marked by the preparation of a formal *contract of sale,* which enumerates the terms to which you and the seller have agreed. You should have already done your perfunctory inspection before starting to negotiate, and finally, getting a signed contract of sale. Now is the time to hire a professional engineer (an inspector) to thoroughly check out the property and give you a report. Note that, today, environmental inspections should be done for all real estate acquisitions, to ensure you're not walking into a potentially contentious situation resulting from hidden environmental abuses.

Usually, the seller instructs his or her attorney to prepare the contract of sale, which comprises:

- The property address and legal descriptions of the property.
- Agreed-upon price and terms (all cash or subject to financing).
- A financing contingency clause; that is, how much time the buyer has to get a loan. Most such clauses have a deadline for a buyer to produce a loan commitment, usually three months in a commercial transaction.
- An inspection contingency clause—how much time the buyer has to physically inspect the property. If it is a commercial property, this would include examination and verification of leases; verification of expenses; zoning and other local restrictions; and physical inspections, including environmental.
- The amount of the *good-faith deposit,* or down payment, on contract. Usually, this amount is 10 percent for home purchases,

subject to conventional financing, or as low as 1 percent of the purchase price (or even less if the home sale is to be financed by a first-time home buyer or similar special program requiring a minimum down payment, such as 3 percent).

In commercial real estate deals subject to financing (or seller-financed; more on that later), the good-faith deposit is usually a percentage of the ultimate down payment after financing (usually one-fourth of the equity).

The good-faith money is held in escrow by the seller's attorney or title insurance company until the closing of the transaction. (Tip: Request that this money be held in an interest-bearing account.)

DEFINITIONS

Conventional financing refers to the normal financing done by lenders usually for no more than 80 percent of the value of the property. The federal government has loan guarantee programs to help small investors; for example, the Federal Housing Administration (FHA) helps first-time home buyers and the Federal Mortgage Association (FMA) helps small apartment building investors. These agencies do not provide funds; they issue guarantees to lenders, encouraging lenders to grant loans to targeted groups.

Escrow is either money or property temporily held in trust. The downpayment on a contract should be held in escrow either until the deal closes—in which case it is used as part of the buyer's investment—or the deal falls apart—in which case it is returned to the buyer.

A *title insurance company* issues to the buyer of a piece of property an insurance policy that guarantees ownership. These companies were created to insure against phony sales. Before issuing a policy, the title company will check the local property records to verify that the seller is "rightful" and thus has the authority to sell. In the process, the title insurance company gathers deeds and mortgages, information on tax arrears, old unpaid mortgages, or other open items that must be cleared up before the closing. The buyer is given an owner's title insurance policy, and most lenders insist on being given a mortgage insurance policy for their loans.

Contingencies

I want to elaborate on the contingencies (which you can regard as deadlines) just mentioned as part of the contract of sale. There are two major types: inspection and financing contingencies.

Inspection Contingencies The deadline for the formal inspection of the property and its accompanying books and records is usually within 30 days following the signing of the contract of sale.

If the property does not pass inspection, or unexpected problems are found, one of three things may happen:

- The buyer may withdraw from the transaction and get the escrow deposit back.
- The seller may agree to correct the problem, but this may require an extension of the closing date.
- The buyer and seller may agree to an adjustment in price. Of course, if the buyer is trying to secure a bank loan, the bank would also have to agree.

Financing Contingencies A formal loan commitment by a lending institution may take 30 to 90 days. Although buyers may have an informal arrangement with a lender with whom they regularly deal, getting a formal loan commitment through the committee system of a financial institution takes time. The financing contingency states the *parameters*, or terms, under which the buyer is willing to borrow: for example, "subject to 80 percent financing at an interest rate of 8 to 9 percent, self-liquidating over 15 years."

If you, the buyer, cannot get a loan according to the financing contingency terms, you have the right to terminate the contract and get your deposit back. You may also be able to withdraw from the deal if you cannot get a formal financing commitment from a financial institution before the financing deadline.

In addition to the contingency clauses and related deadline dates, the closing date is also set in the contract of sale, usually for approximately 30 days after the last deadline has been met. (More on the closing at the end of the chapter.)

Loss of Deposit

It is important to understand that if you, the buyer, do not notify the seller of problems you have with any of the stated contingencies, it will be presumed there are none. If you try to renege later, or if you do not proceed subject to the terms of the contract (or agreement), you probably will lose (*forfeit*) your good-faith deposit. The terms of this happening should also be spelled out in the contract.

The reasons you will forfeit your good-faith deposit for failure to notify the seller prior to contingency deadlines of your intention to withdraw (as a result of the inspections or difficulty in getting financing) are that the seller, by signing a formal contract of sale with you, has:

1. Taken the property "off the market" for a period of time. He or she cannot sell to anyone else before the termination of this contract.
2. Incurred legal and other costs dealing with this prospective buyer.

If you follow the terms of the contract and meet all deadlines and notification requirements, you can usually back out of the deal based on certain contingencies, for example:

- The engineer found severe problems with the property, including those of an environmental nature—the presence of asbestos or water pollution, for example.
- You couldn't get a loan from a lender per the terms of the contract.

Summary of the Negotiation Process

In most real estate transactions, after some typical "backing-and-forthing," you usually will be able to get the deal done at close to the target price you set. If, however, it becomes clear that you cannot get the seller to agree to sell at your realistically determined target price, accept defeat and walk away. A good rule of thumb to follow in this regard is that if you cannot come to an agreement with a seller within a month—two at the most—it is time to walk. But accept defeat graciously, because, as mentioned earlier, the seller may call you back if he or she cannot get another buyer to agree to his or her terms.

For the purposes of this discussion, we're going to assume that you and the seller have agreed to terms—that you've had a contract of sale prepared—and that you are going to proceed with the deal. Now all you need is the money! That's what the next section addresses: the all-important topic of financing your real estate investment.

FINANCING COMMERCIAL REAL ESTATE

At this point in the real estate investment process, you have accumulated your initial cash investment to be used for a down payment and closing costs; you have found a suitable income-producing property; you and the seller have signed a formal contract of sale, which includes, among other pertinent information, subject-to-inspection and subject-to-financing clauses detailing the contingencies described in the previous section; and, finally, you have agreed to a reasonable period of time to get a mortgage commitment (ideally, at least two to three months).

Determining Interest Rates

Interest is simply the cost of money. A bank, in effect, borrows money from individuals (savers) and pays them interest on that money. Therefore, in a bank's accounting records, a savings account is recorded as a debt; that is, it is money payable to a saver. On the saver's side of the equation, a savings account is a receivable from a bank; it is not cash on hand. That is why, when a saver makes a deposit in a bank account, the bank *credits* (or increases the debt or liability) the amount the bank owes to the saver. When a withdrawal is made, it represents a reduction of the bank's debt to the saver and a *debit* (decrease) to the bank's payable account.

Interest charged on mortgage loans and interest paid on savings deposits go up and down together; the usual *spread,* or difference, is 3 percent. Interest is a function of inflation (usually, the inflation rate plus 3 percent) and the demand and supply of money for financing. The benchmark by which interest rates are determined is the *federal funds overnight rate,* the rate at which our central bank, the Federal Reserve, charges or pays banks for overnight balances. All checking transactions go through the Federal Reserve Clearing-house, where they are processed. The Federal Reserve sets the federal funds interest rate, which in turn affects all other interest rates accordingly.

A bank or other lending institution will borrow money from savers at one rate of interest and lend it out to borrowers at a higher rate of interest. The differential is used to cover administrative costs and loss reserves, and, hopefully, leave a profit.

Most banks net approximately a 1 to 2 percent return on total assets. This is made up of:

Interest income (for example)	6%
Less interest costs	(3%)
Gross profit on loans	3%
Less administration costs, bad debts, etc.	(1.3%)
Net income	1.7%

You'll see more clearly how interest rates affect real estate transactions when we discuss the various types of mortgages later in the chapter.

How Mortgages Work

To borrow mortgage money, the owner of a property agrees to give a lender a *lien* (mortgage) on the property in return for the loan. The owner who gives a lender the right to record a mortgage lien is called a *mortgagor*. The lender who accepts a mortgage lien from an owner of a piece of property is called a *mortgagee*.

> **DEFINITION**
>
> A *lien*, in the context of real estate transactions is a legal monetary claim on a property.

Lenders will expect to see copies of leases and service contracts, if any, plus a projected income statement. Other lender requirements include:

- *Biographical data (resume) and financial statements of the buyers.* This includes a credit check on the borrowers by the lenders. A good idea is to do your own credit check on yourself (and the members of your group, if applicable) before the lender does. Don't be unpleasantly surprised by something in your financial past that you or one of the members of your group may have forgotten about but that may impact your being granted financing.

- *Income analysis.* This includes copies of leases, tax bills, insurance policies, and operating costs. All leases should be carefully examined during the inspection period. We go through an income analysis example next.

- *Description of the property.* This is part of a certified appraisal report prepared by a Member of the Appraisal Institute (see Chapter 7) or similar organization. It includes the physical and legal description of the property, an up-to-date survey, and photographs. The survey is submitted by a licensed surveyor. This is a drawing of the legal borders of the property (the length and width, called *metes and bounds* from Old English), any structures, and easements (the right to go on another person's property).

- *Official physical inspections by a professional engineer.* This will include what's called a *Phase I Environmental Inspection*—an overall inspection of the property to ensure that it meets environmental standards. If problems or abuses are found, other inspection phases will ensure full evaluation of the property. These inspections determine whether the property being transferred has, for example, asbestos, underground storage tanks containing dangerous substances, or any other environmental hazards. Most lenders will insist that environmental problems be corrected before they lend money on a property. The cost of correcting anything not meeting environmental safety standards is the responsibility of the seller.

  In addition to the Phase I Environmental Inspection, an inspection should include checking out the overall condition of the property: the roof; electrical wiring and panel boxes; plumbing and drainage systems; heating, ventilation, and air conditioning (HVAC) systems; and so on. A professional inspector or engineer is hired for this, arranged and paid for by the buyer.

All costs of meeting these lender requirements are the responsibility of the borrower.

With those essentials in mind for getting financing, let's go through an example of income analysis:

Selling price of property	$200,000
Net income of property per income statement (after verification)	$ 20,000

Capitalization rate, or rate of return:

$$\frac{\text{Income}}{\text{Selling price}} \quad \frac{\$\ 20,000}{\$200,000} = 10\%$$

Thus, the property would provide a 10 percent return on a cash investment.

Loan requested $150,000

Percentage of loan to value:

$$\frac{\text{Loan}}{\text{Value}} \quad \frac{\$150,000}{\$200,000} = 75\%$$

Most lenders will not lend more than 70 to 80 percent of value unless triple-A tenants are involved and debt coverage (the amount by which the net income covers the *debt service*—or payments—on debt) is at least 1.20 times the amount of the debt. Let us assume we can get the following loan for $150,000.

Interest   8%

Term   25-year self-liquidating

Annual payment $15,000

Debt coverage ratio:

$$\frac{\text{Annual net income}}{\text{Debt service (annual payments)}} \quad \frac{\$20,000}{\$15,000} = 1.33 \text{ times}$$

You can see in this example that the $20,000 annual net income of the property is 1.333 times the annual debt service of $15,000. Significant factors in income analysis of the property are:

- If the current rents are high or low compared to similar properties in the area.
- Expiration dates of the leases—would the leases renew at higher or lower rents?
- Financial strength of the tenants.
- Stability of the tenants—how long have they been there and how successful is their business? You can determine this by spending time at the property on a semi-regular basis during your negotiation period to see the volume of the traffic, and so on.

Environmental Protection

Lenders insist on Phase I Environmental Inspections because, in the event of foreclosure, they do not want to be stuck with a "tainted" property. Banks and institutional lenders are considered by the public to have "deep pockets," that is, plenty of money, and so are vulnerable to lawsuits. To protect themselves from the costs of cleaning up an environmentally unsound property and of potential lawsuits resulting from the infraction, lenders take great care to ensure that properties for which they grant loans are safe from this risk.

No lender will loan money on an environmentally compromised property, so the buyer can:

■ Convince the seller to agree to correct the problems before closing. This will have to be done by a licensed environmental specialist, and will be subject to inspection.

■ Negotiate with the seller for a reduction in price commensurate with the cost of correcting the problem. If lenders refuse to grant a loan to the buyer, the seller may have to agree to finance the buyer.

■ Back out of the deal and have the escrow money returned.

Lenders are usually willing to grant a loan, assuming the following:

■ They have funds to lend.

■ The property meets their loan criteria.

■ The property appraisal confirms the value or approximates the selling price.

■ The income and expense schedule has been checked by the appraiser.

■ The ratio of loan to value does not exceed 70 to 80 percent of property value.

■ The debt coverage is at least 1.2 times. This means the net income from the property is 1.2 times debt service (interest plus amortization), not including escrows.

- The borrower is deemed reliable, based on the traditional "three Cs of credit": character, character, character.

The Commitment or Agreement to Lend

After lenders review this checklist, they give the prospective buyer a letter stating that they are willing to make a loan. But the buyer is not home free yet; often this letter states that the agreement is subject to some additional requirements, which at this juncture include:

- Payment of a commitment fee by the borrower. This fee is usually 1 or 2 percent of the loan. Usually, this fee is refundable if the bank does not go through with the loan; or it may be credited at the closing of the property and related mortgage.
- Updated surveys.
- Appraisals.
- Physical and environmental inspections.
- Title inspection, owner's title, and mortgagee's title insurance.
- Miscellaneous other requirements, such as personal credit checks.

> **NOTE**
>
> Banks today issue either commitment or proposal letters delineating their agreement to make a loan with interest. And, to protect themselves from potential negative surprises, most banks include an extensive listing of requirements in this letter of agreement or proposal. Do not be daunted by this list; by the time you receive it, most of the requirements will have already been met.

A copy of this letter goes to both the buyer's and the seller's attorneys, who work together with the bank's attorney to finish the deal—that is, to address all contingencies in the loan commitment or proposal. Then all three attorneys agree to a *closing,* or settlement, date for the transaction.

Mortgage Payments

Upon borrowing the money, the owner-borrower (mortgagor) gives a lien (mortgage) on the property and a note (which includes the terms of the loan agreement) to the bank (mortgagee). The agreement calls for periodic payments (usually monthly) to the bank. Payments are applied first to interest; the remainder goes to reducing the balance of the loan.

DEFINITION

Amortization is the reduction in the loan balance.

Some mortgages may also call for escrow payments, usually for real estate taxes and insurance, because real estate taxes have legal precedence over mortgages. Nonpayment of real estate taxes may result in foreclosure of the property by the government or subsequent real estate tax lien buyers. Thus, the lender wants the liens to be paid for its own protection. Lenders want the real estate taxes paid along with the mortgage payment to ensure that there will be enough money to pay them. The bank then pays the real estate taxes directly.

NOTE

When a mortgage is paid off, either through normal monthly payments or at a closing, the lender is required to give the borrower a document acknowledging that the loan has been paid off or satisfied. This document is called a *satisfaction of mortgage*, and it must be in "recordable" form for inclusion in county property records.

Legal Order of Liens on Property

Liens on all properties, frequently dating back many years, are recorded in city or town property records, in chronological order, something like the example given in Table 8.1.

You can find this information by doing a title search of the property records. Title insurance companies do this before the closing; they help clear up any problems and provide an insurance policy to the buyer.

Foreclosure

In the event of foreclosure, if the property does not bring in enough money at a foreclosure auction, the difference is called a *shortfall* or *deficiency.* If you have personally guaranteed the mortgage, you are legally responsible for reimbursing the lender for the shortfall.

TABLE 8.1 Sample Property Record

January 1, 1920	Sale by A to B	$10,000
January 1, 1920	First mortgage lien to local bank	$ 8,000
June 30, 1935	Sale from B to C	$30,000
June 30, 1935	Satisfaction of local bank, January 1, 1920 mortgage	($ 8,000)
June 30, 1935	First mortgage lien to new bank	$20,000
July 5, 1936	July 5, 1936 lien against C for	$10,000

To illustrate, we'll use the previous example as a starting point:

Purchase price of property	$200,000
Less mortgage	$150,000
Cash investment or initial equity	$ 50,000
Net income of property	$ 20,000
Less payment of only interest on mortgage	
($150,000 × 8%)	($ 12,000)
Net cash flow after mortgage payments	$ 8,000

An economic downturn or other negative event could result in the following:

Net income of property drops 50% to	$ 10,000
Mortgage payment stays constant at	($ 12,000)
Resulting in an out-of-pocket annual cash loss of	($ 2,000)

As general market rental rates decrease, so do property market values. We'll use a 10 percent rate of return or capitalization rate. Value of income property is the net income divided by the capitalization rate. In this case:

$$\frac{\text{Net income}}{\text{Cap rate}} = \frac{\$10,000}{10\%} = \$100,000$$

The property is now worth	$100,000
The mortgage is still	($150,000)
Shortfall in value	($ 50,000)

The $50,000 shortfall is also known as *negative equity*.

Two things have resulted from a drop in values:

- The income is now less than the amount required to pay the mortgage. If the amount—which in this case is $2,000 per year—is small enough, you might choose to pay it out of the personal funds or other income you have available, the intention being to keep the property and wait until the next upturn. If you cannot afford to make up the $2,000 annual shortfall, you might lose the property to foreclosure, in which case you might still be liable for the deficiency, illustrated as follows:

  Selling price at foreclosure auction $100,000

  Less the amount of the mortgage   ($150,000)

      Shortfall or deficiency   ($ 50,000)

- If the property only sells for $100,000 at a foreclosure auction, and the mortgage is $150,000, the result is a $50,000 shortfall, called a *deficiency*. A borrower who has personally guaranteed a loan is still legally responsible for a deficiency, unless he or she can come to an accommodation with the lender.

The good news is that often during poor economic conditions, when all property values have dropped, banks are willing to defer—or even to forgive—part of the interest payments. Lenders, whether banks or pension plans, generally do not want to take possession of—that is, foreclose—properties, especially in economic downturns, because doing so requires additional cash outlays for management, legal expenses, real estate taxes, insurance, repairs, broker's commissions, and so on. Foreclosing and taking ownership of a property forces the lender to also assume its management responsibilities, and possibly to have to resell the property at a loss. Moreover, foreclosed properties may take a while to sell (though lenders can deduct these losses from tax returns).

Unlike margined stocks, as discussed in the section on leverage and the stock market, it is very difficult for a lender to foreclose (also referred to as *liquidate out*) on a mortgaged property.

In practice, the following is the usual sequence of events preceding a foreclosure:

1. The lender typically will not act until three or more payments have been missed, at which point a form letter goes

NOTE

It is beyond the scope of this book to delve into the legalities of foreclosure. Every state in the country has different laws and procedures. If you ever face foreclosure, it is imperative to seek the advice and services of a competent attorney.

to the borrower advising him or her that he or she will be declared in default unless payments are made or some payment arrangement is entered into. If the borrower ignores the warning letter, the matter is turned over to the lender's attorney, who, in turn, sends a formal default letter to the borrower.

2. If the borrower still takes no action to rectify the matter, the bank's attorneys start a legal foreclosure action. The borrower is "properly served" in the form of an original copy of a document called a *notice of foreclosure*. The borrower generally has 20 to 30 days in which to respond in a court hearing. (There are various legal maneuvers a borrower may engage in to gain additional time, but again, make sure these are undertaken with the advice of a qualified attorney.)

3. A summary judgment hearing date is requested by the lender. The date is usually a function of how backlogged the court calendar is.

4. Assuming no further snags, adjournments, postponements, or other delays, at the final hearing, a judgment is usually rendered on behalf of the lender for:

- The balance of the mortgage
- The accrued interest, and possibly penalty interest if it is provided for in the mortgage
- The disbursements, such as property insurance, real estate taxes, legal fees, and so on paid by the lender
- The attorney's fees and court costs
- Any miscellaneous foreclosure-related expenses

Subsequently, the court sets an auction date for the property. (The address, date, and time of the auction, along with contact

information for the bank representatives, must be as widely advertised as possible to attract as many potential buyers as possible to
the auction—to result in as high a price as possible.) All told, the
foreclosure process can take from four months to well over a year,
depending on the backlog in the courts.

Foreclosure laws are designed not only to protect the lender but
also to give the owner-borrower plenty of time and opportunity to
"cure" or correct the default and to keep his or her property. Usually,
up to the time the gavel drops at the foreclosure auction, if the borrower can come in with the money he or she can redeem the property.

Bankruptcy
During an economic downturn, a borrower-owner always has the
option to declare bankruptcy. In-depth coverage of this topic is
beyond the scope of this book, but for the purposes of this discussion, be aware that there are generally two stages to bankruptcy:

1. *Reorganization.* The court is asked to restructure the debt and
   change the payment terms.
2. *Liquidation, or sale.* If an agreement cannot be reached, or if the
   borrower wants to "clean house," liquidation takes place. If
   there are not enough assets, the lower-ranked creditors lose.

As stated previously, a borrower who has personally guaranteed a loan is still responsible for any deficiency unless he or she
can come to an accommodation with the lender.

Types of Mortgages

There are numerous kinds of loan products. In the process of
researching your mortgage options for your real estate investments,
you'll hear terms such as *adjustable-rate mortgages* (ARMs), *self-
liquidating, fixed-rate, balloon,* and others. In this section, I describe
the most common loans granted to real estate investors, and identify the advantages and disadvantages of each for novice investors.

Self-Liquidating Mortgages
Self-liquidating refers to mortgages whose payments are calculated
so that the loan is completely paid off over a specific period of time.
The mortgage payment includes the interest and enough amortization to pay the loan off by the stated date. For example, for a loan

of $150,000 with a mortgage term of 8 percent that is self-liquidating over 25 years:

Year 1

Payment per amortization table with interest at 8% and a 25-year term (or *payout*)	$15,000
Initially, of that amount, 8% of $150,000, or	$12,000 is interest
Balance applied to loan reduction	$ 3,000

Year 2

Mortgage payment	$15,000
Interest: 8% of loan balance of $147,000 ($150,000 − $3,000)	$11,760
Applied to loan reduction	$ 3,240

Notice that the amount representing change in interest is 8 percent of the prior periods loan reduction ($3,000 × 8% = $240).

Interest year 1	$12,000
Interest year 2	$11,760
Reduction in interest	$ 240

Principal payment year 1	$ 3,000
Principal payment year 2	$ 3,240
Increase in annual loan reduction	$ 240

Year 3

Mortgage payment	$15,000
Interest: 8% of ($147,000 − $3,240) or $143,760 equals	$11,500
Loan reduction	$ 3,500

Summary of year 3 reduction in interest

Interest year 2	$11,760
Interest year 3	$11,500
Loan reduction	$ 260

Principal payment year 3	$ 3,500
Principal payment year 2	$ 3,240
Increase in principal payment	$ 260

As you can see, every year the amount applied to interest decreases as the loan is paid down, and the amount attributable to principal increases as the interest portion drops. As this continues over the life of a self-liquidating mortgage, eventually interest payments drop and principal payments rise to the point where principal payments exceed interest payments until the loan is paid off. Toward the end, virtually all payments go to principal.

The primary advantage of a self-liquidating mortgage is that the borrower knows that he or she is making payments not only on interest, but to reduce the principle of the loan as well. The primary disadvantage is that because it is usually a long-term loan, interest tends to be a little higher than on shorter-term balloon mortgages, described next.

Balloon Mortgages
Balloon mortgages are shorter-term loans that come due (*balloon*) on an established date, meaning the balance must be paid off on that date or the loan is in default. Therefore, it is very important that when you take out a balloon loan you plan from its inception how you will get the money to pay it off when it balloons. You would do this typically by setting aside money from the net income of the property in interest-bearing accounts. Or, if you're investing as part of a group, the members can agree to put up their individual pro rata shares of the amounts at the due date.

Using our previous example:

Mortgage	$150,000
Payable interest only at 8% per annum	$ 12,000
Due date	June 30, 2008

Since no payments on the principle have been made (interest only), on June 30, 2008, the $150,000 must be paid to the lender.

A major advantage of balloon mortgages/loans to novice investors is that, because lenders do not have to tie up the money for a long time, balloon mortgages are usually easier to get and have lower interest rates. Lenders can more easily match up deposits (sources of money) with loan maturities (a practice explained in the upcoming section on sources of mortgages). Furthermore, usually the interest charged and total payments are less than those for a self-liquidating loan, which may provide additional cash flow for the owner-borrower during the term of the loan.

The major disadvantage of this type of loan is that it may come due when the borrower does not have the money to pay it off, or interest rates may have risen. Theoretically, before a balloon loan comes due, the borrower has enough time to negotiate a new loan with the same lender or go to another lender. And most banks usually are willing to extend balloon loans subject to possible modifications, which may include extension fees and a higher interest rate.

Another potential disadvantage of balloon mortgages is that bank lending requirements may change in the interim between the assignment of the loan and its due date, so that banks may no longer want this type of loan in their portfolios and therefore may not be willing to renegotiate the loan if the borrower cannot meet the original payment deadline.

Fixed-Rate Mortgages
Fixed-rate mortgages are those for which the interest rate does not change over the term of the loan. The advantage to borrowers is that they have a fixed, predictable cost. The advantage to lenders is that they can more easily match deposit maturities and loan maturities. The disadvantage to both is the potential negative impact of swings in interest rates.

DEFINITION

Maturity is the date when a financial instrument comes due. In the case of a loan, a maturity is the date by which it must be paid back.

Drop in Interest Rates   If interest rates drop, borrowers may be stuck paying the higher rate. Theoretically, they could do one of two things:

Get a new loan at a lower interest rate and pay off the old loan. The disadvantage of this is that a new loan will entail payment of broker and bank fees, reappraisals, mortgage title insurance, local document taxes, other closing costs, attorneys' fees, possible prepayment penalties, and so on. These could easily add up to 5 percent of the mortgage loan.

DEFINITION

Many lenders, in order to ensure that they will get the benefit of a certain number of years of return on the funds they have set aside for the loan, may charge a *prepayment penalty* if the loan is paid off early. Prepayment penalties are usually a percentage of the loan for a certain number of years (usually under five) or a sliding scale. For example:

One year 5%

Two years 4%

Three years 3%

and so on

Lenders have to look for ways to reinvest the funds. The prepayment fees help them make up for this and would discourage the borrower from paying off the loan ahead of schedule.

Try to renegotiate the interest rate with the existing mortgage holder by threatening to refinance (get a new mortgage) elsewhere and thus pay off the mortgage. The lender may agree to lower the interest rate if you have been a good borrower (made payments on time and expeditiously replied to bank requests for inspections and so on). Also, if you do prepay the lender will have to relend at the lower rates.

Increase in Interest Rates   If interest rates go up, borrowers continue to pay the same fixed interest rate, so lenders lose the opportunity to earn the higher rates.

Self-Liquidating, Fixed-Rate Mortgages
Self-liquidating, fixed-rate mortgages are the best type of mortgages for novice investors. Investors are protected from interest rate fluctuations and the risk of large balloon loan payments coming due at inopportune times.

With self-liquidating, fixed-rate mortgages, investors can feel secure that over a certain period of time the loan will be paid off by the property income (though in temporary economic downturns, borrowers may have to help make payments). Upon maturity of a self-liquidating, fixed-rate loan, investors own the property free and clear, and the money that went to paying off the loan starts representing additional income to the borrower. For example:

Cost	$200,000
Net rental income	$ 20,000
Loan	$150,000
Payments (8% self-liquidating, 25 years)	$ 13,893
Interest is 8% of $150,000	$ 12,000
Loan reduction is	$ 1,893

During an economic downturn, let's say that the net rental income before debt service falls to $10,000 per year, but that debt service remains at $13,893 per year. In this case, we have:

Shortfall: recession income	$10,000
Less mortgage payments	($13,893)
Shortage	($ 3,893)

Remember what I said in Part I: As an investor, you should have enough investment cash reserves to protect you from economic downturns. In this case, you could pay the $3,893 per annum shortage out of your earnings or reserves until the recession passes and rental income goes back up.

I recommend that the maximum length of a self-liquidating mortgage be no more than 15 years, for these reasons:

- You pay off the property faster.
- It is a form of forced savings.

The difference in the payments between various maturities (lengths of mortgages) is relatively small (see Table 8.2 for an example).

The differences between 15 years and 30 years of monthly mortgage payments are shown in Table 8.3.

TABLE 8.2 Self-Liquidating Monthly Payment Table for $100,000

Interest	10 Years	12 Years	15 Years	20 Years	25 Years	30 Years
8%	$1,213.28	$1,082.46	$ 955.68	$839.45	$771.82	$733.77
9%	$1,266.70	$1,138.04	$1,014.27	$899.73	$816.30	$804.63
10%	$1,321.51	$1,195.08	$1,074.61	$965.03	$908.71	$877.58

On a 9 percent mortgage:

15-year monthly payment	$1,014.27
Less 30-year average payment	($ 804.63)
Difference	$ 208.64

Thus, for approximately $210 per month more, or:

$$\frac{\text{Difference}}{\text{30-year payment}} = \frac{208.64}{805.63} = 26\% \text{ more}$$

The loan is paid off 15 years earlier. You would save 15 years, or 180 months, of future mortgage payments. This is an excellent means of "forced" savings.

Increase in monthly payment cost
(15-year versus 30-year mortgage)

Monthly increase in payment	$ 208.64
Number of months (15 years = 180 months)	× 180
Total larger monthly payments of a 15-year mortgage as opposed to a 30-year mortgage	$37,555.20

Years 16–30

30-year mortgage payments average	$805.33 per month
Number of months (15 years × 12)	180
Total future (years 16 to 30) payments for 30-year mortgage	$144,959.40
Less first 15 years' excess payments	($ 37,715.40)
Net cash savings over 30 years	$107,244.00

Thus, if we compare the excess payments for a 15-year mortgage versus a 30-year mortgage (or $37,715.40), the net future

TABLE 8.3 Differences between 15 and 30 Years of Monthly Mortgage Payments

Interest	(A) 30 Years	(B) 15 Years	Difference (A – B) (30 Years – 15 Years)
8%	$733.77	$ 955.68	$221.91
9%	$804.63	$1,014.27	$209.64
10%	$877.58	$1,074.61	$197.09

savings are $107,244. In addition, the faster the mortgage is paid off, the faster the monthly mortgage payment will go to you, the owner (borrower). The best mortgage for a long-term property holder is as short as possible, depending on the operating income of the property. If the mortgage interest is 9 percent, the excess payments result in a savings of 9 percent as they reduce the loan principal. Interest only gets charged on the remaining principal balance; therefore, you are earning 9 percent on your money, compared to what typical bank savings accounts pay.

Some advisors would recommend that you save the excess amount and apply it toward the accumulation of a down payment for another property. I disagree; with a capitalization rate (net income/asset cost) of 10 percent, and commercial interest rates of 9 percent, it pays—literally—to try to pay off the loan as soon as possible. A 10 percent potential return on a new deal versus 9 percent savings from prepaying a loan does not provide enough of a spread (increase in profit) between the two interest rates.

Adjustable-Rate Mortgages

Remember, interest rates are a function of the availability of money. When the money supply is low, or *tight,* a borrower has to pay higher interest; when the money supply is high, interest rates are lower. The national money supply and monetary policy are controlled by the Federal Reserve. As interest fluctuates, so does the interest paid on bank deposits and loans. Since bank deposits comprise the money that banks lend at a profit, if the cost of deposits goes up, banks want to raise their rates accordingly. All this helps explain the existence of adjustable-rate mortgages, more commonly know as ARMs.

ARM interest rates vary in relation to nationally known and accepted *indices* that are easily identifiable. These indices include the Federal Home Loan Bank cost of borrowing money to relend to homeowners, and the *prime rate*—the interest charged by banks for 90-day (short-term) loans to financially strong (prime) borrowers such as major corporations. All loans are tied to these indices. Most mortgages are set at a differential (spread) interest rate above the index rate. Typically, the interest rate on an adjustable-rate mortgage is adjusted annually, based upon one of a combination of both of these indices.

Lenders like ARMs, because the lenders are protected if interest rates (and the interest the lenders have to pay on savings or other sources of funds) go up. Thus, lenders tend to give better terms on ARMs, including low "teaser" interest rates for the first year of the loan and a limit or *cap* on the increase in interest the borrower may have to pay. The disadvantage to borrowers is the effect an increase in interest cost will have on their net income.

Other Financing Options

In addition to the more common types of financing, there are various hybrid types of mortgages and approaches to finance property acquisitions. Remember, lenders need to lend and investors want to borrow. Depending on the nature of the transaction, various types of loans can be made, but most don't apply to small commercial transactions and are beyond the purview of this book. This section covers those that novice real estate investors should familiarize themselves with.

Second Mortgages   A first mortgage is recorded by the title company or the lender's attorney. When you get a mortgage knowing that one already exists on the property, it is subordinate to the first; therefore, it is a *second mortgage*. Third or fourth mortgages may also exist. For example:

Original cost of property 10 years ago	$200,000
Original first mortgage	($150,000)
Equity	$ 50,000
Current value of property (double)	$400,000
Less original first mortgage, assuming no amortization	($150,000)
Equity in 10 years	$250,000

We could, theoretically, get the following additional mortgage:

Equity after first mortgage	$250,000
Second mortgage	($100,000)
Equity after new mortgage	$150,000
Third mortgage	($ 40,000)
Remaining equity ($150,000 − $40,000)	$110,000

To summarize:

Property value	$400,000
Less:	
First mortgage	($150,000)
Second mortgage	($100,000)
Third mortgage	($ 40,000)
Total mortgages	($290,000)
Remaining equity	$110,000

As prior loans are paid, the strength of the underlying second and third mortgages rises. A first-mortgage lender will insist that all existing liens, such as old mortgages, open real estate taxes due, and other liens, be cleared up. Usually these amounts are paid at closing, being deducted from the money due the seller. The seller will get any cash left over after paying off liens, transfer taxes, attorneys' fees (if any), and so on. As soon as the first mortgage is paid off (*satisfied*), the second mortgage becomes the first mortgage and the third mortgage becomes the second. That is the order in which mortgages are recorded in the county or city records.

One type of second mortgage that most homeowners are familiar with is the *equity loan*. The first mortgage stays in place and payments must also be made on the equity loan. In the event of sale, the first mortgage must be paid first, then the equity loan.

Long-Term Leases   An investor with an interested, financially stable tenant (i.e., triple-A) could lease the property from the owner for one price, sublease to the tenant for another higher rent, and keep the difference. This is an alternative to buying. The investor's cash outlay is limited to rent security, insurance, and legal

and other professional fees. The investor's profit is the difference in rent paid to the landlord versus the rent charged to the tenant. In this case, the investor is a *lessee*, and his or her tenant is a *sublessee*.
For example:

Rent paid by triple-A tenant for sublease	$36,000 per annum
Master lease cost (paid by investor-landlord)	($25,000)
Difference retained by real estate investor	$11,000

DEFINITION

The person leasing the property directly from the owner is called the *master tenant* or *lessee.* The tenant who in turn subleases from the master tenant is the *sublessee* or *subtenant.* The primary lease from the property owner to the master tenant is called the *master lease;* the lease from the master tenant to a subordinate tenant is called a *subordinate lease* or *sublease.*

The advantage of long-term leasing to investors is that it minimizes their cash outlay, yet they are in control of a property and make a profit. The advantages to the property owner are that he or she:

- Does not have to sell and pay capital gains tax on profit—maintains ownership of the property
- Is free of management responsibilities

Furthermore, for the owner, the rental income generally is more than the interest earned on the after-tax interest in savings accounts. For example:

Selling price of property	$250,000
Property rental income	$ 25,000

$$\text{Return} = \frac{\$25,000}{\$250,000} \text{ or } 10\%$$

If the property has been owned a very long time and the original cost was, say, $25,000, the following occurs on sale:

Selling price	$250,000
Cost for tax purposes	$ 25,000
Capital gain (profit)	$225,000
Federal capital gains tax say (20%) (assumes no state and local taxes)	$ 45,000

The proceeds of the sale after taxes break downs as follows:

Selling price	$250,000
Less:	
Taxes	$ 45,000
Net after-tax proceeds	$205,000
Return on savings account	$205,000
	× 5½% (CD)
Interest income on savings	$ 11,275
Compared to net lease income	$ 25,000

The lessee, or master tenant—in this case, the investor—should request what is called *right of first refusal.* This means that if the owner decides to sell, he or she gives to the master tenant (you, the investor) the right to match any offer received. This right is usually granted for a very short period of time, such as 15 to 30 days after the landlord decides to sell or receives an offer. This obviously gives the master tenant the opportunity to buy the property.

Options to Buy   Investors use options to buy when they need time to put a deal together before they can close on the property. This may entail finding tenants and/or investment partners, securing financing and government approvals, and so on.

Let's say an investor has a major national tenant interest in a location that is for sale. Most national tenant deals take at least six months to complete because:

- They require market and traffic studies.
- A lease must be proposed—which may be renegotiated by the investor.

■ Local government approvals must be obtained. In addition, if the deal is big enough, the investor may have to get additional backing from other investors and secure mortgage financing.

The advantage to you, the investor, of an option to buy is that you can tie up a property for a fee and have time to get the rest of the deal done (leasing and financing), then close on the property. The disadvantages are (1) the money you pay for the option to buy is nonrefundable: if the deal doesn't go through, you lose it; and (2) the seller, knowing he or she is helping you by giving you extra time to complete the deal, may set the option price high.

Sale Leasebacks   Recall that I introduced the concept of sale leasebacks in Chapter 7 as a source of real estate properties. Sale leasebacks are generated by sellers who want to cash in on the value of a property, yet retain its usage. The property is sold by a seller-user and leased back by him or her from the buyer.

The advantage of a sale leaseback to the seller is fourfold. First, selling and then leasing back frees up working capital (cash). Second, the seller maintains possession (right to use) due to the long-term lease he or she is getting back from the buyer-investor. Third, most sale leasebacks, depending on the financial strength of the seller-lessee, sell at about 10 percent capitalization rates (the rate of return to the investor). The seller may be able to invest the money at a higher rate of return and earn the differential in return. For example:

Business X rate of return	14%
Capitalization rate of property	(10%)
Net increase in profit	4%

To show this in dollar amounts, assume selling proceeds of $300,000:

Business X profit = 14% of $300,000 =	$42,000 per annum
Real estate profit (or rent paid to buyer) 10% of $300,000 =	$30,000
Net increase in profit: (14% − 10% = 4% of $300,000)	$12,000

The fourth advantage of a sale leaseback to a buyer is that, potentially, a tenant (especially triple-A) will add value to a property by occupying it. The main disadvantage to the seller is that he or she forgoes the potential appreciation of the property.

The advantages of sale leasebacks to you, the buyer-investor, are numerous:

- You own an attractive property with a tenant in place (which is another advantage: you don't have to look for and qualify tenants) at a reasonable (say, 10 percent) return on the purchase price.

- You can borrow 70 to 80 percent against the property purchase price and the tenant lease, assuming the tenant is creditworthy and other lender requirements are met.

- You benefit from the future appreciation of the property.

- Although the property may be tied up by a long-term lease, if the location is good, upon expiration or termination of the lease you get it back and can then lease the property to someone else or to the same tenant—ideally at a higher rent.

There are two primary disadvantages of sale leasebacks to you, the buyer-investor. First, sellers usually try to get a higher price than the actual value of the property by offering a higher-than-market rent and capitalizing that amount. For example:

Value of property	$200,000
Market rent ($200,000 at 10%)	$ 20,000
Sale leaseback rent	$ 30,000

$$\text{Selling price is rent capitalized at } 10\% = \frac{\$30,000}{10\%} = \$300,000$$

The seller-tenant is paying $10,000 ($30,000 − $20,000) above market rents to get a higher price for the property—in this case, $100,000 more. If the tenant defaults shortly after purchase, the property may be re-leased only at $20,000 per year, meaning it would be worth $200,000, or $100,000 less than you paid for it.

$$\frac{\$20,000}{10\%} = \$200,000$$

The second potential disadvantage is that very long-term leases will tie up the property at current rents. I have a saying: "Today's high rents are tomorrow's low rents." Since the property value is a function of rent, long-term leasing also keeps the property value low. For example:

Current property value and selling price	$200,000
Rent per sale leaseback ($200,000 at 10%)	
50-year lease; no increases	$ 20,000

Ten years later

Property market value doubles if not rented	$400,000
Property rent (40 years left on lease)	$ 20,000
Rent capitalized at 10% of $20,000	$200,000

That is capitalized value with lease in place. However, as the lease term nears its expiration date, the property value may approach market value, as investors include the anticipated future income in their calculations of current value. This is in anticipation of the near-term potential of re-leasing the property at higher current market rents. The property value would then reflect the new leases.

To prevent—or at least to minimize—the second disadvantage, ensure that all new leases you enter into with a tenant include increases calculated upon either the cost-of-living adjustment (COLA) or a fixed annual percentage increase of 3 to 4 percent. The fixed annual percentage increases should be set at least at the anticipated inflation rate. Also, be assiduous about verifying the creditworthiness of the seller-tenant to assure the strength of the lease. This is particularly important if the property is in a "secondary" location (e.g., a factory) or represents a specialized use. In such a case, you may have difficulty re-leasing in the event of default and vacancy.

There are some basic guidelines you can follow if you are considering a sale leaseback investment:

- Repeat to yourself the real estate mantra: location, location, location.
- Do not overpay. Check the true market value of the property by looking at comparable deals or hiring an appraiser.

- Make sure the return is sufficient to pay for your financing and ensure a positive cash flow.
- Check out the tenant.
- If the lease is going to be long-term, make sure it includes the right to raise the rent over time.

Assumability of Mortgage *Assumability* of a mortgage means that the mortgage loan liability can be taken over by a new buyer of the property; that is, the buyer of the property will continue the mortgage payments of the seller. If the property can be bought with the existing mortgage in place upon sale, the mortgage is called *assumable,* meaning a buyer can take over the loan from the seller. Obviously, this makes the sale easier to accomplish.

Some lenders charge *assumption fees,* a percentage of the loan balance. Lenders may also retain the right to approve the buyer through the usual loan approval process using the same criteria described earlier in this chapter.

The advantages to you, the buyer/seller, of assuming a mortgage are:

- The mortgage is already in place.
- You save the costs and time of applying for a new mortgage.
- The seller may agree to stay on as the original guarantor (if necessary) because he or she has to, or wants to, sell the property quickly. Staying on as guarantor will facilitate the sale; and if the new owner-borrower defaults, the guarantor-seller has the right to take back the property, bring the loan current, and resell to a new buyer.

Assignment of Mortgage Sometimes, mortgages are sold from one lender to another, in which case both lenders must notify the borrower of the sale, informing the borrower of the new lender's name and the address to which future mortgage payments are to be sent. A sale of a mortgage is called an *assignment.*

Mortgage assignments are happening more frequently today as banks increasingly take on the role of loan brokers for big institutional investors such as pension funds and insurance companies.

Buying Mortgages Another type of real estate investment is to buy property mortgages from lenders, hopefully at a discount. Many lenders, due to cash or other requirements, sell mortgages.

The selling price is usually a function of the note's interest rate versus the current market rates of interest for similar securities.

If the buyer cannot raise all the money needed to close the deal, some sellers may agree to hold a mortgage (usually a second mortgage, or sometimes a third mortgage if the preexisting mortgages were assumable) to help facilitate the sale of the property. If, at a later date, they need cash, they may subsequently be willing to sell the notes at a discount from the face value, resulting in a higher return to the buyer due to the higher effective rate of interest plus the amount of the discount. Look at the following example:

Note purchased at face value with a 10-year life (maturity)	$10,000
Market interest rate at time of purchase	6%
Interest income is 6% of $10,000 or	$ 600
Interest rates rise to	10%
Remaining life of note is	10 years
New $10,000 notes would pay 10% of $10,000 or	$ 1,000

What happens to the value of the 6 percent note? Its price drops to reflect the lower interest rate. The discount will reflect the difference, as follows:

Interest earnings of old note $ 600

Price will drop to a formula:

$$\frac{\text{New interest}}{\$1,000} + \frac{\text{Old interest}}{\$600} \text{ divided by } 2 = \frac{(\$1,000 + \$600)}{2} = \$800$$

Since new loans pay 10 percent, the capitalization of the new interest is

$$\frac{\$800}{10\%}$$

and the price of the old note becomes $8,000, a discount of $2,000 from the original face value (called *par*) of $10,000:

$$\frac{\text{Face value} - \text{Price}}{\$10,000 - \$8,000} = \frac{\text{Discount of}}{\$2,000}$$

To recap: The old loan pays interest of $600 per year. The old note will sell for $8,000, or a discount of $2,000. So, $2,000 divided by 10 remaining years equals $200 per year. The annual return then is $800 per year, which is composed of:

Annual interest paid	$600
Plus annual discount	$200
Total return	$800

The 10-year return is:

$$800 \times 10 \text{ years} = \$8,000$$

$$\frac{\text{Total annual return}}{\text{New market price}} = \frac{\$800}{\$8,000} = 10\%$$

Thus, the new market price of the bond brings its total return to match the market rate of interest of 10 percent, as opposed to its original interest of 6 percent.

The interest return comprises the following:

Interest paid (6% of $10,000)	$600
Amortization of $2,000 discount over 10 years to maturity $\dfrac{\$2,000}{10 \text{ years}}$	$200
Total annual return	$800

DEFINITION

Interest paid, plus the amortization of any premium or discount, is called the *yield to maturity.*

Let's take a look at what happens when interest rates drop to 5 percent from 6 percent.

Face value of bond (par) = purchase price	$10,000
Interest paid = 6% of $10,000 (Reflects original market rate)	$ 600

New market rate of interest is 5%

The original bond annually pays	$ 600
The bonds should pay	$ (500)
Excess interest	$ 100

Because new similar bonds pay $500, the following formula applies:

$$\frac{\text{New interest}}{\$500} + \frac{\text{Old interest}}{\$600} \div 2 = \frac{(\$500 + \$600)}{2} = \$550$$

Since the new bonds pay 5 percent, the price of the old bond should be:

$$\frac{\$550}{5\%} \text{ or } \$11,000$$

It will sell at a premium because it pays higher interest ($600 as opposed to $500). Premium equals price minus face value, so $11,000 − $10,000 = $1,000.

To recap: The old bond pays interest of $600. The new price is $11,000, but at maturity (in 10 years) you will only receive $10,000. Thus the premium of $11,000 − $10,000, or $1,000 divided by 2, divided by 10 years, equals $50 ($600 − $50). The net yield is $550, or 5 percent of $11,000 (the new price of the bond). Over the next 10 years, you will receive:

600 × 10 years =	$ 6,000
Plus par value at maturity	$10,000
Total received	$16,000
Less cost of bond	($11,000)
Net interest earned	$ 5,000

$$\frac{\text{Total interest divided by 10 (\$5,000} \div 10)}{\text{Par value}} = \frac{\$500}{\$10,000}$$

$$= 5\% \text{ per annum}$$

Sources of Mortgages

In this section I will introduce you to the various sources of mortgages and the requirements of each.

Savings Banks

Savings banks and savings and loan associations were organized to hold the funds of individual (usually small) depositors and to invest chiefly in home mortgage loans. These institutions also arrange commercial mortgages, however. Typically, the bigger the savings bank, the more commercial properties it has in its loan portfolio.

Commercial Banks

Commercial banks, which are always at risk of sudden withdrawals—especially from checking accounts—prefer to make matching short-term loans to business customers, but they may make mortgages either acting as mortgage broker or as part of an accommodation to a business customer.

Institutional Lenders

Institutional lenders—that is, insurance companies and pension plans—prefer to deal in long-term mortgages, for two reasons: first, unlike banks, they have low risk of sudden withdrawals of deposits; and second, long-term mortgages enable them to profitably meet future obligations to pensioners. They match loan maturities with actuarial cash projections of life expectancy and related payments due to pensioner and annuity owners. For large—usually more than $2 to $3 million—long-term loans, institutional lenders are the best source. They can match long-term, fixed-rate loans to their own long-term obligations to policyholders, pensioners, and annuity owners.

NOTE

Today the gap between the savings and commercial banks is narrowing. Savings banks now offer checking accounts and solicit business customers, while commercial banks solicit small savers to try to sell them other "products" such as stocks, annuities, and so on. Both types of banks are mandated by the federal government's Community Reinvestment Act to "invest" in—that is, to lend to—their communities. Thus, both are sources for commercial real estate loans in the community, and both act as brokers for institutional lenders. With the recent congressional liberalization of the banking laws, banks can now also act as stock brokers and insurance companies.

Private Parties

Banks and institutions are not the only ones to recognize that mortgage lending is a lucrative business. Private parties, in particular financially liquid (cash-rich) individuals or corporations, get into the act. So if you're having difficulty financing a deal, or you need additional capital to close, a private lender may be the answer. The private lender will put up the money and, in lieu of asking for a partnership interest, usually will require a secured high rate of return. Private lenders charge more than banks because they make decisions faster; they are willing to agree to higher-risk loans in return for higher interest, essentially making loans banks turn down; and their terms are more flexible. Private lenders also put in a higher default interest rate that will accrue in the event of default.

Like all lenders, private lenders are protected by a recorded mortgage on the property. Sooner or later they will get either the money or the property back. If they have to foreclose, they can either keep the property or sell it to recoup the investment in the mortgage.

Private lenders could be:

- Retirees with cash to invest and looking for higher returns than banks pay. You can find private mortgage money by asking local real estate brokers or through the commercial real estate sections of most newspapers.
- Private investors.
- Companies, including mortgage brokers, that put lenders and borrowers together for a fee.
- Friends and/or relatives.

The advantages of private mortgages to novice investors are:

- You may get a faster commitment than a bank would give you.
- You circumvent the bureaucratic loan process of the bank or other institutional lender.
- You may save on some bank fees and charges, such as points. If the lender is a friend or relative, this may be beneficial to both of you.

Mortgage Information Online

Many banks and other lenders have Web sites on which customers can start the mortgage process from the comfort of their homes or offices. Most of these lenders will also give you a custom quote online, based on your needs.

You can also find a great deal of information on mortgages in general: definitions, calculators to help you figure out your financing needs, comparisons of mortgages by lenders in your area, and much more. By simply entering in the search engine (Google and Yahoo! are among the most popular) the keywords "real estate mortgages," you will receive hundreds of listings from every state in the country. In addition, Yahoo! Finance provides a questionnaire to help you determine your financial needs.

The disadvantages are that interest rates may be higher than those of a bank; the private lender may foreclose faster than a bank or be less willing to renegotiate. There is also greater risk that a private lender will want to reclaim possession of the property. And, if the lender is a friend or relative and the deal goes bad, it could cause personal problems.

Seller Financing
Sellers sometimes are willing to do their own financing because by doing so they may be able to postpone the bulk of the capital gains tax on their profit. The capital gains tax will be paid as the sales proceeds are received. Seller financing also enables sellers to earn higher interest than on bank deposits, plus interest on the tax money that is postponed (deferred) to the future. To the buyer, the advantage of seller financing is that it is easier and cheaper to arrange than a commercial loan, for example.

Sellers agree to finance deals for the following reasons:

- *To facilitate a sale.* Some properties are sold with seller financing, where the seller holds the mortgage. These include non-income-producing properties such as land or specialty buildings (restaurants, garages, and so on). The seller may also have bought the property with a mortgage from the previous owner, which may be assumable by the buyer.

- *Some properties are difficult to sell and the seller-lender wants to provide an added incentive to a buyer.* The worst that can happen is that the seller-lender has to foreclose, but he or she keeps the down payment and interim monthly payments and gets the property back to keep or resell.

- *Generally, a seller-financed mortgage would pay almost the same interest as banks charge for mortgages.* As stated earlier, this is more than the amount paid to savers on savings accounts. Sellers approaching retirement find this especially attractive. Not only do they get higher interest, but their money is secured by a property they know. Of course, there is the risk that the underlying property may drop in value, but this would be somewhat offset by the buyer's down payment.

Another benefit to a seller with a large profit and potential capital gain tax is that the Internal Revenue Code (IRC) Installment Sale Rule allows a seller of real estate to spread his or her gain over the life of the mortgage he or she gets. This may result in being taxed at a lower bracket, as the profit is reported when received in the future and thus the tax is spread out over the term of the financing.

FOR EXAMPLE:

Selling price	$100,000
Cost to seller	$ 20,000
Profit	$ 80,000
Capital gain tax (20%)	$ 16,000

Net cash after taxes

Selling price	$100,000
Less taxes	$ 16,000
	$ 84,000

If the seller in this case took back a $80,000 mortgage, the result would be:

Selling price	$100,000
Less mortgage (20-year, self-liquidating, paying 8% interest	($ 80,000)
Cash received	$ 20,000
Total profit on sale	$ 80,000

Tax on cash received of $20,000 is based on its prorated percentage of the selling price of $100,000, or:

$$\frac{\text{Cash received}}{\text{Selling price}} \quad \frac{\$20,000}{\$100,000} = 20\%$$

Thus, 20 percent of the $20,000 received, or $4,000, is taxed in the year of sale. Say the capital gains tax on the $4,000 is 20 percent, or $800. In subsequent years, the seller would receive payments of $700 per month, or $8,400 per year. The annual interest portion of 8 percent of $80,000, or $6,400 initially, would be subject to ordinary income tax; and the amortization portion, or approximately $2,000 per year, would be subject to capital gains taxes, as follows:

$$\frac{\text{Cash received}}{\text{Selling price}} = \frac{\$2,000}{\$100,000}, \text{ or } 2\% \text{ of } \$80,000 = \$1,600$$

Thus, $1,600 of the $2,000 principal payment would be subject to federal capital gains tax, or 20% on the $1,600 pro rata share of gain, $320 tax would be paid. Meanwhile, the seller would be earning interest on the tax money he or she didn't pay in the year of sale. To illustrate, on an all-cash deal, the following would have occurred in the year of sale:

Sales proceeds (cash)	$100,000
Less cost	$ 20,000
Profit	$ 80,000
Capital gains tax (20%)	$ 16,000

Net cash received would be $100,000 minus $16,000 tax, or $84,000. On an installment sale with 20 percent down, in the year of sale, cash received equals $20,000, or 20 percent of the sales price ($20,000 is 20 percent of $100,000). The capital gains rate is

20 percent of $16,000, or $3,200 in the year of sale. The net cash received would be $100,000 minus $3,200 tax, or $96,800. Thus, the tax savings in the year of sale are:

Capital Gains Tax on cash sale	$16,000
Tax on installment sale	$ 3,200
Temporary tax savings	$12,800

Of course, this temporary tax saving only represents a postponement, or deferral, of taxes. As the future payments on the $80,000 come in, capital gains tax will be paid on them. But in the meantime, the $12,800 tax money is earning interest for the seller.

Mortgage Brokers

Borrowers hire mortgage brokers to help them find mortgage money. The broker's fee is a percentage of the loan, and is negotiable (in advance). For the novice investor, the advantage of using mortgage brokers is that they are up to date on the current status of the mortgage market and can help them apply for a mortgage. Thus, they can advise borrowers in advance how much a loan will cost, and recommend possible sources of and criteria for such loans.

Moreover, brokers have access to many lenders and know where to place a particular loan, thereby saving you the time of personally applying for a loan at numerous banks. If you are turned down by one lender, you have to start again somewhere else, and this might be risky, depending on the time constraints stated in your contract of sale. It helps to use a broker who can expedite the process.

A mortgage broker also acts as your advisor and as the intermediary between you and the lender while you are negotiating terms of the loan (interest rate, length of loan, escrow requirements for real estate taxes, and miscellaneous other lender requirements). A broker will also assist you in filling out the loan application and with compiling the documentation required by the lender.

In particular for novice investors, the ability of brokers to find funds and expedite the borrowing process more than justifies their fees. And for a long-term investor (that's you, remember) who has intentions of buying more properties in the future, establishing a relationship with a good mortgage broker can prove invaluable. The sole disadvantage is the fee: Usually the borrower is charged 1 or 2 percent.

401(k) or Private Pension Plans
Certain professionals, small businesspeople, or small businesses in general may have accumulated large balances in the pension plans and choose to invest in real estate either by making a direct investment or by granting a loan.

Interest paid to a pension plan is tax deductible to the borrower, and not taxed to the pension plan until future withdrawals are made by the owner of the plan (upon retirement). The retiree-receiver will then pay personal income tax after he or she receives the pension or annuity. The primary disadvantage of using these plans in this way is, obviously, that the investor–plan owner is risking his or her retirement money. For this important reason, investors who choose this option should invest only a portion of the plan, which they can afford to lose.

Of course, you may use a self-directed pension plan as a source of secondary (after first mortgage) debt for your own real estate deals. The interest paid to the pension plan is tax deductible by the property, and tax deferred to the plan, until withdrawn.

THE CLOSING

You've done it! You've secured financing for your first real estate investment. But the property's not yours yet. You still must go through the closing process. The *closing* is the finalization of a real estate transaction. At this point, all parties involved are assumed to have done their homework. The property has passed inspection, the bank has given a formal loan commitment on acceptable terms, and all other contingencies (described earlier in the chapter) have been met. Now it's time to complete the deal.

NOTE

If the deal is complicated, the attorneys may agree to have a "dry run" or "practice" closing in advance of the actual closing date, to iron out and correct any problems. Ideally, the practice closing will expedite the official closing, so that it is simply a matter of making final adjustments, signing documents and exchanging signed documents, and transferring money.

In commercial transactions, usually four groups are involved in a closing, with their respective representatives or attorneys:

- The buyer and his or her attorney
- The seller and his or her attorney
- The lender and his or her attorney
- The title insurance company

The purpose of the closing is essentially to enable the two parties to a transaction to exchange assets with each other. An asset exchanged for another asset is called *consideration*. A consideration need not be money: It could be a service or promise (for example, an engagement ring is consideration). In our case, the consideration—the asset being exchanged—is a piece of property. Let's say for this discussion that the property is being purchased for $100,000 in cash. At the closing, the buyer would pay the seller $100,000 cash. The seller in turn would give the buyer a deed to the property. The $100,000 paid by the buyer to the seller is the buyer's consideration; the property given by the seller to the buyer is the seller's consideration.

At the closing, all documents (described in the next section) and checklists are reviewed to make sure everything is in order or has been adjusted for. After all documents have been signed, the lender issues a check to the seller for the mortgage amount. The buyer then pays the seller the difference between the agreed-upon selling price and the mortgage loan (the bank check). You, the buyer, are responsible for paying all costs of obtaining the loan, which include:

- Bank attorney's fees
- Mortgagee (lender) title insurance
- Mortgage taxes and recording fees
- Any other loan-related costs

In addition, you will pay all other closing expenses attributable to the buyer; the seller will pay his or her selling costs, typically including brokers' commissions and transfer taxes. Then the attorneys and the title company representative will exchange documents, and the seller will get his or her check and arrange to give possession to the buyer.

Documentation

By the date of the closing, the attorneys or representatives of the parties to the transaction have usually examined all the relevant documents in advance and either have agreed to accept them or have negotiated mutually acceptable modifications. These documents include the title report, or abstract of title; the proposed form of deed; and a copy of the mortgage, or deed of trust.

Title Report or Abstract of Title
This is a copy of the *chain of title*—that is, the history of ownership of the property dating back to its original state. A title history includes:

- Purchase dates
- Mortgages and repayments by date
- Other liens and their resolution

The title insurance company gives a title insurance policy to the buyer and a mortgage insurance policy to the lender that ensures so-called clean ownership, or title.

There may be acceptable exceptions to a buyer, such as preexisting mortgage liens, which the buyer may be purchasing "subject to," or is willing to "assume," as explained earlier. Note that "subject to" usually does not imply any personal liability on the part of the buyer, and a lender's approval is not required. In contrast, assumption of a mortgage usually requires lender approval in the form of a personal guarantee or other consideration to the lender.

Proposed Form of Deed
Generally, the seller or his or her attorney will provide a copy (unsigned and stamped "Draft") of the deed being offered to give to the buyer in return for the buyer's money. The buyer or his or her attorney will review this copy to make sure it is acceptable.

Copy of Mortgage or Deed of Trust
The lender prepares the mortgage or *deed of trust* documents and submits copies of them to the buyer or the buyer's attorney for examination. Remember, the borrower gives either a mortgage lien or a deed in trust to a lender in return for the loan. The borrower also signs a loan agreement stating the terms of the loan, which include:

- Amount
- Interest rate
- Repayment terms
- Collateral
- Other lender requirements, such as real estate tax escrows, insurance policies with lender endorsement, maintenance of condition of property, and annual reports of operating results

In the case of commercial real estate transactions, a letter is prepared at the closing for distribution to current tenants at the property. Signed by the seller, it advises tenants of:

- The sale of the property
- The name and address of the new owner
- The address to which to send rent checks in the future
- The name, address, and contact numbers of the new property manager (if different from those of the new owner)

At the Closing

The closing usually takes place at the office of the lender or the lender's attorney. Usually, there is a sign-in sheet where all parties check in and state their official capacity. After initial greetings have been exchanged and everyone involved has been confirmed as present, the closing begins. All the documents are exchanged and examined. A tentative closing statement, with adjustments, is prepared. Usually, the parties work together with the title company representative to verify that the contents of this document are correct. The seller's content includes:

- Selling price.
- List of prepaid expenses to be reimbursed by the buyer or accumulated unpaid bills that will have to be paid by the buyer (but for which the buyer will get credit). Examples include real estate taxes paid in advance by the seller, or unpaid real estate taxes to be paid by the seller. The payer will be credited or reimbursed for any payments made when he or she was the owner. This applies to both buyer and seller.

- Statement of any escrow money held by the seller's attorney.
- List of any brokers' commissions that are the seller's responsibility.
- Other seller responsibilities.

On the buyer's part, the closing statement would include what he or she owes the seller:

- Purchase price.
- Prepaid expenses that have to be reimbursed to the seller.
- Any accumulated portions of unpaid bills on the property, such as estimated real estate taxes, to date. As the new owner, the buyer has to pay the full real estate tax bill when he or she receives it. Part of that bill may have applied to the period before the sale and should be paid by the seller. This is accomplished through a closing adjustment that credits the buyer.
- Other buyer responsibilities.

At the closing, the title insurance company representative reviews the updated title report. He or she usually has someone make a last-minute check of the town property records to ensure that there have been no last-minute changes, such as new liens, and to determine the current status of real estate taxes. Then the title representative records the deed given by the seller to the buyer. The title insurance representative must leave the closing with the signed, recordable deeds and mortgages (or deeds of trust). In turn, he or she:

- Issues title insurance to the buyer and mortgage insurance to the lender
- Issues a title insurance policy to the buyer, which ensures that the buyer is getting good title (ownership) to the property
- Agrees to record against the property record the new deed and the mortgage or deed of trust and the related loan agreement signed by the borrower-buyer and get the recorded documents mailed to the buyer and lender
- Issues a mortgage title insurance policy to the lender to ensure that the mortgage is properly recorded

For completing these tasks, the title insurance company is paid premiums and fees. The title representative issues invoices and collects the fees at the closing, as follows:

Type of fee	Responsible party
Cost of title insurance policy	Buyer
Deed recording fees	Buyer/seller
Cost of mortgage insurance	Borrower/buyer
Mortgage recording fees	Borrower/buyer

It is also customary for the buyer to give the title representative a gratuity at the end of the closing. Your attorney will advise you how much.

It is the responsibility of the title representative to record all the documents as soon as possible and to deliver the recorded documents to the respective parties.

Upon agreeing on the respective closing adjustments, the seller is given his or her selling price, less adjustments, from:

- Escrow or good faith deposit
- Net mortgage proceeds from the lender
- Balance from the buyer in certified funds

For example:

Purchase price	$200,000
Plus seller's net adjustments due buyer	$ 5,000
Thus, the seller should get a total of ($200,000 plus $5,000)	$205,000

This would be paid as follows:

Down payment held in escrow	$ 20,000
Net loan proceeds ($150,000 – $3,000)*	$147,000
Buyer's certified check	$ 38,000
Total paid to seller	$205,000

---

*The $3,000 represents borrower's loan costs.

In addition, the seller pays his or her broker's and attorney's fees, plus other related costs.

The buyer also pays:

- Title insurance fees for his or her deed
- Mortgage title insurance fees for the lender
- Lender's attorney's fees and other costs
- Other loan costs, such as stamps, points, fees, and so on

The seller then symbolically gives a key to the property to the buyer, or they agree to meet to complete the transfer of possession of the property.

Congratulations! You are now the proud owner of a piece of property!

CONCLUSION

You will be feeling relieved and excited once you have been given the keys to your first real estate investment property. But after celebrating, it's time to hunker down again, because there's another important topic to cover to ensure that you will become successful in your new venture: managing your property. That's covered in Chapter 9.

9

Managing Your Real Estate Investment

You have just left the closing and are the proud owner of a real estate property! Give yourself some time to celebrate—and to recover from taking care of all the details of the closing. Then it's time to get back to work, to prepare for the ongoing task of taking care of your investment. Property management is where the chickens come home to roost, so to speak; with real estate, you don't just call your broker and arrange for a computer transfer of money and then wait for the dividend checks to come in. Real estate investment requires you to be involved in a much more hands-on fashion, especially when you're still learning the details of this complex and exciting business. You have to learn to properly manage a property so that it brings you the most return on your investments—which, after all, is the purpose of the process this book describes.

> **NOTE**
>
> Now that you own property, you are considered a landlord, which is the term I appropriately begin using in this chapter.

The purpose of this chapter is to ensure that all the hard work you did in preparation for buying your first property does not go to waste. It covers the best way to manage a first property—with the help of a professional manager—and then moves on to explain insurance, leases, capital improvements and replacements, and tenant improvements, and ends with an overview of how to market your property when you have a vacancy.

PROFESSIONAL MANAGEMENT COMPANIES

I strongly recommend that novice investors hire an outside management company to manage their first property. The primary reason for this is education: the fee you pay an outside manager during the first year of your ownership will come back to you a thousandfold in the form of firsthand knowledge and insight into the workings of the real estate profession. A professional management company has everything you don't at this stage: years of experience, in-place accounting systems, and relationships with tenant brokers, vendors, contractors, and other real estate professionals. Therefore, when you hire a professional, you learn by:

- Overseeing what the manager does
- Reviewing the manager's monthly accountings
- Discussing expenditure requests with the manager
- Preparing budgets
- Negotiating with vendors
- Renewing old leases or writing new ones
- Fulfilling other supervisory management work

Finding a Management Company

Be aware that, in practice, the process of finding an outside management company should begin *before* you buy the property, when you are seeking financing. The reason I did not include this material in the financing section of Chapter 8 is simply because I felt you already had enough new information to learn there.

A good place to find management companies to interview is through your broker or financing institution. Or, if you're an

Internet user, you can also find a wealth of information online on this topic (see the box). It's always best to interview several management companies before you close on your property, and then select the one that you and/or the members of your group are most comfortable with, because the management company's employment should commence immediately following the closing.

All real estate agreements or contracts must be in writing. This includes the agreement or contract with management companies. Before you sign this—or any—agreement, have your attorney review it. And make sure the company you choose is bonded by a major bonding, or surety, firm. That way, if your rent money is lost or stolen, the bonding company will make it good.

Most real estate management contracts have a 30-day cancellation policy, so if you or the members of your group are not satisfied with the performance, you can always fire the first manager and hire another after giving proper (usually 30 days) notice. But the best way to avoid being dissatisfied is to do your homework on this aspect of real estate investing, as you did for all the other steps. Interview at least two or three local management firms, or national firms with strong local offices, to find one that meets your needs. During the interviews, ask to see copies of accounting reports, sample leases, vendor bid solicitation forms, and property inspection checklists; and ask to meet any in-house leasing personnel. Then get details on the following:

- Fees and operations
- Monthly reports
- Billings and collections
- Leasing and tenant relations
- Repairs, capital improvements, and replacements
- Bonding and insurance
- Marketing

Each of these topics is addressed in turn in the following sections.

Management Fees and Operations

In terms of operations—the way the management company structures its processes—the main question you, the property owner,

Management Companies Online

Like most other divisions of the real estate profession, property management companies across the country offer online access to their services. Searching the Internet is without doubt the fastest way to obtain information on the companies in your area. You can do most prescreening online, then winnow down your list to the two or three that you'd like to interview in person. Many offer free consultations online! Just type in the keywords "real estate management" and you'll receive hundreds of listings. A good way to narrow your search, however, is to look up the names of management companies in the phone book in your area and see which ones list Web sites, then go directly to their sites.

Another good way to find area-specific management companies is to log onto the the Institute of Real Estate Management (IREM) Web site (www.irem.org). There you can access IREM's Accredited Management Organization (AMO) Directory, which promises to "help you identify the best real estate management companies available." There are more than 650 AMO headquarters offices and as many branch offices throughout the United States and Canada. All you have to do is click on a location from the map provided, and you're on your way.

More on IREM in the "On Your Own: Your Future in Real Estate" section at the end of the chapter.

should be concerned with is its collections system. Some management companies combine their collections from all the properties they manage—which means the monies for different owners are kept in the same place. The properties' bills are then paid from that one account. I recommend that you work with a company that sets up separate checking accounts for each property, into which all of the property's rent collections would be deposited. After bills are paid, the balance (if any) belongs to the property and its owner(s). There is no danger of financial mix-ups when the management company operates this way.

Another important question to ask is whether you, the owner, would have the right to sign all checks and/or approve all expenditures. In other words, determine how much authority you, the owner, retain.

Inherent in a management company's operations is its fee structure. The management fees should be clearly spelled out in the contract, and you should have your attorney review the contract. Management fees are determined, in part, as a percentage of rent collections (discussed later); usually, this is 4 to 6 percent for smaller properties and 2 to 4 percent for larger properties. Note that residential properties require more work and thus higher fees than commercial properties.

Management fees also cover supervision of construction work or capital improvements made to your property; the management company reviews plans and proposals, negotiates for bids with various contractors, and monitors the actual construction or improvements process. The amount of this fee generally ranges from 5 to 10 percent for jobs under $20,000, and from 3 to 5 percent for jobs above $20,000. More on this in the "Repairs, Replacements, and Capital Improvements" section.

Management companies also earn a leasing commission, that is, a fee for renewing old leases or writing new ones. Usually one fee is established for new leases and a lower one for renewals. (This is discussed more fully in the "Leasing" section.) Often, however, this fee or commission may be shared with a *tenant broker*—a broker who represents tenants looking for space to rent.

Finally, there are miscellaneous reimbursements paid to a management company—for example, property-related out-of-pocket expenses, such as mailings, bank service charges, and so on.

Monthly Reports

The monthly report you and your investment group receive from your management company is very important, as it enables you to literally track the dollars-and-cents activities of your investment. Monthly, the manager should prepare a report that includes:

- Rent analysis, including rent roll, billings, collections, and arrears
- List of checks issued, including check number, payee, amount, and explanation. If your account is separate, a copy of the bank statement

- List of accounts payable: open bills, possible reserves or needs for future major repairs, and so on
- List of accounts receivable, including rent arrears

The report should also provide a written narrative summary, with the following:

- The month's cash flow
- An explanation of arrears and tenant status
- Any significant developments that month
- General recommendations or suggestions

Whether you have invested as part of a group or as an individual, you should set up monthly meetings with your manager to go over the report. Copies should be given to each member far enough in advance of the meeting so that the members have enough time to adequately review the report. At the meeting, the report should be discussed in detail.

Let's take a look at what a typical monthly report from a management company would include. In this case, we'll assume the report was submitted on September 30, 1999:

Balance as of August 31, 1999 (previous month)	$3,235
Plus cash receipts (see attached list)	$3,500
Cash available in September	$6,735

Less disbursements

Check No.	Payee	Purpose	Amount
115	Con Edison	Electric	$ 155
116	Joe's Plumbing	Repair	$ 191
117	First Bank	Mortgage/tax escrow	$2,500
118	Jim Smith	Janitorial service	$ 200
Total disbursements			$3,046
Balance for September 30, 1997			$3,790
Net increase in cash this month ($3,790 – $3,235)			$ 555

The report should also include a rent schedule, which lists for every tenant and in total:

- Previous rental arrears, if any
- September's rent billed
- Rent received in September
- Rent receivable (unpaid rent) as of September 30 (this should be zero)

In addition to the rent schedule, the report should include:

- Accounts payable schedule (unpaid bills), which is a list of vendors to whom the property owes money and how much
- A copy of the bank statement
- A copy of the reconciliation of the bank balance to the balance on the books
- Copies of bills paid
- A memo summarizing the month's operating results and anticipated future events, such as lease expirations, status of lease negotiations, proposed capital improvements and reasons for them, budgets, and any miscellaneous manager's comments

NOTE

There are numerous computer software programs available today to expedite many property management tasks, including billing tenants, paying bills, doing general accounting, sending out repetitious memos, preparing schedules of lease expiration dates, and doing year-end accounting for tax purposes. Ask your manager which system the company uses so that you can become proficient with it as well in case you decide you want to self-manage this property at a later date or another property in the future. Familiarizing yourself with your management company's computer system will also facilitate your management of your management company!

A good source of the latest in property management-related software is the Internet: Just search on "real estate management software."

Rent Collections and Billing

Though management companies will undertake to do the rent collections and billing for their clients, in general I prefer to maintain control over check signing. Rent bills should be sent to tenants approximately a week before the rent is due.

Bank lockbox systems are frequently used for collections of accounts receivable, and they work as well for rent collections. Here's how a lockbox operates for property management:

1. You open a separate bank account for each property.

2. You send or give each tenant a two-part perforated coupon-bill stating his or her rent due, including arrears. This should be done prior to the beginning of the month being billed (toward the end of the previous month). Rent is usually due on the first of every month, unless the lease states otherwise.

3. Include with the coupon a preaddressed envelope with the lockbox number and bank address on it. Your tenants mail their rent checks directly to the bank with the coupon attached.

4. Upon receipt of the bill, the tenant writes the rent check, includes the check with the stub half of the bill in the preaddressed envelope, mails the envelope to the bank, and keeps the main part of the bill for his or her records.

5. The envelope is delivered to the bank box number to which it is addressed; a bank employee opens the envelope, records the stub number on the deposit slip delineating what the check is for, and deposits the check in the proper account. Each day, the bank faxes or e-mails to the owner or management company a list of checks it has received and deposited in the property's account.

TIP

If you or your investment group has a money market checking account, you can earn interest on deposits until the checks issued against them are returned to the bank.

In addition to enabling faster availability of rental income by directing checks directly to the bank, lockboxes also offer a higher level of security. You don't have to worry about the postman delivering numerous checks to your office, with the attendant risks of theft, loss, fire, and so on.

Dealing with Delinquent Payers
As an owner of real estate, at some point you will no doubt have to deal with a slow or nonpaying tenant. This is why you include a 5 percent vacancy factor when you estimate projected profit and loss.

If a tenant hasn't paid the rent by the fifteenth of the month, standard practice is to send a late notice. If the rent still isn't paid the following month, when the new rent bill is sent it will include the previous month's arrears. If the tenant does not respond by the middle of the second month, you start formal legal proceedings to collect the arrears. Eventually, you may have to take action to evict the tenant. Each jurisdiction has its own rules, so you will have to consult your attorney should you ever be in this position.

Leasing

In addition to collecting rent and paying bills, property management includes taking care of leasing. (Note: Leases themselves are explained separately later in the chapter.) As mentioned in the "Management Fees and Operations" section earlier, management companies charge commissions for negotiating leases, usually a percentage of the total amount of the lease, which should be negotiated in advance as part of the original management agreement.

Let's look at an example to illustrate the leasing-commission calculation. Tenant A has signed a five-year lease that breaks out as shown in Table 9.1.

TABLE 9.1   Sample Lease Breakdown

Year	Monthly	Annually
1	$1,000	$12,000
2	$1,050	$12,600
3	$1,100	$13,200
4	$1,150	$13,800
5	$1,200	$14,400
Total rent		$66,000

Total rent under this lease is $66,000. If the leasing commission is 6 percent, the commission due is $3,960. As a rule of thumb, try not to pay more than one month's rent, if it is a renewal of a lease with an existing tenant, or three month's rent, if it is a new lease with a secondary tenant. That said, if the lease is for a triple-A tenant at a good rent, be willing to consider paying a higher commission to an exclusive broker.

TIP

Due to the competitive nature of the industry, real estate brokers are usually willing to be quite flexible in their fees. Take advantage of this situation and negotiate with them.

Tenant Relations

You can't talk about leasing without talking about tenants. It is important to think of your tenants as your customers. That should be your (and your management company's) primary management philosophy. This includes making sure that tenant complaints are responded to and resolved in a timely and respectful way. Though it's true (especially as you become more experienced in real estate) that sometimes you will come in contact with difficult tenants, you will find that most are too busy going about their lives and businesses to be petty and annoying. And, remember, if you have a problem tenant, you can always refuse to renew his or her lease when it expires.

One good way to stay in touch with your tenants and to monitor your management company's work is to introduce yourself to your tenants, first by letter, informing them of the purchase of the property and telling them where to send the rent, and later in person. Taking these actions will go a long way toward easing later interactions.

Insurance

Real estate properties should be insured for their replacement cost or their value, whichever is higher. The property value is determined by your appraiser; determining replacement cost is the responsibility of the engineer. Not surprisingly, insurance on a building is called *property insurance*. It can be divided into two primary categories: comprehensive and liability.

Comprehensive coverage. Ideally, property owners should get what's called *all-risk* or *business owner's policies* (BOPs), comprehensive plans that typically include fire, vandalism, loss of rental income, liability, and theft.

Liability coverage. Basic liability insurance covers the owner against claims of negligence, accidents, and so on. For very large claims, you should also have an *umbrella* policy that kicks in when your regular liability coverage is exhaused.

The cost of insurance coverage should be verified by your insurance broker when you are initially estimating income and loss of a property, and should be included in your projected expenses.

Insurance Adjusters

In the event of a claim for damage to your property that is covered by insurance, an *insurance adjuster* will be sent by the insurance company to evaluate the amount of the damage and to negotiate a settlement with the property owner or the person making the claim (claimant). Because they are being paid by the company, obviously, these adjusters tend to protect their employer by minimizing the amount to be paid. To offset that perspective, there are also public adjusters, who represent the general public or the claimants against insurance companies. They are very knowledgeable about insurance policy terminology and clauses and types of property damages, both short- and long-term. Public adjusters also have many contacts with real estate professionals so that they can obtain estimates to offer in support of the owner's claim, if it is significantly different (read: higher) than the company adjuster's figure. Furthermore, they know how to negotiate with insurance company adjusters on the claimant's behalf.

Public adjusters (ask your insurance broker to recommend one) are paid a percentage fee of the amount collected on the claim. Thus, they have every incentive to try to maximize the amount of the money (the *award*) paid to you, the claimant.

Once you agree to accept a certain amount of money for a claim, the insurance company will request that you sign a receipt, which incorporates a *general release*. This means that you release, or free, the insurance from all other claims in regard to this matter, including future claims. Thus, when negotiating a claim for damage to your property, you should keep in mind the potential future damage that could result. For example:

It Pays to Get the Best

It is important to hire a good property insurance broker, one who is knowledgeable and keeps up to date with changes in the industry. You can choose between independent brokers who deal with many companies and help you shop for the best price and coverage, and affiliated brokers, who represent one insurance company.

It also pays to shop your policies annually with different brokers before the policies expire. One good way to do this is through a company called A.M. Best. Founded in 1899, Best rates the financial strength of insurance companies and the security of each company's debt and preferred stock. Best not only rates past performance, but predicts how the company may be expected to perform in the future. Best rates more than 2,600 property/casualty and 1,700 life/health companies. You should always deal with a company that Best has rated A or better.

To find out more about A.M. Best and the details of its rating system, go to its Web site at www.ambest.com or contact its corporate offices at Ambest Road, Oldwick, NJ 08858, (908) 439-2200.

- A fire may warp or weaken overhead beams.
- HVAC ducts may be compromised.
- Water damage may wet Sheetrock and weaken it.

This is where a good public adjuster is essential. He or she will try to get reimbursement for these potential future damages as part of the negotiated claim.

Repairs, Replacements, and Capital Improvements

Let's begin this section by defining the difference between repairs, replacements, and improvements. A *repair* is the fixing of something that is damaged or broken. A *replacement* is the substitution of a malfunctioning or damaged item with a working—usually more modern—version of it. An *improvement* is the betterment of something, either by modification to the existing item or total replacement with a better unit. The line between replacements and improvements can sometimes be quite fuzzy.

Repairs
The extent of the responsibility of the landlord—or the management company acting as the landlord's agent—with regard to repairs and maintenance depends on the type of property and related leases and lease clauses.

Landlord responsibilities to tenants in apartment buildings are the most extensive. They include:

- Appliance breakdowns (if owned by landlord)
- Plumbing problems
- Painting, for long-term tenants
- Electrical repairs
- Common area cleaning and upkeep

For office buildings, the landlord is responsible for:

- Daily internal office cleaning
- Payment for office and building electricity
- Care and repair of the central heating, ventilation, and air conditioning (HVAC) system
- Replacement of lightbulbs and so on

For retail store leases the landlord is usually not responsible for any internal repair and maintenance. The primary exception to this rule may be the HVAC system.

Common Area Maintenance   Landlords are also responsible for *common area maintenance* (CAM). Common areas are defined as those areas of a property used by everyone, whether tenants or the general public. These areas include hallways and entrances, parking areas, roofs, elevators and stairs, and central HVAC systems. Let's take parking areas as an example of the kind of responsibilities that maintenance of common areas entails. Parking areas have to be well lit, clean, free of snow and ice in winter, resealed and restriped on a regular basis, checked for potholes, and, possibly, patrolled at night.

As a novice property owner, most likely (it is recommended, in fact) you will contract most of these jobs out. Even some owners of numerous and large properties, who could afford to hire full-time crews, prefer to contract these services because doing so tends to be more cost effective and also enables them to reduce their liability if things go wrong. To protect themselves in this way, owners get an insurance policy endorsement that lists them as an additional insured from vendor services, such as cleaning companies, contractors, guard services, and the like.

TIP

Always get three estimates for any service or construction job that must be done on your property.

Replacements

It is a sad reality that all parts of any property eventually have to be replaced. This, of course, is one of the reasons for doing the careful evaluation of the property before you buy it: Unless you have determined that it will be cost effective to buy a run-down building (a "fixer-upper"), generally, you want a building for which you have to do minimal work—initially at least, in particular when you're new to real estate.

If fact, before you make an offer to buy, and even if the property is currently in excellent condition, you need to make allowances for replacement costs or extra maintenance. In addition, you need to set up replacement reserves and establish a program of replacement. Table 9.2 shows a sample replacement program that begins in 1998.

When you set up a replacement program, try to phase in the work periods to enable yourself to pay for them out of cash flow from the property as much as possible.

TABLE 9.2   Sample Replacement Program

Item	Useful Life	Current Age	Cost	Year to Be Done
Roof	15 years	10 years	$10,000	(5 Years) 2003
HVAC	10 years	6 years	$ 5,000	(4 Years) 2002
Parking lot	10 years	9 years	$ 7,000	(1 Year) 1999

> ### NOTE
>
> Some buyers prefer to make all replacements and capital improvements as soon as they buy a property, especially one that is run down. This increases the property's value and related rental rates, makes management easier, and, to the extent the IRS allows, means the buyer is eligible for more tax deductions in the first year of ownership.

Capital Improvements

Capital improvements include:

- Additions to the property
- New facades and/or storefronts to spruce up the property
- Painting or insulating the building to stop leaks and to get HVAC savings
- The addition of elevators to multilevel walk-up buildings
- Replacement with modern, more efficient items

Marketing Space

No matter how well your building is managed and maintained, tenants are bound to come and go, so marketing—publicizing—your property to fill empty space is another important aspect of a new property owner's education and a management company's duties. We've all seen property vacancy advertisements—they're everywhere:

Signage on the building itself. This is remarkably effective because neighborhood businesses and professionals are your most likely tenants. Particularly effective are signs that are lit at night, with the leasing telephone number prominently displayed.

Advertising in newspapers and other publications. Obviously, this type of marketing expands the impact of neighborhood signs and reaches a wider audience.

Include the rental rate in your vacancy publicity. This will limit inquiries to serious potential tenants. And if you want to make it clear up front that you're willing to negotiate, simply add the word *Negotiable* in the ad.

Brokers. In the same way that you perhaps used a broker to find the property you wanted to invest in, tenants use a broker to find a location they want to rent. Prospective tenants go to brokers for the same reasons you did: Brokers can show many appropriate spaces and can help negotiate leases, rental rates, and so on. Often, you, the landlord, will pay the broker's commission (although you can recoup this when you later determine the rental rate). However, in hot rental markets where the supply of available rentals is low, as in New York City apartments, the landlord often insists that the tenant pay the broker.

Note that most major tenants will engage an exclusive broker to find them suitable locations, with the understanding that the broker will be compensated by the landlord. The major tenant in that case would not deal directly with a landlord, but refer the landlord to the broker. Obviously, the landlord would have to negotiate with and pay that broker to get the tenant and the lease.

DEFINITION

Exclusive brokers have the exclusive right, for a certain period of time, to represent someone in a transaction. This can be a seller, an owner-landlord, or a tenant.

Other sources. Real estate organizations and publications are good venues for advertising vacancies. And real estate properties of all kinds are now being marketed over the Internet. You can usually even find listings for a particular location or area simply by typing keywords such as "real estate properties" or "real estate brokers," then clicking through to a state and even to particular counties, cities, or towns.

Preparing for a New Tenant

Once you or your management company has found an appropriate tenant to fill your vacancy, you must get the space ready for occupancy. Generally, what you have to do to ready the space will be specified in the lease.

Office Properties

The details of the preparations for a new tenant are very important components of office building leases. Typically included in such specifications are an agreement by the landlord to alter or build the space being rented to meet the tenants' needs, and an agreement by the tenant to reimburse the landlord for the costs of the tenant improvements (TIs) over the life of the lease, plus 10 percent interest. For example:

Size of space	1,000 sq. ft.
Base rent	$20 per sq. ft.
Total annual base rent	$20,000
Life of lease	5 years
Tenant improvement costs	$15,000
Tenant annual reimbursement: $15,000 amortized over 5 years with interest at 10% per year	$ 3,750
Plus base rent	$20,000
Total initial rent (Plus annual escalations, CAM, etc.)	$23,750

Of course, the landlord would do a credit check on the tenant before agreeing to undertake to spend this $15,000 on improvements on the tenant's behalf. There may also be brokerage commissions involved. Another way to do this would be to give a work letter to the tenant, or a certain amount of "free" rent if the tenant agrees to make his or her own improvements.

Apartment Buildings

Vacated apartments have to be repaired, repainted, cleaned, and readied for the new tenant. These are considered part of the normal operating costs of residential properties.

Retail Properties

Rarely are landlords expected or required to do tenant improvements for retail properties. In general, preparing for a new retail tenant involves cleaning and repairs.

One exception, however, is build-to-suits. Remember from Chapter 3 that a build-to-suit is a property that the owner agrees to build or convert to meet unique requirements of a particular tenant. Thus, unlike the case with most other retail properties, in a build-to-suit the landlord agrees either to undertake new construction or to alter space (including some fixtures) to a tenant's specifications. Needless to say, the owner doesn't do this for nothing; in return, the owner is reimbursed over the lease (as described previously). Build-to-suit leases, by the way, are an excellent way to attract a major tenant to your retail property.

TIP

Some improvements for major tenants can be financed by banks, depending on the quality of the tenant and the amount of the lease. This is another good reason to cultivate a relationship with your bank representative.

LEASES

Let's begin at the beginning: A lease is an agreement by the owner of a property or piece of equipment to grant use of it to someone else in return for money. Pretty much anything can be leased or rented: buildings, cars, machinery, furniture, even employees! The person giving the lease is the *lessor;* the person getting the lease is the *lessee* (also the *tenant*); the money (or other consideration) paid is the *rent;* and the agreement spelling out the respective rights of the tenant and responsibilities of the owner is the *lease.*

Lease agreements include (not necessarily in this order):

- Name of property owner
- Address of property
- Site being leased (e.g., store, apartment, office) and number of square feet

- Name of tenant
- Length of lease
- Rent to be paid (this might appear in a separate schedule, as it may change from year to year)
- Terms of lease (landlord's and tenant's respective rights and responsibilities)
- Additional clauses agreed to (for example, options to renew, right to buy in case of a sale, etc.)
- Date of signing

Most real estate professionals use preprinted *boilerplate* lease forms that have blanks left for filling in the terms. That is why you may have seen nonapplicable clauses crossed out on an apartment or appliance lease that you have signed. You may also have seen other clauses added on a separate page; these are called *addendum clauses*.

NOTE

Most state laws invoke some version of what's called the *Statute of Frauds* to handle disputes, should they arise, between an owner and a tenant. Basically, the Statute of Frauds states that every real estate agreement must be in writing to be valid. In short, if it's not in writing, there is no agreement. This is to prevent impossible-to-prove he said/she said situations regarding promises allegedly made and not kept. Only what is delineated in the lease, including agreed-upon tenant improvements, is binding. Until a lease or purchase agreement is put in writing and signed by both the seller and the buyer, and a good-faith deposit (the consideration) has been paid, there is no agreement—and thus no grounds for dispute.

Addendum clauses usually deal with unique requirements of the landlord (lessor) or tenant (lessee) that are not addressed in the main body of a preprinted lease. In the case of a retail lessee, for example, such clauses may state that the tenant is responsible for cleaning the sidewalk in front of the building, or that the tenant will pay for overtime (after close of business hours) HVAC. In the case of an apartment lessee, addendum clauses will also list additional landlord and/or tenant rights and responsibilities.

Most leases contain a provision that states that six months before the end of the lease the landlord can start marketing the space and showing it to prospective new tenants (see the "Marketing Space" section earlier). To you, the owner (or your management company), this is the "alarm" going off to remind you to approach the current tenant about negotiating a renewal lease. Until the renewal lease is signed, however, you should continue to market the space in case the current tenant doesn't want to meet terms for a renewal. In commercial leases, upon the expiration date, either the tenant and the landlord agree to a renewal (they sign a new lease) or the tenant is expected to vacate the premises, leaving them clean and in the same condition in which they were rented.

> **TIP**
>
> As a novice real estate investor, you should obtain a preprinted, or *boilerplate*, lease agreement and read through it carefully to familiarize yourself with the setup of and terminology used in these documents. A sample lease is provided for your convenience in Appendix C. After you've learned as much as you can on your own, contact your attorney or broker and ask him or her to define the terms or clauses that you do not understand.

Lease Designations

As noted, the subject of leases is complex, and the primary reason for its complexity lies in the fact that real estate laws are set by state and municipalities, not the federal government. Therefore, each state has its own laws—though most have similarities. It is beyond the scope of this book to detail the real estate laws of the 50 United States, but I will address their generalities and similarities as a guideline.

Commercial leases can be divided into four categories: gross, net, land, and triple net.

Gross Lease
Gross leases are defined as those for which the landlord pays all building operating costs and charges rent accordingly. The rent would include the tenants' pro rata share of operating costs. These

leases are considered the most management intensive, as the landlord pays all property-related expenses, including repairs, utilities (depending on the type of property), maintenance of common areas, cleaning (in the case of office buildings), and insurance.

Gross leases are used most commonly for apartment and office buildings. Office leases, in particular, are very volatile; an office tenant can move someplace else easily with minimal business disruption, unlike the case with a neighborhood retail store. And, particularly in office leases, the landlord is held responsible for all building and office costs, including cleaning of offices after hours; utilities; building-related repairs; and maintenance of elevators, hallways, stairwells, and other common areas.

Net Lease

A *net lease* is defined as one for which the tenant pays the operating costs; thus, the rent paid to the landlord is *net*. Under the conditions of this type of lease, the tenant agrees to pay all operating expenses of the space, including real estate taxes, insurance, and fuel. Generally, the landlord is renting the tenant four walls. Not surprisingly, then, net leases are most commonly undertaken with retailers, who develop the inside of the store to suit their needs. Retail tenants also generally do their own repairs and replacements, pay for utilities, and do their own in-house cleaning and maintenance. Net leases specify that tenants must ask the landlord's permission before making changes to the leased space. The tenant supplies the landlord with copies of plans, building permits, and labor compensation insurance for the landlord's approval. The landlord is not responsible for any of this.

Retail properties with net leases are easier to manage; and if they are in good locations, they are less sensitive to the impact of economic changes.

Land Leases

As the name suggests, *land leases* are for land only, and are usually on a net basis to the landlord and for long periods of time.

Triple Net Lease

A *triple net lease* is a form of long-term land lease. The tenant agrees to erect a building on the site and pay for all expenses, so the rent is really net to the landlord. Typical triple net leases are fast-food franchises and gas stations. These leases are easy to manage, but may be too large an investment for novices.

Addendum Clauses

In the section on leasing, I touched briefly on additional clauses to leases, referred to as *addenda,* that extend the boilerplate, or standard, lease as appropriate to the property and the tenant. Addendum clauses typically address common area maintenance (CAM) agreements, rent increases (*escalations*), percentage-of-sales agreements, and relocation agreements. Let's look at each of these common lease addendum issues in turn.

Common Area Maintenance (CAM) Clause
As previously discussed, usually it is the landlord's responsibility to take care of the common areas of his or her property, but some leases may call for reimbursement to the landlord's common area maintenance expenses, usually on a pro rata or other basis. For example, let's take a 5,000-square-foot building whose total CAM for 1996 was $6,150:

$$\text{CAM per sq. ft.} = \frac{\$6,150}{5,000} \text{ sq. ft.} = \$1.23 \text{ per sq. ft.}$$

Tenant A rents 1,000 square feet, and, because it was called for in the lease, pays as additional rent 1,000 square feet times $1.23, which equals $1,230. This is called a *CAM contribution*. This CAM contribution can be either a pro rata share of all CAM or a pro rata share of increases in CAM above a base level or year (usually set at the time the lease is signed). The first example here is of a pro rata share of all CAM.

Building size	5,000 sq. ft.
Store size	1,000 sq. ft.

$$\text{Pro rata} = \frac{1,000}{5,000} = 20\%$$

CAM year 1	$6,130
CAM year 2	$6,450

If the lease provides for a pro rata contribution toward CAM, the tenant pays (in addition to the base rent):

$$\text{Year 1} = \frac{1,000}{5,000} = 20\% \text{ of } \$6,130 = \$1,226$$

$$\text{Year 2} = \frac{1,000}{5,000} = 20\% \text{ of } \$6,450 = \$1,290$$

In the second example, the lease provides for a pro rata share of the increase in CAM over year 1. This is also called an *expense stop*.

CAM year 2	$6,450
Less CAM year 1	6,130
Increase in CAM	$ 320

$$\text{Pro rata share} = \frac{\$1,000}{\$5,000} = 20\% \times \$320 = \$64$$

The tenant pays 20 percent of the $320 increase in CAM, or $64. Now let's look at year 3:

CAM year 3	$6,800
Less CAM year 1	$6,130
Increase in CAM from year 1	$ 670

$$\text{Pro rata share} = \frac{\$1,000}{\$5,000} = 20\% \times \$670 = \$134$$

So, in year 3, the tenant pays 20 percent of the $670 increase in CAM over year 1—or $134—in addition to the base rent.

A CAM contribution passes along the costs of operating the property to the tenant. This protects the landlord from inflationary cost increases versus long-term, fixed-rent leases. CAM contributions are fairer to tenants, too, as they only pay for actual pro rata costs and/or increases thereof, as opposed to set rent increases that may be more or less than inflation.

Rent Increase Clause

Increases in base rent from year to year are called *escalations*. They can be a certain amount, as shown here:

Monthly rent	Increase
Year 1 $1,000	
Year 2 $1,050	$50
Year 3 $1,110	$60
Year 4 $1,175	$65
Year 5 $1,250	$75

Or they can be a straight percentage—for example, a 5 percent increase per annum—as in the following example:

Monthly rent	Increase
Year 1 $1,000	
Year 2 $1,050	($1,000 + 5%)
Year 3 $1,100	($1,000 + 5% for 2 years)
Year 4 $1,150	($1,000 + 5% for 3 years)
Year 5 $1,200	($1,000 + 5% for 4 years)

The 5 percent increase could be compounded, producing the following result:

Monthly rent
Year 1 $1,000.00
Year 2 $1,050.00
Year 3 $1,102.50
Year 4 $1,157.63
Year 5 $1,215.50

Percentage-of-Sales Clause

Some leases provide for the landlord to get a percentage of sales, in particular when dealing with a major tenant, as defined earlier, such as a supermarket or department store that demanded—and was given—a low base rent. If the store is highly profitable, the percentage of sales:

- Makes up the low rent to the owner.

- Is justified to the tenant by the higher-than-expected profit, if sales turn out to be greater than projected at the time the lease is signed.

- Is very beneficial to the landlord in the event of superinflation; the tenant loses nothing either, as sales will be up in such an economic period.

There are two ways to do a percentage of sales: straight percentage of all sales and higher-percentage-of-sales provision compared to the base rent, whichever is higher. We'll go through a straight percentage of all sales example first:

Year 1 base rent	$500,000 per annum, plus 3% of sales
Year 1 sales	$10 million
Percentage	× 3%
Amount as percentage of sales	$300,000
Total rent paid ($500,000 base, plus $300,000 as a percentage of sales)	$800,000
Year 2 base rent	$500,000 per annum plus 3% of sales
Year 2 sales	$11 million
Percentage	× 3%
Amount	$330,000
Total rent paid ($500,000 base, plus $330,000 as 3% of sales)	$830,000

The alternative is to include in the lease a higher-percentage-of-sales provision compared to the base rent, whichever is higher. Here's an example:

Year 1 base rent	$500,000, or 6% of sales, whichever is higher
Sales year 1	$8 million
Percentage	× 6%
Amount	$480,000

Which is higher? Obviously, $500,000, the base rent. Thus, $500,000 rent would be paid for year 1. Now let's look at year 2:

Base rent	$500,000
Sales year 2	$9 million
Percentage	× 6%
Amount	$540,000

Here, the $540,000 is higher, based on the percentage of sales, so in year 2, $540,000 would be the rent paid. Now for year 3:

Base rent	$500,000
Sales year 2	$8.25 million
Percentage	× 6%
Amount	$495,000

In this case, the $500,000 base rent is higher than the $495,000, so the rent for year 3 would be $500,000.

In practice, the way the higher-percentage-of-sales provision works is that the tenant pays the base rent monthly during the year—in this case, $500,000 ÷ 12 months, for $41,667 per month. The tenant does its year-end closing of its books and determines its sales for the year. This usually takes three or four months (the deadline date should be specified in the lease). The percentage of sales is then computed. In our example:

- Year 1: No (0) additional rent is due.
- Year 2: $540,000 versus $500,000, or $40,000 additional rent is due.

- Year 3: No (0) additional rent is due.

Other Clauses

You may see various other lease clauses, depending on the needs of
the landlord and tenant.

> *Demolition clauses.* In some cities, older buildings scheduled for
> future destruction may have demolition clauses, which typi-
> cally call for termination of the lease upon advance notice of
> demolition. Demolition clauses may also call for reimburse-
> ment to the tenant for the unamortized (undepreciated)
> portion of previously agreed-upon improvement costs, relo-
> cation costs, and possible other compensation. The advantage
> to the landlord is that if a major developer comes along and is
> willing to pay top dollar to buy and demolish the building to
> put up a new, bigger building, the landlord can invoke the
> demolition clause, reimburse the tenants per their respective
> leases, and deliver the building vacant to the developer.
>
> *Relocation clauses.* If the lease has a relocation clause, and tenant
> A wants to expand, but tenant B is in the adjacent space nec-
> essary for the expansion, the landlord has the right to move
> tenant B to another similar office/store in the building. In
> such a case, the landlord would typically pay tenant B's costs
> of preparing the new space, all unamortized move-in costs,
> utility installation, and some downtime reimbursements.
> The advantage of relocation clauses to the landlord is that
> they enable him or her to accommodate the growth of ten-
> ants' businesses and to keep these growing tenants by giving
> them the additional space they need.

Lease Summary

To summarize, a lease is an agreement between a landlord (the
lessor), who gives the lease, and a tenant (the lessee), who gets the
lease. Lease clauses are a function of location, negotiations, local
market conditions, local rent regulations, and other agreements
between landlords and tenants. To familiarize yourself with these
important documents, review the sample leases included in
Appendix C. That process, plus all-important experience, will
result in lease negotiating ability.

ON YOUR OWN: YOUR FUTURE IN REAL ESTATE

One of the best aspects of real estate investing is that it's never boring. There's always more to learn and farther you can go to expand your skills and knowledge—and your financial growth! Though it is beyond the scope of this primer in real estate investing to go into detail on the more professional side of real estate involvement, I want to give you a taste of all that awaits if you decide to continue in this exciting field of investment.

For starters, after you and/or your group have owned the property for at least a year, and you have carefully monitored and learned from your professional management company, you can consider undertaking the management yourself. By doing so, you and/or the group will reduce costs, gain more direct control over the property, and continue to supplement your learning process and develop management expertise. But note that if you do this as part of a group, unless the work is shared equally, the group should set up a system that compensates the members who do the accounting, lease preparation, showing and inspection, tenant visits, and so forth. A good way to investigate this possibility is to contact the Institute of Real Estate Management (IREM), mentioned earlier. It is a comprehensive source for information on education and accreditation in real estate management. IREM describes itself as providing "training, information, research, analysis, and practical advice for professionals managing all types of income-producing real estate at all career levels." Its services "are designed to support our members' commitment to maximizing the value of the real estate entrusted to them and to safeguarding the people who live, work, and shop in the properties they manage."

And if you continue to buy real estate—let's say you have three or more properties—you may even consider setting up your own management company. This could take the form of sole proprietorship, a partnership, a limited liability company (LLC), or a C or S corporation. Your own management company could charge each property you own the normal management fees. In turn, it could pay you a salary, provide medical benefits, provide you with a pension plan, and enable you to get liability and other insurance.

On a personal development note, you might also want to consider becoming either a real estate associate or eventually a broker. Most real estate licensing laws provide that an active buyer and owner of properties can qualify to apply for a real estate broker's license after a certain number of years or deals. Or you can become a certified property manager (CPM). Whatever your personal growth plan in real estate, the point is to keep your eye on the prize: financial benefit. In real estate, it is always useful to have one more certificate or license. To become a licensed professional, you need to acquire a combination of education (including passing any required exams) and experience. There's no time like the present to get started in this exciting field!

APPENDIX

A

Additional Deals

PROPERTY RENOVATIONS: "NO MONEY DOWN"

Another way to make money in real estate is to buy distressed, broken-down property, renovate it, and sell it for substantial profits. Infomercials, especially, claim that with "no money down" you can pick up properties, fix them, and sell or rent them. Fallacies in pronouncement, are that you need money for:

- Closing costs, especially to record deeds and mortgages
- Monthly mortgage payments, utility deposits, monthly bills, and insurance until the property is sold or rented
- Purchasing materials, labor, permits, drawings, and so on
- Leaving the property vacant until it is completed

It generally takes a minimum of four to six months to turn around a distressed single-family home and more time to sell or refinance it. You must be able to carry (pay) the monthly costs during the period it is vacant.

Sharpen your pencil and make real projections that allow for real costs before going into a deal on a shoestring and running out of money before completing it.

I learned this lesson the hard way. In 1977, while operating our garden-apartment complex, my partners and I were offered a package of 10 buildings in Park Slope, Brooklyn, which was beginning to become gentrified. There was a partnership dispute, as it turned out that one of the partners (the promoter), a real estate broker, had convinced a wealthy backer to fund the purchase and renovations of the properties. The financier was to be a silent partner. The broker was to do all of the work, which included finding and renovating suitable properties, then renting and financing or selling them. What profit-sharing arrangement they had between them I didn't know.

At that point, the package consisted of 10 small buildings of four to five stories with six to ten apartments each. Some buildings were vacant; others were partially occupied. The renovations were incomplete.

The partners were in litigation. The financier claimed that the broker was overcharging for the renovations. Apparently, actual costs far exceeded original guesstimates, and the financier grew tired of coming up with more money all the time.

We were offered all 10 buildings for $300,000, with a $30,000 down payment. However, we realized that we didn't have the money to buy, renovate, make mortgage payments, and so on, for all 10 buildings. We selected two of them. One was a five-story walk-up apartment building with two stores on street level. We bought it for $60,000, with $10,000 in cash.

We vacated the apartments and began renovations. My partners decided to do the renovations themselves, even though they had no experience. They thought that by hiring cheap day laborers and cutting other corners they could save money.

They had told me the renovations were to take two months and cost $30,000. It was to be financed by not paying the garden-apartment mortgage for those two months, then making it up. After two months, practically nothing had been done. At my urging, we then hired an outside contractor to finish the job.

Good, efficient contractors are worth the 10 to 20 percent margin (on bigger jobs, the margin is less than 10 percent): They have the capability of bringing to the project a skilled, experienced pool of laborers; good subcontractors with whom they have worked before;

the ability to buy materials at a discount; experience in reviewing plans, the knowledge needed to deal with architects and building inspectors; and the desire to finish the job as quickly and as expeditiously as possible in order to get paid and thus earn a profit.

Before starting a major renovation, it is a good idea to estimate labor, time, and materials costs. You can do this yourself from experience or hire an engineering consultant architect. This preliminary estimate can be used as the basis of comparison with any bids received.

The most important thing is the contractor's reputation. Get recommendations from friends and business associates for three or more contractors, show them the drawings and specifications (if necessary), and get their bids. The lowest bidder is not necessarily the best one to choose.

When I was operating 1 million square feet of office building in Houston and spending more than $1 million per year in office renovations (build-outs) I always had three contractors, and would spread the work among them to keep them all interested, competitive, and honest.

By the time construction was completed, we were four months behind in mortgage payments on our garden apartments. We rented the renovated apartments at decent rents, and renewed the store leases with increases. This justified a $100,000 refinance. With the proceeds of this loan we were able to pay back the $50,000 mortgage from the seller, catch up on our mortgage payments on the garden-apartment mortgage, and get back our $10,000 down payment. The cash flow from the five-story building then looked like this:

Income apartments

8 apartments @ $500 per month, over 12 months	$48,000
2 stores @ $750 per month, over 12 months	$18,000
Gross annual rental income	$64,000
Less annual expenses	
Real estate taxes	$ 6,000
Heating	$ 6,000
Insurance	$ 1,500
Electricity	$ 1,000
Repairs	$ 3,000

Porter (part-time)	$ 1,200
Miscellaneous	$ 1,300
Total annual expenses	$20,000
Cash flow before mortgage (64,000 – 20,000)	$44,000
Less $100,000 mortgage at 8 percent for 15 years	$14,000 (est.)
Approximate annual net cash flow	$30,000

A year after acquisition and a lot of hard work we had annual cash income of $30,000.00!

Along with gentrification, regenerating, and rebuilding of old city neighborhoods came the condominium craze. Landlords were able to sell apartments to the residents as condominiums, or *condos*. We sold our eight apartments for an average of $75,000 each, or a total of $600,000 over three years in the mid-1980s. We kept the stores, and we currently net $60,000 a year in rents. Thus, our original cash investment of $10,000 generated over $600,000 in condo sales 10 years later, and currently produces $60,000 in net rental income. At a 10 percent return, the stores are worth:

$$\frac{\text{Income}}{\text{Return}} = \frac{\$60,000}{10\%} \quad \text{or} \quad \$600,000$$

The total return was $600,000 in condo sales, a current value of another $600,000 for the condo stores, or over $1.2 million, plus net rental income from the apartments before they were sold.

WEST 42ND STREET TENEMENT BUILDINGS: INTRODUCTION TO MANHATTAN DEVELOPMENT

In 1983, I found a package of three adjacent tenement buildings on a 75- by 100-foot lot on West 42nd Street near Times Square in Manhattan. The selling price was $1.2 million, with $400,000 in cash and 15-year payments at 6 percent interest, self-liquidating. A *tenement* is a walk-up apartment building containing only basic amenities, often originally built to house immigrant labor. There were a total of 39 apartments, most of which were rent-controlled, many of which housed senior citizens. Each building had about 13 small apartments and a store on the ground floor. I bought these buildings on behalf of our clients.

The most valuable piece of real estate in a very densely built area like midtown Manhattan is an empty lot. Therefore, I gradually started vacating the buildings. As apartments emptied, I sealed them off. As the store leases expired, I wrote new ones with demolition clauses. A demolition clause states that, in the event the building is to be demolished (usually for new construction), the lease automatically terminates; most old-building leases in Manhattan contain that clause. Some make provision for reimbursing the tenant.

In 1986, I was offered $6 million for the site as is! We had paid $1.2 million with $400,000 cash four years earlier. Of course, due to process of vacating, we had to subsidize the building to the extent of $100,000 per year. Thus, the results of the deal were:

Selling price	$6,000,000
Mortgage balance	$ 675,000
Cash proceeds from sale	$5,325,000
Down payment	($ 400,000)
Subsidies (100,000 per year for 4 years)	($ 400,000)
Total Cash Investment	($ 800,000)
Net Profit	$4,625,000

This on an investment of $800,000 in four years!

The value of land is based on what can be built on it, and the related potential income. Thus, rural land whose potential income is based on sales of crops, obviously has a much lower value than a lot in a busy area on which can be built a multistory building that can command high rents.

Many municipalities control the development of land within their boundaries by enacting zoning laws. Certain parts of town may be set aside, or *zoned* as residential zones, others may be zoned for manufacturing and industrial, other zones may be both residential and commercial. A town needs commercial zones because these basics are needed to provide a certain quality of life:

- Jobs
- Retail services (e.g., supermarkets, pharmacies, small stores)
- Professional services (e.g., doctors, lawyers, accountants, bankers)

In addition to supplementing the residential part of the community, commercially zoned properties pay much more in real estate taxes than residential zones do. Real estate taxes are used to pay for municipal services, with the major part of most municipalities' budgets being derived therefrom. Each community must decide between a certain quality of life for its residents, and paying for it. That is one reason why commercial developments are encouraged.

Of course the zoning laws are different everywhere. The value of land is a function of its future value with building on it, minus the cost of construction, minus a reasonable developer's profit. To put this into numbers:

Value of completed building was 10 times net rental income of $60,000 per year	$600,000
Construction cost for 5,000-sq.-ft. building @ $70 per ft.	($350,000)
Soft costs (interest during construction, legal, engineering, architectural, etc.)	($ 70,000)
	($420,000)
Developer's profit (15% of $420,000)	($ 63,000)
Net land value before construction	$117,000

Thus, if one could buy land in the path of development, like farmland, cheaply, wait for development, and get a change of zoning to upgrade the land, big profits can be made.

Now, to get back to Manhattan. In 1986, Manhattan residential and office space rented at an average $40 per square foot per year. It cost $250 per square foot to build. Thus, the value of a square foot of buildable land:

Net rental income of $40 @ 10%	$400
Less construction cost per square foot	($250)
	150
Soft cost, including interest, during construction (15% of construction cost)	($ 40)
	110
Allowable Developer's profit (10% of 400) 10% of building value	($ 40)
Net land value per buildable foot	$ 70.00

In a high-density area like Manhattan you are allowed to build up to 12 to 16 times your land area. Thus, one square foot of land can be built 12 to 16 times, or 12 to 16 buildable feet, giving one square foot of property a value of $840 (12 floors × $70 per foot up to 16 floors × $70 per foot) or $1120 per foot.

Thus, the land under the West 42nd Street property of 7,500 square feet had a potential value of $9 million (7,500 feet × $1,200 per foot), which is why we were able to sell it in 1988 (at the peak of the real estate boom) for $6 million!

RETAIL OUTLET

By 1983, I was becoming more involved with real estate. I had been licensed as a real estate sales associate (salesman), and was working out of my real estate partner's (a real estate broker) office since 1974. Because of the amount of time needed to teach 12 credits per week of college courses, handle my lucrative CPA practice, and transact real estate, I decided to give up teaching to free up my time for clients, deals, and personal investments.

If you start on a savings, pension, and real estate investment program in your twenties, by your mid-fifties you should be in good financial shape. You might take early retirement, with real estate providing supplemental income and a possible second career.

Because I had nearly 10 years of experience and numerous deals under my belt and had taken the mandatory 90 hours of course work in New York, I passed the exam for my New York state real estate broker's license and set up an office in an apartment in one of our properties.

A foreigner approached me with the following proposal: His wife owned a factory in Greece and they wanted to open a chain of retail outlets in the United States. The first building purchased was a two-story retail building, 20 feet by 60 feet, in a very busy retail area, costing $320,000.

I set up two corporations: the owner corporation to buy and own the building, and the retail corporation to lease the building from the owner corporation and to operate the retail store.

Based on the location of the building, the retail corporation lease, and my personal guarantee, I was able to get a mortgage of $240,000 ((75%) of cost) at 8 percent for 20 years, self-liquidating. Thus, the deal shaped up as follows:

Cost of building	$320,000
Less bank mortgage (75%)	($240,000)
Cash equity	$ 80,000
Building renovation cost	$100,000
Total cash investment	$180,000

The retail corporation operated the retail store and paid the mortgage instead of rent.

Five years later, in 1988, when we were offered $850,000 cash for the building, we decided to sell, resulting in the following:

Selling price	$850,000
Less mortgage balance	($200,000)
Net proceeds of sale	$650,000

Thus, on an initial cash investment of $180,000 (including store renovations) we got five years of use as a retail store and cash proceeds of $650,000, or a profit of $470,000, more than two and a half times our $180,000 investment.

MANHATTAN ASSEMBLAGE: TRIBECA

Another interesting deal was the assemblage I helped put together on a block-front in Tribeca (Triangle below Canal) in lower Manhattan. An *assemblage* is a group of adjacent buildings on a large enough land area to make them suitable for demolition and replacement by a large, new building. A *block-front* is a site that fronts a main thoroughfare from one corner to the next, or the whole block. Clients of an attorney I know owned a coffee shop on the south corner of Murray and Church Streets in lower Manhattan.

Their lease was coming due, and they wanted to try to buy the building. Every successful small business should try to buy the building in which it is located for long-term security, appreciation, and future salability. In the future, the owners could sell the business with a lease on the building as part of the deal. The building was five stories, 176 feet long on Church Street and 25 feet wide, with stores on the ground floor and offices above.

I started to negotiate the purchase of 125 Church Street. The owners' attorney had a minority interest in the building with the right of first refusal, which gave him the right to match my offer. The attorney stated that the building was not for sale to us, and that he intended to exercise his right of first refusal by matching our offer, neither selling it to us or giving us a good lease extension. His long-term plans were to develop the building; at one point in our meeting, he said that he would like to own an office building in Manhattan.

Meanwhile, I had met the manager of the adjacent building (building 2), who informed me that the owner of the building wanted to sell. I told my partners that we should look into it as a backup position. In the event that the lease renewal terms were too onerous, we could move the coffee shop next door, keeping our regular customers.

The asking price was $850,000 for the building, plus notes of $130,000 in lieu of rent arrears for the store. The ground floor of the building was an aquarium running from Murray Street straight through to Warren Street, 176 feet long by 25 feet wide, or more than 4,000 square feet; upstairs were lofts. It had been operated by the building owner until the late 1950s, when he decided to retire in Hawaii.

The manager, a CPA, was left in charge of the building and the business. He had religiously sent financial statements and money every month for close to 30 years. He was also getting ready to retire. The aquarium business had been sold for notes and a lease calling for $3,000 per month in rent. The current rental value was $6,000 per month, or $3,000 more. The store buyer hadn't made note payments or paid rent in about two years, for a total of $130,000.

For a $130,00 note secured by a third mortgage on the building, I took over the arrears. My strategy was to sue him for payment and use his payment to pay off the note. If he vacated, I would rent to the next tenant for $6,000 per month and pay off the notes over five years. The deal was financed as follows:

Selling price	$850,000
Note and rent arrears	$130,000
Total paid	$980,000
First mortgage from a bank	$650,000
Second mortgage from the owner	$100,000

Third mortgage note	$130,000
Net cash required	$100,000
Total	$980,000

After the closing, we started legal processing against the tenants, who left. We then put the store up for rent at $6,000 per
month. Meanwhile, it was costing us $6,000 a month to carry the
buildings, which included operating expenses and mortgage payments. The building was commercial, with the ground floor store
and four floors of lofts, two per floor. These were occupied by
artists as work and residence quarters. From them we collected
about $5,000 a month in rents.

The corner building (building 1), had been appraised at $2.3
million. I had estimated the value of building 2 at $1.5 million. The
bank's appraiser agreed with me! Thus, I now had equity computed as follows:

Appraised value of building 2	$1,500,000
Less: First mortgage	$ (650,000)
Second mortgage	$ (100,000)
Third mortgage	$ (130,000)
Total debt	$ (880,000)
Net equity in building 2	$ 620,000

This, on a cash investment of $100,000! Thus, we were already
making a profit of:

Equity	$620,000
Cash down payment	($100,000)
Profit	$520,000

Our equity was now six times our cash investment of $100,000!

After taking over the building, I was approached by the owner
of buildings 3 and 4, who also wanted to sell. I said I would pay the
same price I paid for building 2. We finally agreed on a price of
$950,000 per building to avoid paying the New York state tax on

buildings selling for over $1 million. I now needed $1.9 million in cash, as the owner wouldn't take notes. The purchase was finalized with a first mortgage on buildings 3 and 4 and a new fourth mortgage on building 2, for total financing of $1.9 million from another bank. In other words, no cash down! I put up all three buildings as collateral.

When I had signed the purchase contract I had approached the attorney who owned building 1 and offered to sell him building 2 and my contract to purchase buildings 3 and 4. He would then control a 176- by 100-foot (17,600-square-foot) site, with 211,000 buildable feet (17,600 × 12). After vacating the tenants and demolishing the building, the resulting lot would have a value of approximately $10,000,000 (211,000 × $50 = $10 million).

The attorney refused to buy, apparently thinking that I didn't have the financial resources to complete the deal. I was hoping to avoid the closing costs, including payment of a 1 percent fee (a point) to a mortgage broker.

By that time, I had invested more than $250,000 cash, between the down payment of $100,000, out-of-pocket carrying cost, and legal and other fees. My partners, who had assured me they would carry their part of the deal, suddenly had no money. I agreed to carry the whole load in return for 15 percent interest on my money and a 50 percent share of profits (as opposed to one-third). They agreed.

A week before the closing, the lender announced that he wanted $200,000 of the $1.9 million loan to be held in escrow until buildings 3 and 4 were rented and could carry themselves. The buildings were completely occupied and used by the seller. Even though I had anticipated and budgeted $100,000 for closing costs, I did not have the $200,000!

Meanwhile, as I was looking for the money, the attorneys (mine and the seller's) decided to conduct a dry run, making sure the paperwork was in order, ironing out any problems, and making for a smoother closing. The purchase contract had called for immediate possession of buildings 3 and 4 by the buyers right after closing. The seller's attorney stated they needed 90 days to sell their inventory and move out.

I stated that, because the buildings weren't paying rent, I had to set aside $200,000 in escrow. Would he hold a second mortgage for the escrow and closing costs? He agreed, as long as the interest rate was the same as that charged by the bank. I agreed, and also agreed not to charge any rent for the 90 days.

The seller took back a second mortgage of $300,000, which is how I bought buildings 3 and 4 with no money down!

However, my monthly out-of-pocket carrying costs for the three buildings were now $35,000. I estimated that I could make this up by renting the empty space. Before doing this, however, I decided to give my neighbor (the attorney) a call. I told him that I had just closed. Since most of the buildings were vacant, it would be relatively easily to completely vacate them in their present condition if he were to buy them now. If he didn't buy them, I would be forced to start renting and it would cost much more in the future to vacate. He said, let's meet.

I sold him the whole package, buildings 2, 3, and 4, for $4 million cash, with three months to close. He made a down payment, on contract, of $150,000. Because my mortgage payments were $35,000 per month, and I had to keep the buildings vacant, the buyer agreed to let me use this escrow money to make the monthly payments on the mortgages.

Apparently, he started looking for backers. Three months later, he called to say that he needed more time to put an investment group together. I agreed to give him until the end of the year (it was then March) as long as I received $40,000 per month to cover my out-of-pocket costs. He agreed.

He found backers and, on December 23, 1986, we closed. The significance of this date was that it was just before the Tax Reform Act of 1986. The Tax Reform Act extended depreciation lives on buildings from 20 years to 39.5 years, no matter how old the building was. The buyers wanted to take advantage of grandfathered IRS real estate rules before the new law came into effect. To summarize the sale:

Selling price, cash	$4,000,000
Less: Closing costs	$ (150,000)
First mortgage, building 2	$ (650,000)
Second mortgage, building 2	$ (100,000)
Third mortgage note, building 2	$ (100,000)
First Mortgage, buildings 3 and 4	$(1,900,000)

Total deductions	$ 2,900,00
Net cash proceeds	$1,100,000
Total cash invested over a three year period:	$ 300,000

Thus, $300,000 became $1.1 million over three years. The money was divided as follows:

Return of cash invested by me	$ 300,000
Interest, 15% for 3 years	$ 135,000
Subtotal	$ 435,000
$1,100,000 − $435,000 = $665,000 ÷ 2	$ 332,500
Total due me	$ 767,500
Partner A (25% × $665,000)	$ 166,250
Partner B (25% × $665,000)	$ 166,250
Total cash proceeds	$1,100,000

To explain, the first $300,000 went to reimburse me for the money I had laid out over three years. I was also entitled to 15 percent annual interest during that period, and 15 percent of $300,000 is $45,000 per year times three years, which equals $135,000. Up to that point, I got $435,000. There remained:

Cash proceeds	$1,100,000
Paid to me for loans with interest of 15%	$ 435,000
Leftover, net profit	$ 665,000

665,000 divided as follows:

Me (50% × 665,000)	$ 332,500
Partner A (25% × 665,000)	$ 166,250
Partner B (25% × 664,000)	$ 166,250
	$ 665,000

Thus, I received a total of $435,000 for loans and interest, and $332,500 representing 50 percent of the remaining profits, for a total of $767,500 in three years, on an investment of $300,000 and a lot of hard work. My partners each received $166,250 for finding the deal and helping me put it together. However, they lied to me about their original cash holdings and the ability to help carry the buildings.

The problem with no-money-down deals is that you still need enough money to close, renovate if necessary, and pay mortgage and operating costs until the property is either sold or rented.

After this deal I always made sure my partners put up their share of the money before proceeding with any partnership.

B

Understanding Taxes and Real Estate

If you take into account the income tax benefits, combined with appreciation and the ability to take advantage of leverage, real estate becomes even a more lucrative investment. That's the good news. The bad news is that the Internal Revenue Code (IRC), with its related rules and regulations, is a very complex subject.

> **NOTE**
>
> This appendix is not intended to be a comprehensive guide to real estate tax information. Perhaps in this area more than any other in real estate investing, you must be sure to hire competent professional help to help you navigate the rough waters. The goal of this chapter is to introduce you to the potential tax benefits of owning real estate, so that you will be able to plan accordingly.

This appendix is divided into two main sections: home ownership and commercial real estate ownership. Recall from Chapter 1 that I recommend that the first real estate investment should always be a home. The process of buying and owning a home is the ideal training ground for the greater complexities involved in commercial real estate investments. So, as in the body of the text, here too we begin with home ownership.

TAX BENEFITS OF HOME OWNERSHIP

Simply put, real estate tax payments and interest paid on home mortgages are deductible against your personal income for tax purposes (adjusted gross income). For example:

Cost of home	$110,000
Mortgage	$100,000
Mortgage payments at 8% self-liquidating interest for 15 years	$ 1,075.64
Plus real estate taxes of $2,400/year / 12 months	$ 200
Total monthly payment	$ 1,275
Yearly payments ($1,275 × 12 =)	$ 15,300

Your annual payments for the home mortgage, including escrows for taxes, total $15,300. Of that, the following are tax deductible:

Interest portion of the mortgage (8% of $100,000)	$ 8,000
Real estate taxes	$ 2,400
Total tax deductions	$10,400

For the purposes of this discussion, we're going to assume that you are in a combined federal and local income tax bracket of 30 percent.

DEFINITION

Being in a *tax bracket* means that a percentage of your income above a certain level will be paid to the government in taxes (in this case 30 percent).

Tax deductions from the example	$10,400
Tax bracket is	30%
Savings on income taxes are 30% of $10,400, or	$ 3,120

Total mortgage payments	$15,300
Minus tax savings	($ 3,120)
Net out-of-pocket (or cash) cost for home mortgage	$12,180

Next we'll take into account the *amortization,* or amount of the mortgage payment, that will go to pay off the loan:

Mortgage payments (excluding $2,400 escrowed for taxes)	$12,900
Mortgage interest (8% of $100,000)	($ 8,000)
Amount applied to pay off the mortgage (amortization)	$ 4,900

In addition, we have *appreciation* of the home—assuming a conservative 5 percent per annum compounded. In this case:

$$\text{Original cost of } \$110,000 \times 5\% = \underline{\underline{\$5,500}}$$

To summarize:

	Monthly	*Annually*
Total mortgage payments	$1,275	$15,300

Now we subtract:

Income tax benefit based on 30% bracket	($ 3,120)
Amortization (or payoff) of mortgage	($ 4,900)
Appreciation (increase in value) of home	($ 5,500)
Total subtractions	($13,520)
Net cost of home ownership less tax benefits, amortization of loan, and appreciation (increase in value) of home ($15,300 − $13,520)	$1,780 per year

Appreciation

Appreciation, or increase in value, is not taxed until you sell your home. There are additional tax benefits when you sell your home. As of January 1, 1999, as long as you have lived in a primary residence for at least two years, the following profits are exempt from taxes:

Marital status	Tax-free profit
Single	$250,000
Married	$500,000

Remember, we are talking about profits, not cost! In addition, you can repeat this procedure every two years as long as you live in the house as your primary residence. You can keep "trading up"—assuming you can carry the higher mortgage— to more expensive homes every two years and build up even more equity. And, to lower the mortgage payments on a more expensive home, you can possibly make a higher down payment from the cash proceeds of the sale of the previous home.

Thus, the net after-tax cost of home ownership in this example is $1,780 per year. Of course, this does not take into consideration repairs, insurance, and so on.

To summarize, the income tax benefits of home ownership are:

- Mortgage interest is tax deductible.
- Real estate taxes are tax deductible.
- On sale, the profits are exempt from tax up to a certain point.
- The net after-tax effects make mortgage payments cheaper than renting.

TAX BENEFITS OF COMMERCIAL REAL ESTATE OWNERSHIP

As I've mentioned throughout the book, you can take advantage of significant income tax benefits when you invest in commercial real estate. The primary tax benefit, or source of tax savings, is the tax deductibility of "depreciation." According to the Internal Revenue Code, you are permitted to deduct the amount that each capital (business-related) asset depreciates each year.

Depreciation

Depreciation is the decrease in price or value of an asset due to aging, technological obsolescence, wear and tear, and other factors. There are several ways to compute depreciation, but for purposes of this discussion, I limit it to straight-line depreciation based on cost minus scrap divided by the estimated life of the property. There are other, accelerated methods of computing depreciation, but for the purpose of this book, we will use the simple, straight-line approach, which provides for equal annual depreciation amounts. Here's the basic equation for straight-line depreciation:

$$\frac{\text{Total cost} - \text{land value (land does not depreciate per the IRC)}}{\text{Number of years}}$$

The Internal Revenue Code has guidelines that list the Internal Revenue Service's estimated useful life of assets. For real estate, per the IRC, the depreciation life of a residential building is 27.5 years, and that of a commercial property is 39.5 years. This means that after 39.5 years of depreciation, a commercial building is worth zero. We have offset original building costs against building income over the 39.5 years.

As an example:

Net income of property	$ 20,000
Cost of property	$200,000

We must subtract the portion to be allocated to land. The Internal Revenue Service will generally accept one-sixth, which in this case equals $33,000.

Allocated to building: $200,000 − $33,000 = $166,667

Using the Internal Revenue Code useful life of 39.5 years:

$$\text{Depreciation} = \frac{\text{Building cost } \$166,667}{\text{Useful life of 39.5 years}} = \$4,219 \text{ per year}$$

Cash Purchase

If we paid all cash for the property, the income of the property without mortgage payments would be $20,000 per year; the annual depreciation expense would be $4,219; and the net taxable income of the property would be $15,781 (although the net income is $20,000 per year, only $15,781 is taxed!). Assuming again that you are in the 30 percent tax bracket, your income taxes on the property would be 30 percent of $15,781, which is $4,734. To summarize:

Property income	$20,000
Less depreciation	($ 4,219)
Taxable income	$15,781

Income taxes would be 30 percent of the $15,781, or $4,734.

Net income before taxes	$20,000
Less income taxes	($ 4,734)
Cash flow after taxes	$15,266

$$\frac{\text{Cash flow after tax}}{\text{Investment}} = \frac{\$15,266}{\$200,000} = 7.63\% \text{ tax-free!}$$

Effects of Leverage

Now let's examine the tax effects of leverage. Remember, leverage is the use of debt, meaning we didn't pay all cash for the property.

Property net income before depreciation	$ 20,000

Property cost	$200,000
Mortgage of $150,000 at 8%, interest only	$150,000
Equity or down payment	$ 50,000

For tax purposes:

Property net income (before debt service and depreciation)	$20,000
Less interest expense of 8% × $150,000	($12,000)
	$ 8,000

Less depreciation (see preceding)	($4,219)
Taxable income	$3,781
Income tax (30% of $3,781)	$1,134

To summarize, this deal with an 8 percent interest-only mortgage would look like this:

Net income (cash flow) before debt service	$20,000
Less debt service (8% of $150,000)	($12,000)
Income after debt service	$ 8,000
Less income taxes (after interest and depreciation deductions; see preceding)	($ 1,134)
Net cash flow after interest and taxes	$ 6,866

$$\frac{\text{Net cash flow}}{\text{Net investment or down payment}} = \frac{\$6,866}{\$50,000} = 13.73\% \text{ tax-free!}$$

That's a 13.73 percent return! But what did we leave out here? Appreciation! Assuming a conservative rate of appreciation of 5 percent per year, the appreciation of this property would be 5 percent of the cost ($200,000), which equals $10,000 per year. Thus:

Net cash flow after taxes	$ 6,866
Plus appreciation in value based on 5% of $200,000 per year	$10,000
Total profit	$16,866

$$\frac{\text{Total profit}}{\text{Investment (down payment)}} \frac{\$16,866}{\$50,000} = 33.73\%!$$

That's a 33.73 percent annual tax-deferred return on a relatively conservative investment. Let's see Wall Street beat that! That said, I would be remiss if I didn't remind you that real estate is more management-intensive than stocks or mutual funds. With the latter, you buy them, then put them away for future appreciation; you have few related responsibilities. Nevertheless, the potential additional return of real estate is worth the extra effort.

Maximizing the Depreciation Deduction
So far, remember, we have proceeded with the normal straight-line depreciation life of 39.5 years of the building cost. In our example:

Total cost $200,000

Allocated to land (1/6 of $200,000) $ 33,333

Net depreciable building cost $166,667

$$\frac{\text{Allocation building cost}}{\text{Depreciation life}} = \frac{\$166,667}{39.5 \text{ years}} = \$4,219 \text{ per year}$$

Thus, the annual straight-line depreciation is $4,219.

Component Depreciation

The previous example assumes that the building is an empty shell—four walls, a floor, and a roof. Now what about the service components? These are shown in Table B.1.

When you had your property inspected before you bought it, the inspector/engineer gave you a breakdown of the evaluation, which should have included:

- The significant building components (as listed in Table B.1)
- Current value of those components in their as-is condition
- Current age and remaining useful life of those components

Table B.2 shows what the component depreciation schedule looks like:

The components of the building, according to this sample engineer's report, are currently worth $36,000. So, for tax purposes:

Total depreciable building cost $166,667

Less current value of components ($ 36,000)

Net building cost (as a shell) $130,667

TABLE B.1 Service Components

Component	Estimated Life (Years)
Built-up roofs	15
HVAC systems	10
Electrical lines	20
Walls (temporary)	10
Plumbing	50
Flooring	5

TABLE B.2   Sample Component Depreciation Schedule

Component	(A) Estimated Value	(B) Useful Life	(C) Age	(D) Life Left (B) – (C)	(E) Depreciation (A) ÷ (D)
Roof	$10,000	15 years	10 years	15 – 10 = 5	$\dfrac{\$10,000}{5 \text{ years}} = \$2,000$
HVAC	$ 6,000	10 years	4 years	10 – 4 = 6	$\dfrac{\$6,000}{6 \text{ years}} = \$1,000$
Elevator	$15,000	20 years	10 years	20 – 10 = 10	$\dfrac{\$15,000}{10 \text{ years}} = \$1,500$
Flooring	$ 5,000	5 years	3 years	5 – 3 = 2	$\dfrac{\$5,000}{2 \text{ years}} = \$2,500$
Totals	$36,000				$7,000

Depreciation of the $200,000 purchase would be as shown in Table B.3.

Using component depreciation, our depreciation expense and tax deduction is $10,308. Recall that the previous building straight-line depreciation was:

$$\frac{\$166,667}{39.5 \text{ years}} = (4,219)$$

Thus, our depreciation write-off (deduction) is now $10,308 or $6,089 more (10,308 minus 4,219). The $6,089 additional tax deduction, at a 30 percent tax bracket, represents additional tax savings of $6,089 times 30 percent, or $1,827 per year more than ordinary straight-line depreciation on the building alone.

Replacement Reserves
The truth of the matter is that component depreciation more properly reflects the importance of setting up reserves for replacement.

TABLE B.3   Depreciation on a Sample $200,000 Purchase

Composed of	Component	Depreciation %	Amount
Land	$33,333	0	0
Building	$130,667	39.5 years	$3,308
Components	$36,000	Various (see Table A.2)	$7,000
Totals	$200,000		$10,308

You should take this into account when analyzing the net income of the building and *before* agreeing to purchase it. Hypothetically, the analysis would be as follows:

Gross income (after analysis of leases)	$40,000
Less operating expenses:	
Real estate taxes	$ 3,000
Insurance	$ 1,500
Utilities (gas and electric)	$ 1,000
Water and sewer	$ 1,000
Repairs	$ 2,000
Maintenance	$ 600
Management	$ 2,400
Miscellaneous	$ 1,500
Total operating expenses	$13,000
Net income before reserves (40,000 – 13,000)	$27,000
Less reserves for replacement (see Table B.2)	($ 7,000)
Net operating income	$20,000

Other Expenditures

In addition to the tax deductibility of your annual replacement reserves, total expenditures of under $19,000 per year can be deducted immediately. For example:

New HVAC system	$10,000
Tax deduction (under a certain amount)	$10,000
Tax savings (30% bracket – 30% of $10,000 =	($ 3,000)
Net cost of new system after tax	$ 7,000

In this way, not only do you improve your property—and raise its value—by installing the new HVAC system, but you benefit tax-wise as well. And note that it is these types of improvements—installation of energy-saving lighting, HVAC systems, and so on—that are particularly beneficial, because:

- You are modernizing your property.

- The property operates more efficiently (read: more cheaply).
- You get tax benefits.

Tenant Improvements

Recall from Chapter 9 in the section on how to market vacant space in a building that I discussed tenant improvements—that is, preparations for a new tenant. Tenant improvements, too, reap tax savings for you, the owner. Annual total building improvements or equipment purchases that cost up to a certain amount can be written off immediately. Those costing over that amount can be depreciated over either the actual estimated useful life, per the Internal Revenue Service, or the life of lease, whichever is shorter. The IRC includes a list of guidelines that delineate the IRS estimated useful depreciation deduction.

Here's an example for an improvement that costs $30,000. Let's say in this case that the Internal Revenue Service determines the useful life of the improvement to be 10 years. Here's that calculation:

$$\frac{\$30,000}{10 \text{ years}} = \text{depreciation of } \$3,000 \text{ per year}$$

For the second calculation, if the life of lease in this case were 5 years, the annual depreciation deduction would be:

$$\frac{\$30,000}{5 \text{ years}} = \text{depreciation of } \$6,000 \text{ per year}$$

Obviously, we would deduct the $6,000 (the higher of the two depreciation amounts).

TAX EFFECTS OF VARIOUS OWNERSHIP CATEGORIES

In Chapter 6, I described the various forms of ownership an investment group might agree on for the purposes of structuring and controlling its activities. In this section, you'll see those forms of ownership described in terms of the tax benefits attached to each one. Again, keep in mind that this information is intended as an overview of complex tax implications; it is by no means comprehensive, and the details of your property ownership should be put in the hands of your trusted tax accountant.

Individual or Joint

If you (or you and another or others) own an investment property, you will report the income and expenses (including depreciation) on Schedule E of Form 1040 every year. Schedule E, Part I is for listing income and expenses for each property owned jointly or individually. The net income or loss shown on Schedule E is carried forward to the first page of Form 1040 "rental real estate, royalties, partnerships, S corporations, trusts, etc." Attached to Schedule E is Form 4562 for depreciation expenses (described more fully in the following text). The total depreciation expense is then transposed to Schedule E, and from Schedule E to page 1 of Form 1040.

The tax advantage of personal ownership of real estate is that the net profit or loss (after depreciation) is reflected on the owner's personal tax return. The disadvantage is, of course, the personal liability of the owner.

Joint Ventures

A joint venture is a simple type of partnership. The property's income statement is prepared, and the profits and losses are divided among the members of the venture. No separate tax form is prepared. Each member of the joint venture attaches a copy of the joint venture income statement to his or her tax return and reports his or her share of profit and loss.

Partnerships

A partnership annually files Form 1065 (the partnership return) with the Internal Revenue Service. This form is where you list the income, expenses, and profits or losses of a partnership. The first page is an income and expense schedule. The expenses include depreciation, which is analyzed on Form 4562 (depreciation schedule). On this form you list all the properties you own, along with the depreciation for each. This form is attached to all tax returns on which depreciation is taken as an expense.

The net income or loss is divided up among the partners, based on the partnership agreement. Each partner's share is shown on Form K-1, "Partner's Share of Income, Credits, Deductions, etc." The last column on the right of this form tells you where on Form

1040 to show the different sums received or accrued from the partnership. The taxpayer (partner) includes the property partnership tax results with his or her other income.

If the property shows a profit, the partners' shares are added to their other income on Form 1040. If the K-1 shows losses, these are deducted from the partners' other income on Form 1040.

The tax advantage of the partnership form of real estate ownership is that each partner's respective share of profits and losses is carried through to the partner's personal tax return. The partnership itself pays no tax. The primary disadvantage of partnership ownership is that if deductible "losses" exceed a partner's income, he or she may lose the tax benefit of the net negative balance.

Limited Partnerships
For tax purposes, limited partnerships are treated the same as regular partnerships.

C Corporations
A C corporation annually files Form 1120 with the Internal Revenue Service. A regular corporation does not prepare K-1s showing each stockholder's share of profits and losses; it pays its own corporate taxes. Subsequent payments to the stockholders are called *dividends* and are taxed to the stockholders receiving them. This taxing of corporate profit and then taxing the dividends is called *double taxation*. If there is a profit, a C corporation is taxed; if there is a loss, obviously the corporation will not pay tax that year. However, the loss can be carried forward for up to 15 years to offset future profits.

There are a couple of major tax advantages associated with being a C corporation. First, a C corporation pays its own taxes. If the shareholders are in high tax brackets, and the corporation's net income is low, the C corporation's tax bracket could be lower than that of the shareholders, resulting in lower taxes. For example:

Net income of property in C corporation	$20,000
C corporation tax bracket is 15%; tax is	$ 3,000
	(15% of $20,000)
Shareholder bracket is 30%; tax is	$ 6,000
	(30% of $20,000)

Thus, the corporation would pay lower taxes than an individual owner would.

The second advantage of a C corporation is that tax losses can be carried forward. Let's say your corporation buys a run-down property, and you project that there will be extensive remodeling and vacancies in the first year of ownership. This will result in a significant operating loss, including depreciation and write-offs. This loss can be carried forward to later years to offset future profits. The tax then will be the future profits minus the losses that were carried forward times your tax bracket. Let's look at a year 1 example:

Price of property (5,000 square feet)	$100,000
Projected income (partial occupancy)	$ 15,000
Less operating expense	($ 25,000)
Building depreciation $\dfrac{\$90,000}{30}$	($ 3,000)
Improvements of:	
HVAC write-off	($10,000)
Painting write-off	($ 3,000)
Wiring write-off	($ 5,000)
Total deductions	($46,000)
Net taxable income (loss)	($31,000)

Because the individual improvements total under $19,000 each, we elect to deduct them immediately. The taxable loss is $31,000; thus, no tax is due. But, remember, the loss has tax benefits, as illustrated in the following text.

Let's look at year 2; at this point, the property is fully leased at $10 per square foot:

Income:	
5,000 sq. ft. at $10 per year	$50,000
Less	
Operating expenses	($25,000)
Depreciation	($ 3,000)
Net income (ordinarily this would be taxed)	$22,000

Less tax losses carried forward from year 1	($31,000)
Taxable income or loss ($22,000 profit, less $31,000 loss) to be carried forward	($ 9,000)

Not only is there no tax to pay in year 2 on the $25,000 prede-preciation profits, but the remaining $9,000 net loss can be carried forward.

Here's how year 3 shapes up:

Income (5,000 sq. ft. @ $10 per year; no increases)	$50,000
Less:	
Operating expenses	($25,000)
Depreciation	($ 3,000)
Net income	$22,000
Less prior year's operating loss carried forward	($ 9,000)
Net taxable income	$13,000

Only the $13,000 would get taxed in year 3. Of course, from that point forward, without the carry-forward loss, all the net income (i.e., the $22,000) would be fully taxed.

What have you accomplished? You have improved your property. The Internal Revenue Service has partially subsidized you by allowing deductions of certain capital imrovements and by enabling you to carry forward the resulting first-year losses to off-set future profits and partially protect them from tax.

The main tax disadvantage for a C corporation is *double taxation*. This refers to the fact that, first, the corporation pays income tax on its profits. (Taxes must be paid before dividends are paid.) Then, if the board of directors decides to pay some of the after-tax profits to the shareholders (dividends), the shareholders must include those dividends on their personal tax return Form 1040 and pay tax on them. Hence, double taxation. However, a stock-holder-manager can draw a salary or fees and business-related expense reimbursements, all of which are tax deductible by the corporation.

Subchapter S Corporations

Subchapter S corporations file a Form 1120 S, a hybrid of a Partnership Form 1065 and a C (or regular) Corporation Tax Return Form 1120. Page 1 is income and expense resulting in a profit or loss, which is divided up among the shareholders based on the shareholder agreement and the number of shares owned. The shareholders' shares of profit or losses are shown again on Schedule K-1, as for a partnership. That K-1 number is transposed to Schedule E of Form 1040.

The tax advantages and disadvantages for this category are the same as those of a partnership.

> **NOTE**
>
> Remember, owners of a partnership are called *partners.* Owners of a corporation are called *stockholders* or *shareholders.*

Limited Liability Companies

A limited liability company (LLC) is a recently created type of business entity designed to give a small business the benefits of corporate ownership (i.e., limited liability) plus the tax advantage of a partnership.

The shareholders' respective shares of the profit and loss are carried over to reflect on their individual tax returns. An LLC is taxed similarly to an S corporation.

CONCLUSION

In addition to profits from cash returns on a down payment, paying off the mortgage, and appreciation, you can reap significant tax benefits from your real estate investments. The deductibility of depreciation as an expense serves to help reduce the taxable income and related tax liability. Various business structures earn different tax benefits, so be sure to discuss them in detail with your accountant or attorney before you organize.

C

Common Real Estate-Related Forms and Documents

The forms and documents supplied in this appendix should be regarded as *samples only*. As I mentioned in the body of the text, each state in this country has its own laws and regulations that apply to the real estate industry; therefore, though similar in many ways, forms and documents will differ depending on where you live. I have included these to give you an idea of what to expect in the form of paperwork that you will have to complete as you proceed through the real estate investment process.

CAUTION:

Be sure to consult with an attorney before you enter into any legal agreement (that is, sign any legal form or document).

The forms in this appendix, in order of their presentation, are:

- Contract for sale and purchase (Figure C.1)
- Settlement (closing) statement (Figure C.2)
- Deed (indenture) (Figure C.3)
- Warranty deed (from corporate owner) (Figure C.4)
- Balloon mortgage (Figure C.5)
- Installment note (Figure C.6)
- Business lease (Figure C.7)
- Apartment residential lease (Figure C.8)

CONTRACT FOR SALE AND PURCHASE FLORIDA ASSOCIATION OF REALTORS® AND THE FLORIDA BAR

PARTIES: _____ ("Seller"),

of _____ (Phone) _____ ,

and _____ ("Buyer"),

of _____ (Phone) _____ ,

hereby agree that Seller shall sell and Buyer shall buy the following described real property and personal property (collectively "Property") pursuant to the terms and conditions of this Contract for Sale and Purchase and any riders and addenda ("Contract"):

I. DESCRIPTION:

(a) Legal description of the Real Property located in _____ County, Florida:

_____

_____

(b) Street address, city, zip, of the Property is: _____

(c) Personal Property: _____

_____

II. PURCHASE PRICE .... $ _____

PAYMENT:

(a) Deposit held in escrow by _____ (Escrow Agent) in the amount of $ _____

(b) Additional escrow deposit to be made to Escrow Agent within _____ days after Effective Date (see Paragraph III) in the amount of $ _____

(c) Subject to AND assumption of existing mortgage in good standing in favor of _____

having an approximate present principal balance of .... $ _____

(d) New mortgage financing with a Lender (see Paragraph IV) in the amount of.......................... $ _____

(e) Purchase money mortgage and note to Seller (see rider for terms) in the amount of.................... $ _____

(f) Other: .... $ _____

(g) Balance to close by U.S. cash or LOCALLY DRAWN cashier's or official bank check(s), subject to adjustments or prorations .... $ _____

III. TIME FOR ACCEPTANCE OF OFFER; EFFECTIVE DATE; FACSIMILE: If this offer is not executed by and delivered to all parties OR FACT OF EXECUTION communicated in writing between the parties on or before _____, the deposit(s) will, at Buyer's option, be returned and this offer withdrawn. For purposes of delivery or notice of execution, parties include Buyer and Seller or each of the respective brokers or attorneys. The date of Contract ("Effective Date") will be the date when the last one of the Buyer and Seller has signed this offer. A facsimile copy of this Contract and any signatures hereon shall be considered for all purposes as an original.

IV. FINANCING:

[ ] (a) This is a cash transaction with no contingencies for financing;

[ ] (b) This Contract is conditioned on Buyer obtaining a written loan commitment within _____ days after Effective Date for (CHECK ONE ONLY): [ ] a fixed; [ ] an adjustable; or [ ] a fixed or adjustable rate loan in the principal amount of $ _____, at an initial interest rate not to exceed _____ %, discount and origination fees not to exceed _____ % of principal amount, and for a term of _____ years. Buyer will make application within _____ days (5 days if left blank) after Effective Date and use reasonable diligence to obtain a loan commitment and, thereafter, to satisfy terms and conditions of the commitment and close the loan. Buyer shall pay all loan expenses. If Buyer fails to obtain a commitment or fails to waive Buyer's rights under this subparagraph within the time for obtaining a commitment or, after diligent effort, fails to meet the terms and conditions of the commitment by the closing date, then either party thereafter, by written notice to the other, may cancel this Contract and Buyer shall be refunded the deposit(s); or

[ ] (c) The existing mortgage, described in Paragraph II(c) above, has: [ ] a variable interest rate; or [ ] a fixed interest rate of _____ % per annum. At time of title transfer, some fixed interest rates are subject to increase; if increased, the rate shall not exceed _____ % per annum. Seller shall furnish a statement from each mortgagee stating the principal balance, method of payment, interest rate and status of mortgage or authorize Buyer or Closing Agent to obtain the same. If Buyer has agreed to assume a mortgage which requires approval of Buyer by the mortgagee for assumption, then Buyer shall promptly obtain the necessary application and diligently complete and return it to the mortgagee. Any mortgage charge(s) not to exceed $ _____ (1% of amount assumed if left blank), shall be paid by Buyer. If Buyer is not accepted by mortgagee or the requirements for assumption are not in accordance with the terms of this Contract or mortgage makes a charge in excess of the stated amount, Seller or Buyer may rescind this Contract by written notice to the other party unless either elects to pay the increase in interest rate or excess mortgage charges.

V. TITLE EVIDENCE: At least _____ days before closing date, (CHECK ONLY ONE): [ ] Seller shall, at Seller's expense, deliver to Buyer or Buyer's attorney; or [ ] Buyer shall at Buyer's expense obtain (CHECK ONLY ONE): [ ] abstract of title; or [ ] title insurance commitment (with legible copies of instruments listed as exceptions attached thereto) and, after closing, an owner's policy of title insurance.

VI. CLOSING DATE: This transaction shall be closed and the closing documents delivered on _____, unless modified by other provisions of this Contract.

VII. RESTRICTIONS; EASEMENTS; LIMITATIONS: Buyer shall take title subject to: comprehensive land use plans, zoning, restrictions, prohibitions and other requirements imposed by governmental authority; restrictions and matters appearing on the plat or otherwise common to the subdivision; outstanding oil, gas and mineral rights of record without right of entry; public utility easements of record (easements are to be located contiguous to real property lines and not more than 10 feet in width as to the rear or front lines and 7 1/2 feet in width as to the side lines, unless otherwise stated herein); taxes for year of closing and subsequent years; assumed mortgages and purchase money mortgages, if any (if additional items, see addendum); provided, that there exists at closing no violation of the foregoing and none prevent use of the Property for _____ purpose(s).

VIII. OCCUPANCY: Seller warrants that there are no parties in occupancy other than Seller; but if Property is intended to be rented or occupied beyond closing, the fact and terms thereof and the tenant(s) or occupants shall be disclosed pursuant to Standard F. Seller shall deliver occupancy of Property to Buyer at time of closing unless otherwise stated herein. If occupancy is to be delivered before closing, Buyer assumes all risks of loss to Property from date of occupancy, shall be responsible and liable for maintenance from that date, and shall be deemed to have accepted Property in its existing condition as of time of taking occupancy unless otherwise stated herein.

IX. TYPEWRITTEN OR HANDWRITTEN PROVISIONS: Typewritten or handwritten provisions, riders and addenda shall control all printed provisions of this Contract in conflict with them.

X. RIDERS: (CHECK those riders which are applicable AND are attached to this Contract):

[ ] COMPREHENSIVE RIDER	[ ] HOMEOWNERS' ASSN.	[ ] COASTAL CONSTRUCTION CONTROL LINE
[ ] CONDOMINIUM	[ ] "AS IS"	[ ] INSULATION
[ ] VA/FHA	[ ] LEAD-BASED PAINT	[ ] _____

XI. ASSIGNABILITY: (CHECK ONLY ONE): Buyer [ ] may assign and thereby be released from any further liability under this Contract; [ ] may assign but not be released from liability under this Contract; or [ ] may not assign this Contract.

XII. DISCLOSURES:

(a) Radon is a naturally occurring radioactive gas that when accumulated in a building in sufficient quantities may present health risks to persons who are exposed to it over time. Levels of radon that exceed federal and state guidelines have been found in buildings in Florida. Additional information regarding Radon or Radon testing may be obtained from your County Public Health unit.

(b) Buyer acknowledges receipt of the Florida Building Energy-Efficiency Rating System Brochure.

(c) If the real property includes pre-1978 residential housing then a lead-based paint rider is mandatory.

(d) If Seller is a "foreign person" as defined by the Foreign Investment in Real Property Tax Act, the parties shall comply with that Act.

(e) If Buyer will be obligated to be a member of a homeowners' association, BUYER SHOULD NOT EXECUTE THIS CONTRACT UNTIL BUYER HAS RECEIVED AND READ THE HOMEOWNERS' ASSOCIATION DISCLOSURE.

XIII. MAXIMUM REPAIR COSTS: Seller shall not be responsible for payments in excess of:

(a) $ _____ for treatment and repair under Standard D (if blank, then 2% of the Purchase Price).

(b) $ _____ for repair and replacement under Standard N (if blank, then 3% of the Purchase Price).

XIV. SPECIAL CLAUSES; ADDENDA: If additional terms are to be provided, attach addendum and CHECK HERE [ ].

XV. STANDARDS FOR REAL ESTATE TRANSACTIONS: Standards A through W on the reverse side or attached are incorporated as a part of this Contract.

THIS IS INTENDED TO BE A LEGALLY BINDING CONTRACT. IF NOT FULLY UNDERSTOOD, SEEK THE ADVICE OF AN ATTORNEY PRIOR TO SIGNING.

THIS FORM HAS BEEN APPROVED BY THE FLORIDA ASSOCIATION OF REALTORS AND THE FLORIDA BAR.

Approval does not constitute an opinion that any of the terms and conditions in this Contract should be accepted by the parties in a particular transaction. Terms and conditions should be negotiated based upon the respective interests, objectives and bargaining positions of all interested persons.

COPYRIGHT 1998 BY THE FLORIDA BAR AND THE FLORIDA ASSOCIATION OF REALTORS

_____ (Date) _____ _____ (Date) _____

(Buyer)   (Seller)

Social Security or Tax I.D. # _____   Social Security or Tax I.D. # _____

_____ (Date) _____ _____ (Date) _____

(Buyer)   (Seller)

Social Security or Tax I.D.# _____   Social Security or Tax I.D. # _____

Deposit under Paragraph II (a) received; IF OTHER THAN CASH, THEN SUBJECT TO CLEARANCE. _____ (Escrow Agent)

BROKER'S FEE: The brokers named below, including listing and cooperating brokers, are the only brokers entitled to compensation in connection with this Contract:

Name: _____

Cooperating Brokers, if any   Listing Broker

FAR/BAR-5   Revised 8/98

Figure C.1   Contract for sale and purchase.

STANDARDS FOR REAL ESTATE TRANSACTIONS

A. EVIDENCE OF TITLE: (1) An abstract of title prepared or brought current by a reputable and existing abstract firm (if not existing then certified as correct by an existing firm) purporting to be an accurate synopsis of the instruments affecting title to the real property recorded in the public records of the county wherein the real property is located through Effective Date. It shall commence with the earliest public records, or such later date as may be customary in the county. Upon closing of this Contract, the abstract shall become the property of Buyer, subject to the right of retention thereof by first mortgagee until fully paid. (2) A title insurance commitment issued by a Florida licensed title insurer agreeing to issue Buyer, upon recording of the deed to Buyer, an owner's policy of title insurance in the amount of the purchase price, insuring Buyer's title to the real property, subject only to liens, encumbrances, exceptions or qualifications provided in this Contract and those to be discharged by Seller at or before closing. Seller shall convey marketable title subject only to liens, encumbrances, exceptions or qualifications provided in this Contract. Marketable title shall be determined according to applicable Title Standards adopted by authority of The Florida Bar and in accordance with law. Buyer shall have 5 days from date of receiving evidence of title to examine it. If title is found defective, Buyer shall within said 5 days notify Seller in writing specifying the defect(s). If defect(s) render title unmarketable, Seller will have 30 days from receipt of notice to remove the defects, failing which Buyer shall, within five (5) days after expiration of the thirty (30) day period, deliver written notice to Seller either: (1) extending the time for a reasonable period not to exceed 120 days within which Seller shall use diligent effort to remove the defects; or (2) requesting a refund of deposit(s) paid which shall be immediately returned to Buyer. If Buyer fails to so notify Seller, Buyer shall be deemed to have accepted the title as it then is. Seller shall, if title is found unmarketable, use diligent effort to correct defect(s) within the time provided therefor. If Seller is unable to timely correct the defects, Buyer shall either waive the defects, or receive a refund of deposit(s), thereby releasing Buyer and Seller from all further obligation under this Contract. If evidence of title is delivered to Buyer less than 5 days prior to closing, Buyer may extend closing date so that Buyer shall have up to 5 days from date of receipt of evidence of title to examine same in accordance with this Standard.

B. PURCHASE MONEY MORTGAGE; SECURITY AGREEMENT TO SELLER: A purchase money mortgage and mortgage note to Seller shall provide for a 30-day grace period in the event of default if a first mortgage and a 15-day grace period if a second or lesser mortgage; shall provide for right of prepayment in whole or in part without penalty; shall permit acceleration in event of transfer of the real property; shall require all prior liens and encumbrances to be kept in good standing and forbid modifications of or future advances under prior mortgage(s); shall require Buyer to maintain policies of insurance containing a standard mortgagee clause covering all improvements located on the real property against fire and all perils included within the term "extended coverage endorsements" and such other risks and perils as Seller may reasonable require, in an amount equal to their highest insurable value; and the mortgage, note and security agreement shall be otherwise in form and content required by Seller; but Seller may only require clauses and coverage customarily found in mortgages, mortgage notes and security agreements generally utilized by savings and loan institutions or state or national banks located in the county wherein the real property is located. All personal property and leases being conveyed or assigned will, at Seller's option, be subject to the lien of a security agreement evidenced by recorded financing statements. If a balloon mortgage, the final payment will exceed the periodic payments thereon.

C. SURVEY: Buyer, at Buyer's expense, within time allowed to deliver evidence of title and to examine same, may have the real property surveyed and certified by a registered Florida surveyor. If the survey discloses encroachments on the real property or that improvements located thereon encroach on setback lines, easements, lands of others or violate any restrictions, Contract covenants or applicable governmental regulation, the same shall constitute a title defect.

D. TERMITES/WOOD DESTROYING ORGANISMS: Buyer, at Buyer's expense, within the time allowed to deliver evidence of title, may have the Property inspected by a Florida Certified Pest Control Operator ("Operator") to determine if there is any visible active termite infestation or visible damage from termite infestation, excluding fences. If either or both are found, Buyer shall have 4 days from date of written notice thereof within which to have cost of treatment, if required, estimated by the Operator and all damage inspected and estimated by a licensed builder or general contractor. Seller shall pay valid costs of treatment and repair of all damage up to the amount provided in Paragraph XIII(a). If estimated costs exceed that amount, Buyer shall have the option of canceling this Contract within 5 days after receipt of contractor's repair estimate by giving written notice to Seller or Buyer may elect to proceed with the transaction, and receive a credit at closing on the amount provided in Paragraph XIII(a). "Termites" shall be deemed to include all wood destroying organisms required to be reported under the Florida Pest Control Act, as amended.

E. INGRESS AND EGRESS: Seller warrants and represents that there is ingress and egress to the real property sufficient for its intended use as described in Paragraph VII hereof, title to which is in accordance with Standard A.

F. LEASES: Seller shall, not less than 15 days before closing, furnish to Buyer copies of all written leases and estoppel letters from each tenant specifying the nature and duration of the tenant's occupancy, rental rates, advanced rent and security deposits paid by tenant. If Seller is unable to obtain such letter from each tenant, the same information shall be furnished by Seller to Buyer within that time period in the form of a Seller's affidavit, and Buyer may thereafter contact tenant to confirm such information. Seller shall, at closing, deliver and assign all original leases to Buyer.

G. LIENS: Seller shall furnish to Buyer at time of closing an affidavit attesting to the absence, unless otherwise provided for herein, of any financing statement, claims of lien or potential lienors known to Seller and further attesting that there have been no improvements or repairs to the real property for 90 days immediately preceding date of closing. If the real property has been improved or repaired within that time, Seller shall deliver releases or waivers of construction liens executed by all general contractors, subcontractors, suppliers and materialmen in addition to Seller's lien affidavit setting forth the names of all such general contractors, subcontractors, suppliers and materialmen, further affirming that all charges for improvements or repairs which could serve as a basis for a construction lien or a claim for damages have been paid or will be paid at the closing of this Contract.

H. PLACE OF CLOSING: Closing shall be held in the county wherein the real property is located at the office of the attorney or other closing agent ("Closing Agent") designated by Seller.

I. TIME: In computing time periods of less than six (6) days, Saturdays, Sundays and state or national legal holidays shall be excluded. Any time periods provided for herein which shall end on a Saturday, Sunday, or a legal holiday shall extend to 5:00 p.m. of the next business day. **Time is of the essence in this Contract.**

J. CLOSING DOCUMENTS: Seller shall furnish the deed, bill of sale, construction lien affidavit, owner's possession affidavit, assignments of leases, tenant and mortgagee estoppel letters and corrective instruments. Buyer shall furnish closing statement, mortgage, mortgage note, security agreement and financing statements.

K. EXPENSES: Documentary stamps on the deed and recording of corrective instruments shall be paid by Seller. Documentary stamps and intangible tax on the purchase money mortgage and any mortgage assumed, mortgagee title insurance commitment with related fees, and recording of purchase money mortgage to Seller, deed and financing statements shall be paid by Buyer. Unless otherwise provided by law or rider to this Contract, charges for the following related title services, namely title or abstract charge, title examination, and settlement and closing fee, shall be paid by the party responsible for furnishing the title evidence in accordance with Paragraph V.

L. PRORATIONS; CREDITS: Taxes, assessments, rent, interest, insurance and other expenses of the Property shall be prorated through the day before closing. Buyer shall have the option of taking over existing policies of insurance, if assumable, in which event premiums shall be prorated. Cash at closing shall be increased or decreased as may be required by prorations to be made through day prior to closing, or occupancy, if occupancy occurs before closing. Advance rent and security deposits will be credited to Buyer. Escrow deposits held by mortgagee will be credited to Seller. Taxes shall be prorated based on the current year's tax with due allowance made for maximum allowable discount, homestead and other exemptions. If closing occurs at a date when the current year's millage is not fixed and current year's assessment is available, taxes will be prorated based upon such assessment and prior year's millage. If current year's assessment is not available, then taxes will be prorated on prior year's tax. If there are completed improvements on the real property by January 1st of year of closing, which improvements were not in existence on January 1st of prior year, then taxes shall be prorated based upon prior year's millage and at an equitable assessment to be agreed upon between the parties; failing which, request shall be made to the County Property Appraiser for an informal assessment taking into account available exemptions. A tax proration based on an estimate shall, at request of either party, be readjusted upon receipt of tax bill on condition that a statement to that effect is signed at closing.

M. SPECIAL ASSESSMENT LIENS: Certified, confirmed and ratified special assessment liens as of date of closing (not as of Effective Date) are to be paid by Seller. Pending liens as of date of closing shall be assumed by Buyer. If the improvement has been substantially completed as of Effective Date, any pending lien shall be considered certified, confirmed or ratified and Seller shall, at closing, be charged an amount equal to the last estimate or assessment for the improvement by the public body.

N. INSPECTION, REPAIR AND MAINTENANCE: Seller warrants that the ceiling, roof (including the fascia and soffits) and exterior and interior walls, foundation, seawalls (or equivalent) and dockage do not have any Visible Evidence of leaks, water damage or structural damage and that the septic tank, pool, all appliances, mechanical items, heating, cooling, electrical, plumbing systems and machinery are in Working Condition. The foregoing warranty shall be limited to the items specified unless otherwise provided in an addendum. Buyer may, at Buyer's expense, have inspections made of those items within 20 days after the Effective Date, by a firm or individual specializing in home inspections and holding an occupational license for such purpose (if required) or by an appropriately licensed Florida contractor, and Buyer shall, prior to Buyer's occupancy but not more than 20 days after Effective Date, report in writing to Seller such items that do not meet the above standards as to defects. Unless Buyer timely reports such defects, Buyer shall be deemed to have waived Seller's warranties as to defects not reported. If repairs or replacements are required to comply with this Standard, Seller shall cause them to be made and shall pay up to the amount provided in Paragraph XIII(b). Seller is not required to make repairs or replacements of a Cosmetic Condition unless caused by a defect Seller is responsible to repair or replace. If the cost for such repair or replacement exceeds the amount provided in Paragraph XIII(b), Buyer or Seller may elect to pay such excess, failing which either party may cancel this Contract. If Seller is unable to correct the defects prior to closing, the cost thereof shall be paid into escrqw at closing. Seller shall, upon reasonable notice, provide utilities service and access to the Property for inspections, including a walk-through prior to closing, to confirm that all items of personal property are on the real property and, subject to the foregoing, that all required repairs and replacements have been made and that the Property, including, but not limited to, lawn, shrubbery and pool, if any, has been maintained in the condition existing as of Effective Date, ordinary wear and tear excepted. For purposes of this Contract: (a) "Working Condition" means operating in the manner in which the item was designed to operate; (b) "Cosmetic Condition" means aesthetic imperfections that do not affect the working condition of the item, including, but not limited to: pitted marcite; missing or torn screens; fogged windows; tears, worn spots, or discoloration of floor coverings, wallpaper, or window treatments; nail holes, scratches, dents, scrapes, chips or caulking in ceilings, walls, flooring, fixtures, or mirrors; and minor cracks in floors, tiles, windows, driveways, sidewalks, or pool decks; and (c) cracked roof tiles, curling or worn shingles, or limited roof life shall not be considered defects Seller must repair or replace, so long as there is no evidence of actual leaks or leakage or structural damage, but missing tiles will be Seller's responsibility to replace or repair.

O. RISK OF LOSS: If the Property is damaged by fire or other casualty before closing and cost of restoration does not exceed 3% of the assessed valuation of the Property so damaged, cost of restoration shall be an obligation of Seller and closing shall proceed pursuant to the terms of this Contract with restoration costs escrowed at closing. If the cost of restoration exceeds 3% of the assessed valuation of the Property so damaged, Buyer shall have the option of either taking the Property as is, together with either the 3% or any insurance proceeds payable by virtue of such loss or damage, or of canceling this Contract and receiving return of the deposit(s).

P. PROCEEDS OF SALE; CLOSING PROCEDURE: The deed shall be recorded upon clearance of funds. If an abstract of title has been furnished, evidence of title shall be continued at Buyer's expense to show title in Buyer, without any encumbrances or change which would render Seller's title unmarketable from the date of the last evidence. All closing proceeds shall be held in escrow by Seller's attorney or other mutually acceptable escrow agent for a period of not more than 5 days after closing date. If Seller's title is rendered unmarketable, through no fault of Buyer, Buyer shall, within the 5-day period, notify Seller in writing of the defect and Seller shall have 30 days from date of receipt of such notification to cure the defect. If Seller fails to timely cure the defect, all deposit(s) and closing funds shall, upon written demand by Buyer and within 5 days after demand, be returned to Buyer and, simultaneously with such repayment, Buyer shall return the personal property, vacate the real property and reconvey the Property to Seller by special warranty deed and bill of sale. If Buyer fails to make timely demand for refund, Buyer shall take title as is, waiving all rights against Seller as to any intervening defect except as may be available to Buyer by virtue of warranties contained in the deed or bill of sale. If a portion of the purchase price is to be derived from institutional financing or refinancing, requirements of the lending institution as to place, time of day and procedures for closing, and for disbursement of mortgage proceeds shall control over contrary provision in this Contract. Seller shall have the right to require from the lending institution a written commitment that it will not withhold disbursement of mortgage proceeds as a result of any title defect attributable to Buyer-mortgagor. The escrow and closing procedure required by this Standard shall be waived if the title agent insures adverse matters pursuant to Section 627.7841, F.S., as amended.

Q. ESCROW: Any escrow agent ("Agent") receiving funds or equivalent is authorized and agrees by acceptance of them to deposit them promptly, hold same in escrow and, subject to clearance, disburse them in accordance with terms and conditions of this Contract. Failure of funds to clear shall not excuse Buyer's performance. If in doubt as to Agent's duties or liabilities under the provisions of this Contract, Agent may, at Agent's option, continue to hold the subject matter of the escrow until the parties hereto agree to its disbursement or until a judgement of a court of competent jurisdiction shall determine the rights of the parties, or Agent may deposit same with the clerk of the circuit court having jurisdiction of the dispute. Upon notifying all parties concerned of such action, all liability on the part of Agent shall fully terminate, except to the extent of accounting for any items previously delivered out of escrow. If a licensed real estate broker, Agent will comply with provisions of Chapter 475, F.S., as amended. Any suit between Buyer and Seller wherein Agent is made a party because of acting as Agent hereunder, or in any suit wherein Agent interpleads the subject matter of the escrow, Agent shall recover reasonable attorney's fees and costs incurred with these amounts to be paid from and out of the escrowed funds or equivalent and charged and awarded as court costs in favor of the prevailing party. The Agent shall not be liable to any party or person for misdelivery to Buyer or Seller of items subject to the escrow, unless such misdelivery is due to willful breach of the provisions of this Contract or gross negligence of Agent.

R. ATTORNEY'S FEES; COSTS: In any litigation, including breach, enforcement or interpretation, arising out of this Contract, the prevailing party in such litigation, which, for purposes of this Standard, shall include Seller, Buyer and any brokers acting in agency or nonagency relationships authorized by Chapter 475, F.S., as amended, shall be entitled to recover from the non-prevailing party reasonable attorney's fees, costs and expenses.

S. FAILURE OF PERFORMANCE: If Buyer fails to perform this Contract within the time specified, including payment of all deposits, the deposit(s) paid by Buyer and deposit(s) agreed to be paid, may be recovered and retained by and for the account of Seller as agreed upon liquidated damages, consideration for the execution of this Contract and in full settlement of any claims; whereupon, Buyer and Seller shall be relieved of all obligations under this Contract; or Seller, at Seller's option, may proceed in equity to enforce Seller's rights under this Contract. If for any reason other than failure of Seller to make Seller's title marketable after diligent effort, Seller fails, neglects or refuses to perform this Contract, Buyer may seek specific performance or elect to receive the return of Buyer's deposit(s) without thereby waiving any action for damages resulting from Seller's breach.

T. CONTRACT NOT RECORDABLE; PERSONS BOUND; NOTICE: Neither this Contract nor any notice of it shall be recorded in any public records. This Contract shall bind and inure to the benefit of the parties and their successors in interest. Whenever the context permits, singular shall include plural and one gender shall include all. Notice given by or to the attorney for any party shall be as effective as if given by or to that party.

U. CONVEYANCE: Seller shall convey title to the real property by statutory warranty, trustee's, personal representative's or guardian's deed, as appropriate to the status of Seller, subject only to matters contained in Paragraph VII and those otherwise accepted by Buyer. Personal property shall, at the request of Buyer, be transferred by an absolute bill of sale with warranty of title, subject only to such matters as may be otherwise provided for herein.

V. OTHER AGREEMENTS: No prior or present agreements or representations shall be binding upon Buyer or Seller unless included in this Contract. No modification to or change in this Contract shall be valid or binding upon the parties unless in writing and executed by the party or parties intended to be bound by it.

W. WARRANTY: Seller warrants that there are no facts known to Seller materially affecting the value of the Property which are not readily observable by Buyer or which have not been disclosed to Buyer.

Buyer (__________) (__________) and Seller (__________) (__________) acknowledge receipt of a copy of this page.

FAR/BAR-5 Rev. 8/98 COPYRIGHT 1998 THE FLORIDA BAR AND THE FLORIDA ASSOCIATION OF REALTORS®

Figure C.1 *(Continued)*

A. Settlement Statement

U.S. Department of Housing and Urban Development

OMB No. 2502-0265

B. Type of Loan

1.☐ FHA 2.☐ FmHA 3.☐ Conv. Unins	6. File Number	7. Loan Number	8. Mortgage Insurance Case Number
4.☐ VA 5.☐ Conv. Ins.			

C. NOTE: This form is furnished to give you a statement of actual settlement costs. Amounts paid to and by the settlement agent are shown. Items marked "(p.o.c.)" were paid outside the closing; they are shown here for informational purposes and are not included in the totals

D. NAME OF BORROWER:

ADDRESS OF BORROWER:

E. NAME OF SELLER:

ADDRESS OF SELLER:

F. NAME OF LENDER:

ADDRESS OF LENDER:

G. PROPERTY LOCATION:

H. SETTLEMENT AGENT: HARPER, KYNES, GELLER, WATSON & BUFORD, P.A., ATTORNEYS AT LAW
2560 GULF TO BAY BLVD., CLEARWATER, FL 33765
PLACE OF SETTLEMENT: 2560 GULF TO BAY BLVD., CLEARWATER, FL 33765

I. SETTLEMENT DATE:

J. SUMMARY OF BORROWER'S TRANSACTION		K. SUMMARY OF SELLER'S TRANSACTION	
100.GROSS AMOUNT DUE FROM BORROWER		400.GROSS AMOUNT DUE TO SELLER	
101.Contract sales price		401.Contract sales price	
102.Personal property		402.Personal property	
103.Settlement charges to borrower (line 1400)		403.	
104.		404.	
105.		405.	
Adjustments for items paid by seller in advance		Adjustments for items paid by seller in advance	
106.City/town taxes to		406.City/town taxes to	
107.County taxes to		407.County taxes to	
108.Assessments to		408.Assessments to	
109. to		409. to	
110. to		410. to	
111. to		411. to	
112. to		412. to	
120.GROSS AMOUNT DUE FROM BORROWER ▶		420.GROSS AMOUNT DUE TO SELLER ▶	
200.AMOUNTS PAID BY OR IN BEHALF OF BORROWER		500.REDUCTIONS IN AMOUNT DUE TO SELLER	
201.Deposit or earnest money		501.Excess deposit (see instructions)	
202.Principal amount of new loan(s)		502.Settlement charges to seller(line 1400)	
203.Existing loan(s) taken subject to		503.Existing loan(s) taken subject to	
204.		504.Payoff of first mortgage loan	
205.		505.Payoff of second mortgage loan	
206.Principal amount of seller financing		506.Principal amount of seller financing	
207.		507.	
208.		508.	
209.		509.	
209a		509a	
209b		509b	
Adjustments for items unpaid by seller		Adjustments for items unpaid by seller	
210.City/town taxes to		510.City/town taxes to	
211.County taxes to		511.County taxes to	
212.Assessments to		512.Assessments to	
213. to		513. to	
214. to		514. to	
215. to		515. to	
216. to		516. to	
217. to		517. to	
218. to		518. to	
219. to		519. to	
220.TOTAL AMOUNTS PAID BY OR IN BEHALF OF BORROWER ▶		520.TOTAL REDUCTIONS IN AMOUNT DUE SELLER ▶	
300.CASH AT SETTLEMENT FROM/TO BORROWER		600.CASH AT SETTLEMENT TO/FROM SELLER	
301.Gross amount due from borrower (line 120)		601.Gross amount due to seller (line 420)	
302.Less amounts paid by/for borrower (line 220)		602.Less reductions in amount due seller (line 520)	
303.CASH ☒ From ☐ To BORROWER ▶		603.CASH ☒ To ☐ From SELLER ▶	

Figure C.2 Settlement (closing) statement.

L. Settlement Charges		Paid From Borrower's Funds At Settlement	Paid From Seller's Funds At Settlement
700. TOTAL SALES/BROKER'S COM. based on price @ % =			
Division of Commission (line 700) as follows:			
701. to			
702. to			
703. Commission paid at Settlement			
704. to			
800. Items Payable In Connection With Loan			
801. Loan Origination Fee % to			
802. Loan Discount % to			
803. Appraisal Fee to			
804. Credit Report to			
805. Lender's Inspection Fee to			
806. Mortgage Insurance Application Fee to			
807. to			
808. to			
809. to			
810. to			
811. to			
812. to			
813. to			
814. to			
815. to			
900. Items Required By Lender To Be Paid In Advance			
901. Interest from to @ /day			
902. Mortgage Insurance Premium for months to			
903. Hazard Insurance Premium for years to			
904. years to			
905. years to			
1000. Reserves Deposited With Lender			
1001. Hazard insurance months@ per month			
1002. Mortgage insurance months@ per month			
1003. City property taxes months@ per month			
1004. County property taxes months@ per month			
1005. Annual assessments months@ per month			
1006. months@ per month			
1007. months@ per month			
1008. months@ per month			
1009.			
1100. Title Charges			
1101. Settlement or closing fee to			
1102. Abstract or title search to			
1103. Title examination to			
1104. Title insurance binder to			
1105. Document preparation to			
1106. Notary fees to			
1107. Attorney's fees to			
(includes above items numbers:			
1108. Title insurance to			
(includes above items numbers:			
1109. Lender's coverage: Risk Premium INS AMT:			
1110. Owner's coverage: Risk Premium INS AMT:			
1110a			
1111. to			
1112. to			
1113. to			
1200. Government Recording and Transfer Charges			
1201. Recording Fees: Deed ; Mortgage(s) ; Mortgage(s) ; Releases			
1202. City/County tax/stamps: Deed ; L-Mortgage(s) ; S-Mortgage(s)			
1203. State tax/stamps: Deed ; L-Mortgage(s) ; S-Mortgage(s)			
1204.			
1205.			
1300. Additional Settlement Charges			
1301. Survey to			
1302. Pest Inspection to			
1303. Roof Inspection to			
1304. to			
1305. to			
1306. to			
1307. to			
1308. to			
1309. to			
1400. Total Settlement Charges (enter on lines 103, Section J and 502, SectionK) ▶			

CERTIFICATION DATE:
I have carefully reviewed the HUD - 1 Settlement Statement and to the best of my knowledge and belief, it is a true and accurate statement of all receipts and disbursements made on my account or by me in this transaction. I further certify that I have received a copy of the HUD - 1 Settlement Statement.

_____ Borrower By: _____ Seller

_____ Borrower By: _____ Seller

The Hud-1 Settlement Statement which I have prepared is a true and accurate account of this transaction. I have caused the funds to be disbursed in accordance with this statement.   HARPER, KYNES, GELLER, WATSON & BUFORD, P.A. ATTORNEYS AT LAW

Settlement Agent   Date
WARNING: It is a crime to knowingly make false statements to the United States on this or any other similar form. Penalties upon conviction can include fine and imprisonment. For details see: Title 18 U.S. Code Section 1001 and Section 1010.

Figure C.2 *(Continued)*

TUTBLANX REGISTERED U S PAT OFFICE
TUTTLE LAW PRINT PUBLISHERS RUTLAND VT 05701

This Indenture,

Wherever used herein, the term "party" shall include the heirs, personal representatives, successors and/or assigns of the respective parties hereto; the use of the singular number shall include the plural, and the plural the singular; the use of any gender shall include all genders; and, if used, the term "note" shall include all the notes herein described if more than one.

Made this   day of   A. D. 19
          Between

of the County of   in the State of
party of the first part, and

of the County of   in the State of
party of the second part,

Witnesseth, that the said party of the first part, for and in consideration of the sum of
                                                                    Dollars,
to him in hand paid by the said party of the second part, the receipt whereof is hereby acknowledged, has granted, bargained and sold to the said party of the second part his heirs and assigns forever, the following described land, situate lying and being in the County of   ,
State of Florida, to wit:

And the said party of the first part does hereby fully warrant the title to said land, and will defend the same against the lawful claims of all persons whomsoever.

In Witness Whereof, the said party of the first part has hereunto set his hand and seal the day and year first above written.

Signed, Sealed and Delivered in Our Presence:

_____   _____ L.S.

_____   _____ L.S.

_____   _____ L.S.

_____   _____ L.S.

State of Florida)
County of   )

I Hereby Certify That on this day personally appeared before me, an officer duly authorized to administer oaths and take acknowledgments,

to me well known and known to me to be the individual   described in and who executed the foregoing deed, and   acknowledged before me that   executed the same freely and voluntarily for the purposes therein expressed.

          Witness my hand and official seal at   County
of   , and State of Florida, this   day of
          , A. D. 19

My Commission Expires _____

          _____
                    Notary Public

Figure C.3   Deed (indenture).

This Warranty Deed *Made and executed the*　　　*day of*　　　*A. D. 19*　　*by*

a corporation existing under the laws of　　　*, and having its principal place of business at*
hereinafter called the grantor, to

whose postoffice address is

hereinafter called the grantee:

(Wherever used herein the terms "grantor" and "grantee" include all the parties to this instrument and the heirs, legal representatives and assigns of individuals, and the successors and assigns of corporations)

Witnesseth: *That the grantor, for and in consideration of the sum of $　　　and other valuable considerations, receipt whereof is hereby acknowledged, by these presents does grant, bargain, sell, alien, remise, release, convey and confirm unto the grantee, all that certain land situate in County, Florida, viz:*

Together *with all the tenements, hereditaments and appurtenances thereto belonging or in anywise appertaining.*

To Have and to Hold, *the same in fee simple forever.*

And *the grantor hereby covenants with said grantee that it is lawfully seized of said land in fee simple; that it has good right and lawful authority to sell and convey said land; that it hereby fully warrants the title to said land and will defend the same against the lawful claims of all persons whomsoever; and that said land is free of all encumbrances*

(CORPORATE SEAL)

In Witness Whereof *the grantor has caused these presents to be executed in its name, and its corporate seal to be hereunto affixed, by its proper officers thereunto duly authorized, the day and year first above written.*

ATTEST:...
　　　　　　　　　　Secretary

....

Signed, sealed and delivered in the presence of:

....

By..
　　　　　　　　　　　　　　　　　　President

....

STATE OF
COUNTY OF

I HEREBY CERTIFY that on this day, before me, an officer duly authorized in the State and County aforesaid to take acknowledgments, personally appeared

well known to me to be the　　　President and　　　respectively of the corporation named as grantor in the foregoing deed, and that they severally acknowledged executing the same in the presence of two subscribing witnesses freely and voluntarily under authority duly vested in them by said corporation and that the seal affixed thereto is the true corporate seal of said corporation.

WITNESS my hand and official seal in the County and State last aforesaid this　　　day of　　　, A. D. 19

This Instrument prepared by:

Address

Figure C.4　Warranty deed (from corporate owner).

Form 1146   Florida   MORTGAGE DEED——(Balloon)

TUTBLANX REGISTERED U. S. PAT. OFFICE
TUTTLE LAW PRINT, PUBLISHERS, RUTLAND, VT. 05701

This Indenture,

THIS IS A BALLOON MORTGAGE AND FINAL PAYMENT OR THE BALANCE DUE UPON MATURITY IS $————————. TOGETHER WITH ACCRUED INTEREST, IF ANY, AND ALL ADVANCEMENTS MADE BY MORTGAGEE UNDER THE TERMS OF THIS MORTGAGE.

(Wherever used herein the terms "mortgagor" and "mortgagee" include all the parties to this instrument and the heirs, legal representatives and assigns of individuals, and the successors and assigns of corporations; and the term "note" includes all the notes herein described if more than one.)   Wherever used the singular number shall include the plural and the plural the singular, and the use of any gender shall include all genders.)

Made this   *day of*   *,A. D. 19*

Between

called the Mortgagor, and

called the Mortgagee,

Witnesseth,   *That the said Mortgagor, for and in consideration of the sum of*
Dollars,
to him in hand paid by the said Mortgagee, the receipt whereof is hereby acknowledged,
granted, bargained and sold to the said Mortgagee, the
following described land situate, lying and being in the County of
State of   *to wit:*

and the said Mortgagor does hereby fully warrant the title to said land, and will defend the same against the lawful claims of all persons whomsoever.

Provided Always,   *That if said Mortgagor shall pay to the said Mortgagee a certain promissory note, a copy of which is on the reverse side hereof, and shall perform and comply with each and every stipulation, agreement and covenant of said note and of this mortgage, then this mortgage and the estate hereby created shall be void, otherwise the same shall remain in full force and virtue. And the said Mortgagor covenants to pay the interest and principal promptly when due; to pay the taxes and assessments on said property; to carry insurance against fire on the building   on said land for not less than $; and windstorm insurance in amount of $, approved by the Mortgagee, with standard mortgage loss clause payable to Mortgagee, the policy to be held by the Mortgagee, to keep the building   on said land in proper repair; and to waive the homestead exemption.*

Should any of the above covenants be broken, then said note and all moneys secured hereby shall without demand, if the Mortgagee so elects, at once become due and payable and the mortgage be foreclosed, and all costs and expenses of collection of said moneys by foreclosure or otherwise, including solicitor's fees shall be paid by the Mortgagor, and the same are hereby secured.

Figure C.5   Balloon mortgage.

In Witness Whereof, *The said Mortgagor hereunto sets his hand and seal the day and year first above written.*

THIS IS A BALLOON MORTGAGE AND FINAL PAYMENT OR THE BALANCE DUE UPON MATURITY IS $——————. TOGETHER WITH ACCRUED INTEREST, IF ANY, AND ALL ADVANCEMENTS MADE BY MORTGAGEE UNDER THE TERMS OF THIS MORTGAGE.

Signed, Sealed and Delivered in Presence of Us;

_____   _____ L.S.

_____   _____ L.S.

_____   _____ L.S.

_____   _____ L.S.

State of Florida,

County of

I HEREBY CERTIFY, *That on this day personally appeared before me, an officer duly authorized to administer oaths and take acknowledgments,*

to me well known and known to me to be the person   described in and who executed the foregoing mortgage; and   acknowledged before me that executed the same for the purposes therein expressed.

WITNESS *my hand and official seal at*
County of , *and State of Florida, this*
day of , *A. D. 19*

*My Commission Expires*_____   *Notary Public* _____

Date

TO

𝔐𝔬𝔯𝔱𝔤𝔞𝔤𝔢 𝔇𝔢𝔢𝔡

Figure C.5 *(Continued)*

Form A230 Installment Note

INSTALLMENT NOTE

$ Dated: , 19

Principal Amount   State of

FOR VALUE RECEIVED, the undersigned hereby jointly and severally promise to pay to the order of
                                                                          , the sum of

Dollars ($), together with interest thereon at the rate of   % per annum
on the unpaid balance. Said sum shall be paid in the manner following:

All payments shall be first applied to interest and the balance to principal. This note may be prepaid, at any time, in whole or in part, without penalty. All prepayments shall be applied in reverse order of maturity.

This note shall at the option of any holder hereof be immediately due and payable upon the occurrence of any of the following:

1. Failure to make any payment due hereunder within   days of its due date.

2. Breach of any condition of any security interest, mortgage, pledge agreement or guarantee granted as collateral security for this note.

3. Breach of any condition of any security agreement or mortgage, if any, having a priority over any security agreement or mortgage on collateral granted, in whole or in part, as collateral security for this note.

4. Upon the death, insolvency dissolution or liquidation of any of the undersigned, or any endorser, guarantor or surety hereto.

5. Upon the filing by any of the undersigned of an assignment for the benefit of creditors, bankruptcy, or for relief under any provisions of the Bankruptcy Code; or by suffering an involuntary petition in bankruptcy or receivership not vacated within thirty (30) days.

In the event this note shall be in default, and placed with an attorney for collection, then the undersigned agree to pay all reasonable attorney fees and costs of collection. Payments not made within five (5) days of due date shall be subject to a late charge of   % of said payment. All payments hereunder shall be made to such address as may from time to time be designated by any holder hereof.

The undersigned and all other parties to this note, whether as endorsers, guarantors or sureties, agree to remain fully bound hereunder until this note shall be fully paid and waive demand, presentment and protest and all notices thereto and further agree to remain bound, notwithstanding any extension, renewal, modification, waiver, or other indulgence by any holder or upon the discharge or release of any obligor hereunder or to this note, or upon the exchange, substitution, or release of any collateral granted as security for this note. No modification or indulgence by any holder hereof shall be binding unless in writing; and any indulgence on any one occasion shall not be an indulgence for any other or future occasion. Any modification or change of terms, hereunder granted by any holder hereof, shall be valid and binding upon each of the undersigned, notwithstanding the acknowledgement of any of the undersigned, and each of the undersigned does hereby irrevocably grant to each of the others a power of attorney to enter into any such modification on their behalf. The rights of any holder hereof shall be cumulative and not necessarily successive. This note shall take effect as a sealed instrument and shall be construed, governed and enforced in accordance with the laws of the State first appearing at the head of this note. The undersigned hereby execute this note as principals and not as sureties.

Signed in the presence of:

_____   _____

_____   _____

(See Reverse for Guaranty)

c. E-Z Legal Forms

Figure C.6 Installment note.

𝕭𝖚𝖘𝖎𝖓𝖊𝖘𝖘 𝕷𝖊𝖆𝖘𝖊

THIS AGREEMENT, entered into this   day of   , 19

between

, hereinafter called the lessor,

party of the first part, and

of the County of   and State of

hereinafter called the lessee or tenant, party of the second part:

    WITNESSETH, That the said lessor does this day lease unto said lessee, and said lessee does hereby hire and take as tenant   under said lessor Room   or Space

No.

situate in   Florida, to be used and occupied by the lessee as

and for no other purposes or uses whatsoever, for

the term of   , subject and conditioned on the provisions of

clause ten of this lease beginning the   day of   ,

19   , and ending the   day of   , 19   ,

at and for the agreed total rental of

Dollars, payable as follows:

all payments to be made to the lessor on the first day of each and every month in advance without demand at the office of   in the City of

or at such other place and to such other person, as the lessor may from time to time designate in writing.

    The following express stipulations and conditions are made a part of this lease and are hereby assented to by the lessee:

    FIRST: The lessee shall not assign this lease, nor sub-let the premises, or any part thereof nor use the same, or any part thereof, nor permit the same, or any part thereof, to be used for any other purpose than as above stipulated, nor make any alterations therein, and all additions thereto, without the written consent of the lessor, and all additions, fixtures or improvements which may be made by lessee, except movable office furniture, shall become the property of the lessor and remain upon the premises as a part thereof, and be surrendered with the premises at the termination of this lease.

    SECOND: All personal property placed or moved in the premises above described shall be at the risk of the lessee or owner thereof, and lessor shall not be liable for any damage to said personal property, or to the lessee arising from the bursting or leaking of water pipes, or from any act of negligence of any co-tenant or occupants of the building or of any other person whomsoever.

    THIRD: That the tenant_____shall promptly execute and comply with all statutes, ordinances, rules, orders, regulations and requirements of the Federal, State and City Government and of any and all their Departments and Bureaus applicable to said premises, for the correction, prevention, and abatement of nuisances or other grievances, in, upon, or connected with said premises during said term; and shall also promptly comply with and execute all rules, orders and regulations of the Southeastern Underwriters Association for the prevention of fires, at_____own cost and expense.

    FOURTH: In the event the premises shall be destroyed or so damaged or injured by fire or other casualty during the life of this agreement, whereby the same shall be rendered untenantable, then the lessor shall have the right to render said premises tenantable by repairs within ninety days therefrom. If said premises are not rendered tenantable within said time, it shall be optional with either party hereto to cancel this lease, and in the event of such cancellation the rent shall be paid only to the date of such fire or casualty. The cancellation herein mentioned shall be evidenced in writing.

    FIFTH: The prompt payment of the rent for said premises upon the dates named, and the faithful observance of the rules and regulations printed upon this lease, and which are hereby made a part of this covenant, and of such other and further rules or regulations as may be hereafter made by the lessor, are the conditions upon which the lease is made and accepted and any failure on the part of the lessee to comply with the terms of said lease, or any of said rules and regulations now in existence, or which may be hereafter prescribed by the lessor, shall at the option of the lessor, work a forfeiture of this contract, and all of the rights of the lessee hereunder, and thereupon the lessor, his agents or attorneys, shall have the right to enter said premises, and remove all per-

Figure C.7   Business lease.

sons therefrom forcibly or otherwise, and the lessee thereby expressly waives any and all notice required by law to terminate tenancy, and also waives any and all legal proceedings to recover possession of said premises, and expressly agrees that in the event of a violation of any of the terms of this lease, or of said rules and regulations, now in existence, or which may hereafter be made, said lessor, his agent or attorneys, may immediately re-enter said premises and dispossess lessee without legal notice or the institution of any legal proceedings whatsoever.

SIXTH: If the lessee shall abandon or vacate said premises before the end of the term of this lease, or shall suffer the rent to be in arrears, the lessor may, at his option, forthwith cancel this lease or he may enter said premises as the agent of the lessee, by force or otherwise, without being liable in any way therefor, and relet the premises with or without any furniture that may be therein, as the agent of the lessee, at such price and upon such terms and for such duration of time as the lessor may determine, and receive the rent therefor, applying the same to the payment of the rent due by these presents, and if the full rental herein provided shall not be realized by lessor over and above the expenses to lessor in such re-letting, the said lessee shall pay any deficiency, and if more than the full rental is realized lessor will pay over to said lessee the excess of demand.

SEVENTH: Lessee agrees to pay the cost of collection and ten per cent attorney's fee on any part of said rental that may be collected by suit or by attorney, after the same is past due.

EIGHTH: The lessee agrees that he will pay all charges for rent, gas, electricity or other illumination, and for all water used on said premises, and should said charges for rent, light or water herein provided for at any time remain due and unpaid for the space of five days after the same shall have become due, the lessor may at its option consider the said lessee tenant at sufferance and immediately re-enter upon said premises and the entire rent for the rental period then next ensuing shall at once be due and payable and may forthwith be collected by distress or otherwise.

NINTH: The said lessee hereby pledges and assigns to the lessor all the furniture, fixtures, goods and chattels of said lessee, which shall or may be brought or put on said premises as security for the payment of the rent herein reserved, and the lessee agrees that the said lien may be enforced by distress foreclosure or otherwise at the election of the said lessor, and does hereby agree to pay attorney's fees of ten percent of the amount so collected or found to be due, together with all costs and charges therefore incurred or paid by the lessor.

TENTH: It is hereby agreed and understood between lessor and lessee that in the event the lessor decides to remodel, alter or demolish all or any part of the premises leased hereunder, or in the event of the sale or long term lease of all or any part of the_____; requiring this space, the lessee hereby agrees to vacate same upon receipt of sixty (60) days' written notice and the return of any advance rental paid on account of this lease.

It being further understood and agreed that the lessee will not be required to vacate said premises during the winter season: namely, November first to May first, by reason of the above paragraph.

ELEVENTH: The lessor, or any of his agents, shall have the right to enter said premises during all reasonable hours, to examine the same to make such repairs, additions or alterations as may be deemed necessary for the safety, comfort, or preservation thereof, or of said building, or to exhibit said premises, and to put or keep upon the doors or windows thereof a notice "FOR RENT" at any time within thirty (30) days before the expiration of this lease. The right of entry shall likewise exist for the purpose of removing placards, signs, fixtures, alterations, or additions, which do not conform to this agreement, or to the rules and regulations of the building.

TWELFTH: Lessee hereby accepts the premises in the condition they are in at the beginning of this lease and agrees to maintain said premises in the same condition, order and repair as they are at the commencement of said term, excepting only reasonable wear and tear arising from the use thereof under this agreement, and to make good to said lessor immediately upon demand, any damage to water apparatus, or electric lights or any fixture, appliances or appurtenances of said premises, or of the building, caused by any act or neglect of lessee, or of any person or persons in the employ or under the control of the lessee.

THIRTEENTH: It is expressly agreed and understood by and between the parties to this agreement, that the landlord shall not be liable for any damage or injury by water, which may be sustained by the said tenant or other person or for any other damage or injury resulting from the carelessness, negligence, or improper conduct on the part of any other tenant or agents, or employees, or by reason of the breakage, leakage, or obstruction of the water, sewer or soil pipes, or other leakage in or about the said building.

FOURTEENTH: If the lessee shall become insolvent or if bankruptcy proceedings shall be begun by or against the lessee, before the end of said term the lessor is hereby irrevocably authorized at its option, to forthwith cancel this lease, as for a default. Lessor may elect to accept rent from such receiver, trustee, or other judicial officer during the term of their occupancy in their fiduciary capacity without effecting lessor's rights as contained in this contract, but no receiver, trustee or other judicial officer shall ever have any right, title or interest in or to the above described property by virtue of this contract.

FIFTEENTH: Lessee hereby waives and renounces for himself and family any and all homestead and exemption rights he may have now, or hereafter, under or by virtue of the constitution and laws of the State of Florida, or of any other State, or of the United States, as against the payment of said rental or any portion hereof, or any other obligation or damage that may accrue under the terms of this agreement.

SIXTEENTH: This contract shall bind the lessor and its assigns or successors, and the heirs, assigns, administrators, legal representatives, executors or successors as the case may be, of the lessee.

SEVENTEENTH: It is understood and agreed between the parties hereto that time is of the essence of this contract and this applies to all terms and conditions contained herein.

EIGHTEENTH: It is understood and agreed between the parties hereto that written notice mailed or delivered to the premises leased hereunder shall constitute sufficient notice to the lessee and written notice mailed or delivered to the office of the lessor shall constitute sufficient notice to the Lessor, to comply with the terms of this contract.

NINETEENTH: The rights of the lessor under the foregoing shall be cumulative, and failure on the part of the lessor to exercise promptly any rights given hereunder shall not operate to forfeit any of the said rights.

TWENTIETH: It is further understood and agreed between the parties hereto that any charges against the lessee by the lessor for services or for work done on the premises by order of the lessee or otherwise accruing under this contract shall be considered as rent due and shall be included in any lien for rent due and unpaid.

TWENTY-FIRST: It is hereby understood and agreed that any signs or advertising to be used, including awnings, in connection with the premises leased hereunder shall be first submitted to the lessor for approval before installation of same.

Figure C.7 *(Continued)*

IN WITNESS WHEREOF, the parties hereto have hereunto executed this instrument for the purpose herein expressed, the day and year above written.

Signed, sealed and delivered in the presence of:

_____   _____ (Seal

_____   _____ (Seal
     As to Lessor   Lessor

_____   _____ (Seal

_____   _____ (Seal
     As to Lessee   Lessee

STATE OF FLORIDA,   }

County of_____

Before me, a Notary Public in and for said State and County, personally came_____

_____to me

well known and known to be the person_____ named in the foregoing lease, and_____

acknowledged that_____executed the same for the purpose therein expressed.

IN WITNESS WHEREOF, I have hereunto set my hand and affixed my official seal the_____

day of_____, 19_____.

                                _____

My commission expires_____   _____
                                   Notary Public, State of Florida at Large.

This Instrument prepared by:

Address

Figure C.7   *(Continued)*

(For A Term Not To Exceed One Year)

INSTRUCTIONS:

1. Agent: Give this disclosure to the Landlord prior to your assisting with the completion of the attached Lease.

2. Agent: As the person assisting with the completion of the attached form, insert your name in the first (5) blank "Name" spaces below.

3. Agent: **SIGN** the disclosure below.

4. Landlord and Tenant: Check the applicable provision regarding English contained in the disclosure and **SIGN** below.

5. Agent, Landlord and Tenant: Retain a copy for your files.

       *   *   *   *   *

DISCLOSURE:

_____ told me that he/she is not a lawyer and may not give
           (Name)
legal advice or represent me in court.

_____ told me that he/she may only help me fill out a form
           (Name)
approved by the Supreme Court of Florida. _____ may only help me
                                        (Name)
by asking me questions to fill in the form. _____ may also tell me
                                     (Name)
how to file the form.

_____ told me that he/she is not an attorney and cannot tell
           (Name)
me what my rights or remedies are or how to testify in court.

Tenant: Landlord:

_____ I can read English.   _____ I can read English.
_____ I cannot read English but this   _____ I cannot read English but this
       notice was read to me by   notice was read to me by

_____   _____
              (Name)   (Name)
in _____   in _____
             (Language)   (Language)

_____   _____   _____
     (Agent)   (Landlord)   (Tenant)

RLAU-1 9/92

Figure C.8 Apartment residential lease.

(FOR A TERM NOT TO EXCEED ONE YEAR)
(Not To Be Used For Commercial, Agricultural, or Other Residential Property)

WARNING: IT IS VERY IMPORTANT TO READ ALL OF THE LEASE CAREFULLY. THE LEASE IMPOSES IMPORTANT LEGAL OBLIGATIONS. AN ASTERISK (∗) OR A BLANK SPACE (_____) INDICATES A PROVISION WHERE A CHOICE OR A DECISION MUST BE MADE BY THE PARTIES. NO CHANGES OR ADDITIONS TO THIS FORM MAY BE MADE UNLESS A LAWYER IS CONSULTED.

I.   **TERM AND PARTIES.** This is a lease ("the Lease") for a period of _____ months (the "Lease Term"), beginning _____ [number] [month, day, year] and ending _____, between _____ [month, day, year] [name of owner of the property] and _____ (In the Lease, the owner, whether one or more, of the [name(s) of person(s) to whom the property is leased] property is called "Landlord." All persons to whom the property is leased are called "Tenant.")

II. **PROPERTY RENTED.** Landlord leases to Tenant the apartment no. _____ in the building located at _____. [street address] known as _____, _____, Florida _____, [name of apartment] [city] [zip code] together with the following furniture and appliances: _____

_____

[List all furniture and appliances. If none, write "none."] (In the Lease the property leased, including furniture and appliances, if any, is called "the Premises.")

III. **COMMON AREAS.** Landlord grants to Tenant permission to use, along with others, the common areas of the building and the development of which the Premises are a part.

IV. **RENT PAYMENTS AND CHARGES.** Tenant shall pay rent for the Premises in installments of $ _____ each on the _____ day of each _____. (A "Rental Installment Period," as used in the Lease, shall be a month if rent is paid monthly, [month, week] and a week if rent is paid weekly.) Tenant shall pay with each rent payment all taxes imposed on the rent by taxing authorities. The amount of taxes payable on the beginning date of the Lease is $ _____ for each installment. The amount of each installment of rent plus taxes ("the Lease Payment"), as of the date the Lease begins, is $ _____. Landlord will notify Tenant if the amount of the tax changes. Tenant shall pay the rent and all other charges required to be paid under the Lease by cash, valid check, or money order. Landlord may appoint an agent to collect the Lease Payment and to perform Landlord's obligations.

∗   The Lease Payments must be paid in advance / in arrears **(circle one)** beginning _____ [date]

∗ V. **DEPOSITS, ADVANCE RENT, AND LATE CHARGES.** In addition to the Lease Payments described above, Tenant shall pay the following: (check only those items that apply)

_____ a security deposit of $ _____ to be paid upon signing the Lease.

_____ advance rent in the amount of $ _____ for the Rental Installment Periods of _____ to be paid upon signing the Lease.

_____ a pet deposit in the amount of $ _____ to be paid upon signing the Lease.

_____ a late charge in the amount of $ _____ for each Lease Payment made more than _____ number of days after the date it is due.

_____ a bad check fee in the amount of $ _____ (not to exceed $20.00, or 5% of the Lease Payment, whichever is greater) if Tenant makes any Lease Payment with a bad check. If Tenant makes any Lease Payment with a bad check, Landlord can require Tenant to pay all future Lease Payments in cash or by money order.

VI. **SECURITY DEPOSITS AND ADVANCE RENT.** If Tenant has paid a security deposit or advance rent the following provisions apply:
A.   Landlord shall hold the money in a separate interest-bearing or noninterest-bearing account in a Florida banking institution for the benefit of Tenant. If Landlord deposits the money in an interest-bearing account, Landlord must pay Tenant interest of at least 75% of the annualized average interest paid by the bank or 5% per year simple interest, whichever Landlord chooses. Landlord cannot mix such money with any other funds of Landlord or pledge, mortgage, or make any other use of such money until the money is actually due to Landlord; or
B.   Landlord must post a surety bond in the manner allowed by law. If Landlord posts the bond, Landlord shall pay Tenant 5% interest per year.

At the end of the Lease, Landlord will pay Tenant, or credit against rent, the interest due to Tenant. No interest will be due Tenant if Tenant wrongfully terminates the Lease before the end of the Lease Term.

If Landlord rents 5 or more dwelling units, then within 30 days of Tenant's payment of the advance rent or any security deposit, Landlord must notify Tenant in writing of the manner in which Landlord is holding such money, the interest rate, if any, that Tenant will receive, and when such payments will be made.

VII. **NOTICES.** _____ is Landlord's Agent. All notices to Landlord and [name] all Lease Payments must be sent to Landlord's Agent at _____ [address] unless Landlord gives Tenant written notice of a change. Landlord's Agent may perform inspections on behalf of Landlord. All notices to Landlord shall be given by certified mail, return receipt requested, or by hand delivery to Landlord or Landlord's Agent.

Any notice to Tenant shall be given by certified mail, return receipt requested, or delivered to Tenant at the Premises. If Tenant is absent from the Premises, a notice to Tenant may be given by leaving a copy of the notice at the Premises.

Figure C.8   *(Continued)*

VIII.   **USE OF PREMISES.** Tenant shall use the Premises only for residential purposes. Tenant also shall obey, and require anyone on the Premises to obey, all laws and any restrictions that apply to the Premises. Landlord will give Tenant notice of any restrictions that apply to the Premises.
*   Landlord may / may not **(circle one)** adopt, modify, or repeal rules and regulations for the use of common areas and conduct on the Premises during the Lease Term. If adoption, modification, or repeal of additional rules and regulations is not permitted, they must be reasonable and in the best interest of the development in which the Premises are located.
*   Occasional overnight guests are / are not **(circle one)** permitted. An occasional overnight guest is one who does not stay more than _____ nights
*   in any calendar month. Landlord's written approval is / is not **(circle one)** required to allow anyone else to occupy the Premises.
*   Tenant may / may not **(circle one)** keep or allow pets or animals on the Premises without Landlord's approval of the pet or animal in writing.
         Tenant shall not keep any dangerous or flammable items that might increase the danger of fire or damage on the Premises without Landlord's consent. Tenant shall not create any environmental hazards on or about the Premises.
         Tenant shall not destroy, deface, damage, impair, or remove any part of the Premises belonging to Landlord, nor permit any person to do so.
*   Tenant may / may not **(circle one)** make any alterations or improvements to the Premises without first obtaining Landlord's written consent to the alteration or improvement.
         Tenant must act, and require all other persons on the Premises to act, in a manner that does not unreasonably disturb any neighbors or constitute a breach of the peace.

IX.   **MAINTENANCE.** Landlord and Tenant agree that the maintenance of the Premises must be performed by the person indicated below:
         A. Landlord's Required Maintenance. Landlord will comply with applicable building, housing, and health codes relating to the Premises. If there are no applicable building, housing, or health codes, Landlord shall maintain and repair the roofs, porches, windows, exterior walls, screens, foundations, floors, structural components, and steps, and keep the plumbing in reasonable working order.
*   B. Elective Maintenance. Fill in each blank space in this section with Landlord or Tenant to show who will take care of the item noted. If a space is left blank, Landlord will be required to take care of that item.

_____ Smoke detectors	_____ Running water	_____ Appliances
_____ Extermination of rats, mice, roaches, ants, wood-destroying organisms, and bedbugs	_____ Hot water	_____ Fixtures
	_____ Lawn	_____ Pool (including filters, machinery, and equipment)
_____ Locks and keys	_____ Heat	
_____ Clean and safe condition of outside areas	_____ Air conditioning	_____ Heating and air conditioning filters
	_____ Furniture	_____ Other: _____
_____ Garbage removal and outside garbage receptacles		_____

*   Tenant's responsibility, if any, indicated above, shall / shall not **(circle one)** include major maintenance or major replacement of equipment.

         Landlord shall be responsible for major maintenance or major replacement of equipment, except for equipment for which Tenant has accepted responsibility for major maintenance or major replacement in the previous paragraph.

         Major maintenance or major replacement means a repair or replacement that costs more than $ _____ .

         Tenant shall be required to vacate the Premises on 7 days' written notice, if necessary, for extermination pursuant to this subparagraph. When vacation of the Premises is required for extermination, Landlord shall not be liable for damages but shall abate the rent.

         Nothing in this section makes Landlord responsible for any condition created or caused by the negligent or wrongful act or omission of Tenant, any member of Tenant's family, or any other person on the Premises with Tenant's consent.
         C. Tenant's Required Maintenance. At all times during the Lease Term, Tenant shall:
            1. comply with all obligations imposed upon tenants by applicable provisions of building, housing, and health codes;
            2. keep the Premises clean and sanitary;
            3. remove all garbage from the dwelling unit in a clean and sanitary manner;
            4. keep all plumbing fixtures in the dwelling unit clean, sanitary, and in repair; and
            5. use and operate in a reasonable manner all electrical, plumbing, sanitary, heating, ventilating, air conditioning, and other facilities and appliances, including elevators.

X.   **UTILITIES.** Tenant shall pay all charges for hook-up, connection, and deposit for providing all utilities and utility services to the Premises during this lease except
         _____, which Landlord agrees to provide at Landlord's expense.
         (Specify any utilities to be provided and paid for by Landlord such as water, sewer, oil, gas, electricity, telephone, garbage removal, etc.).

XI.   **LANDLORD'S ACCESS TO PREMISES.** Landlord or Landlord's Agent may enter the Premises in the following circumstances:
         A. At any time for the protection or preservation of the Premises.
         B. After reasonable notice to Tenant at reasonable times for the purpose of repairing the Premises.
         C. To inspect the Premises; make necessary or agreed-upon repairs, decorations, alterations, or improvements; supply agreed services; or exhibit the Premises to prospective or actual purchasers, mortgagees, tenants, workers, or contractors under any of the following circumstances:
            1. with Tenant's consent;
            2. in case of emergency;
            3. when Tenant unreasonably withholds consent; or
            4. if Tenant is absent from the Premises for a period of at least one-half a Rental Installment Period. (If the rent is current and Tenant notifies Landlord of an intended absence, then Landlord may enter only with Tenant's consent or for the protection or preservation of the Premises.)

XII.   **PROHIBITED ACTS BY LANDLORD.**
         A. Landlord cannot cause, directly or indirectly, the termination or unreasonable interruption of any utility service furnished to Tenant, including, but not limited to, water, heat, light, electricity, gas, elevator, garbage collection, or refrigeration (whether or not the utility service is under the control of, or payment is made by, Landlord).
         B. Landlord cannot prevent Tenant's access to the Premises by any means, including, but not limited to, changing the locks or using any bootlock or similar device.
         C. Landlord cannot remove the outside doors, locks, roof, walls, or windows of the Premises except for purposes of maintenance, repair, or replacement. Landlord cannot remove Tenant's personal property from the Premises unless the action is taken after surrender, abandonment, or a lawful eviction. If provided in a written agreement separate from the Lease, upon surrender or abandonment by Tenant, Landlord shall not be liable or responsible for storage or disposition of Tenant's personal property. (For the purposes of this section, abandonment means Tenant is absent from the Premises for at least one-half a Rental Installment Period without paying rent or giving Landlord reasonable notice of Tenant's absence.)

XIII.   **CASUALTY DAMAGE.** If the Premises are damaged or destroyed other than by wrongful or negligent acts of Tenant or persons on the Premises with Tenant's consent, so that the use of the Premises is substantially impaired, Tenant may terminate the Lease within 30 days after the damage or destruction and Tenant will immediately vacate the premises. If Tenant vacates, Tenant is not liable for rent that would have been due after the date of termination. Tenant may vacate the part of the Premises rendered unusable by the damage or destruction, in which case Tenant's liability for rent shall be reduced by the fair rental value of the part of the Premises that was damaged or destroyed.

XIV.   **DEFAULT.**
         A. Landlord's Default. Except as noted below, Landlord will be in default if Landlord fails to comply with Landlord's required maintenance obligations under Section IX(A) or fails to comply with other material provisions of the Lease and such failure continues for more than 7 days after Tenant delivers a written notice to Landlord that tells Landlord how Landlord has violated the Lease.

         If Landlord's failure to comply is due to causes beyond the Landlord's control and if Landlord has made, and continues to make, every reasonable effort to correct the problem, the Lease may be altered by the parties, as follows:
            1. If Landlord's failure to comply makes the Premises uninhabitable and Tenant vacates, Tenant shall not be liable for rent during the period the Premises remains uninhabitable.
            2. If Landlord's failure to comply does not make the Premises uninhabitable and Tenant continues to occupy the Premises, the rent for the period of noncompliance will be reduced by an amount in proportion to the loss of rental value caused by the noncompliance.

Figure C.8   *(Continued)*

B. Tenant's Default. Tenant will be in default if any of the following occur:
1. Tenant fails to pay rent when due and the default continues for 3 days, excluding Saturday, Sunday, and legal holidays, after delivery of written demand by Landlord for payment of the rent or possession of the Premises.
2. Tenant fails to perform its obligations under the Lease, and the failure is such that Tenant should not be given an opportunity to correct it or the failure occurs within 12 months of a written warning by Landlord of a similar failure. Examples of such failures which do not require an opportunity to correct include, but are not limited to, destruction, damage, or misuse of Landlord's or other Tenant's property by an intentional act or a subsequent or continued unreasonable disturbance.
3. Except as provided above, Tenant fails to perform any other obligation under the Lease and the default continues for more than 7 days after delivery of written notice to Tenant from Landlord specifying the default.
C. Waiver of Default. If Landlord accepts rent knowing of Tenant's default or accepts performance by Tenant of any provision of the Lease different from the performance required by the Lease, or if Tenant pays rent knowing of Landlord's default or accepts performance by Landlord of any provision of the Lease different from the performance required by the Lease, the party accepting the rent or performance or making the payment shall not have the right to terminate the Lease or to bring a lawsuit for that default, but may enforce any later default.

XV. REMEDIES AND DEFENSES.
A. Tenant's Remedies.
1. If Landlord has defaulted under the Lease and if Tenant has given Landlord a written notice describing the default and Tenant's intention to withhold rent if the default is not corrected within 7 days, Tenant may withhold an amount of rent equal to the loss in rental value caused by the default. If Tenant's notice advises Landlord that Tenant intends to terminate the lease if the default is not cured within 7 days and the default is not cured within the 7 days, Tenant may terminate the Lease.
2. If Tenant has given the notice referred to in subparagraph (1) above, and if Landlord has not corrected the default within 7 days, Tenant may, in addition to withholding the applicable amount of rent, file a lawsuit in county court to require Landlord to correct the default and for damages.
3. If Landlord's default makes the Premises uninhabitable, and if Tenant has given Landlord a notice describing the default and informing Landlord that Tenant intends to terminate the Lease, then if Landlord does not cure the default within the 7-day period, Tenant may terminate the Lease at the end of the 7 days.
4. If Landlord violates the provisions of section XII, Landlord shall be liable to Tenant for actual and consequential damages or 3 months' rent, whichever is greater, for each violation.
B. Landlord's Remedies.
1. If Tenant remains on the Premises after expiration or termination of the Lease without Landlord's permission, Landlord may recover possession of the Premises in the manner provided for by law. Landlord also may recover double rent for the period during which Tenant refuses to vacate the Premises.
2. If Tenant defaults under the Lease by failing to pay rent, as set forth in section XIV(B)(1), Landlord may terminate Tenant's rights under the Lease and Tenant shall vacate the Premises immediately. If Tenant defaults under the Lease for any other reason, as set forth in sections XIV(B)(2) or (3) above, Landlord may terminate Tenant's rights under the Lease and Tenant shall vacate the Premises within 7 days of delivery of the notice of termination.
3. If Tenant fails to cure a default within the time specified in the notice to Tenant, Landlord may recover possession of the Premises as provided by law.
4. Landlord shall not recover possession of the Premises except:
   a. in a lawsuit for possession;
   b. when Tenant has surrendered possession of the Premises to Landlord; or
   c. when Tenant has abandoned the Premises. Absent actual knowledge of abandonment, the Premises shall be considered abandoned if Tenant is absent from them for at least one-half a Rental Installment Period, the rent is not current, <u>and</u> Tenant has not notified Landlord, in writing, of an intended absence.
5. If Tenant has defaulted under the Lease and Landlord has obtained a writ of possession, if Tenant has surrendered possession of the Premises to Landlord, or if Tenant has abandoned the Premises, Landlord may:
   a. treat the Lease as terminated, retake possession for Landlord's own account, and any further liability of Tenant will be ended;
   b. retake possession of the Premises for Tenant's account. Tenant will remain liable for the difference between rent agreed to be paid under the Lease and rent Landlord is able to recover in good faith from a new tenant; or
   c. do nothing, and Tenant will be liable for the rent as it comes due.
6. If Landlord retakes possession of the Premises for Tenant's account, Landlord must make a good faith effort to re-lease the Premises. Any rent received by Landlord as a result of the new lease shall be deducted from the rent due from Tenant. For purposes of this section, "good faith" in trying to re-lease the Premises means that Landlord shall use at least the same efforts to re-lease the Premises as were used in the initial rental or at least the same efforts as Landlord uses in attempting to lease other similar property. It does not require Landlord to give a preference in leasing the Premises over other vacant properties that Landlord owns or has the responsibility to rent.
C. Other Remedies. Each party also may have other remedies available at law or in equity.
D. Defenses. In a lawsuit by Landlord for possession of the Premises based upon nonpayment of rent or in a lawsuit by Landlord seeking to obtain unpaid rent, Tenant may assert as a defense Landlord's failure to perform required maintenance, as set forth in Section VIII(A) above. Landlord's failure to provide elective maintenance, as set forth in Section VIII(B) above, shall not be a defense to any lawsuit by Landlord for possession of the Premises unless otherwise provided by the Lease or applicable law. Tenant may also raise any other defense, whether legal or equitable, that Tenant may have, including the defense or retaliatory conduct.
E. Payment of Rent to Court. In any lawsuit by Landlord for possession of the Premises, if Tenant raises any defense other than payment, Tenant must pay into the registry of the court the past due rent set forth in Landlord's complaint, or an amount determined by the court, and the rent which comes due during the lawsuit, as it comes due. Failure of Tenant to pay the rent into the registry of the court will be a waiver of Tenant's defenses other than payment.
F. Attorney's Fees. In any lawsuit brought to enforce the Lease or under applicable law, the party who wins may recover its reasonable court costs and attorneys' fees from the party who loses.

* XVI. ASSIGNMENT AND SUBLEASING. Tenant may / may not **(circle one)** assign the Lease or sublease all or any part of the Premises without first obtaining Landlord's written approval and consent to the assignment or sublease.

* XVII. RISK OF LOSS. Landlord shall / shall not **(circle one)** be liable for any loss by reason of damage, theft, or otherwise to the contents, belongings, and personal effects of the Tenant, or Tenant's family, agents, employees, guests, or visitors located in or about the Premises, or for damage or injury to Tenant or Tenant's family, agents, employees, guests, or visitors. Landlord shall not be liable if such damage, theft, or loss is caused by Tenant, Tenant's family, agents, employees, guests, or visitors. Nothing contained in this provision shall relieve Landlord or Tenant from responsibility for loss, damage, or injury caused by its own negligence or willful conduct.

XVIII. SUBORDINATION. The Lease is subordinate to the lien of any mortgage encumbering the fee title to the Premises from time to time.

XIX. LIENS. Tenant shall not have the right or authority to encumber the Premises or to permit any person to claim or assert any lien for the improvement or repair of the Premises made by Tenant. Tenant shall notify all parties performing work on the Premises at Tenant's request that the Lease does not allow any liens to attach to Landlord's interest.

* XX. APPROVAL CONTINGENCY. The Lease is / is not **(circle one)** conditioned upon approval of Tenant by the association that governs the Premises.

XXI. RENEWAL/EXTENSION. The Lease can be renewed or extended only by a written agreement signed by both Landlord and Tenant, but **no renewal may extend the term to a date more than 1 year after the lease begins.** A new lease is required for each year.

XXII. MISCELLANEOUS.
A. Time is of the essence of the Lease.
B. The Lease shall be binding upon and for the benefit of the heirs, personal representatives, successors, and permitted assigns of Landlord and Tenant, subject to the requirements specifically mentioned in the Lease. Whenever used, the singular number shall include the plural or singular and the use of any gender shall include all appropriate genders.
C. The agreements contained in the Lease set forth the complete understanding of the parties and may not be changed or terminated orally.
D. No agreement to accept surrender of the Premises from Tenant will be valid unless in writing and signed by Landlord.
E. All questions concerning the meaning, execution, construction, effect, validity, and enforcement of the Lease shall be determined pursuant to the laws of Florida.
F. The place for filing any suits or other proceedings with respect to the Lease shall be the county in which the Premises is located.
G. Landlord and Tenant will use good faith in performing their obligations under the Lease.
H. As required by law, Landlord makes the following disclosure: "RADON GAS." Radon is a naturally occurring radioactive gas that, when it has accumulated in a building in sufficient quantities, may present health risks to persons who are exposed to it over time. Levels of radon that exceed federal and state guidelines have been found in buildings in Florida. Additional information regarding radon and radon testing may be obtained from your county public health unit.

Figure C.8 *(Continued)*

Glossary

This glossary is designed to give brief definitions of common terms you are likely to come across as you start investing in real estate.

Abstract of title. A history of all that affects the title, or ownership, of a piece of property; includes posted sales, mortgages, liens, and so on.

Acre. A measurement of land, 43,560 square feet.

Addendum. A page of additional clauses added to a real estate contract or lease. It should be signed or initialed by all parties involved.

Amortization of debt. Scheduled payoff of a debt.

Appraisal. Evaluation.

Appraisal report. A written document indicating evaluation and methods used.

As is. What you see is what you get.

Assessed valuation. The evaluation of a property by the local government for real estate tax purposes. The assessed value may or may not approximate market value.

Assessment. Real estate tax or fee charged by a municipality against a property.

Assumption. Taking over an existing mortgage on a piece of property you are buying. The lender (or mortgagee) may or may not have to agree, depending on the terms of the original mortgage.

Balloon. A mortgage on which the balance comes due at a certain date—not self-liquidating.

Boilerplate. Standard clauses in legal documents.

Broker. An intermediary who helps a transaction to take place, in return for a fee called a commission. There are various types: real estate brokers, mortgage brokers, and so on.

Building codes. Local or state regulations regarding the status of a piece of property.

Cancellation clause. A clause in a contract or an agreement allowing one side to cancel it under certain conditions.

Caveat emptor. "Let the buyer beware."

Closing. The meeting of all interested parties in order to complete a deal. Parties could include the seller, buyer, lender, title company, and their attorneys or representatives.

Closing costs. Necessary costs to close a deal. These may include attorney's fees, transfer stamp fees, title insurance costs, and mortgage costs.

Closing statement. An accounting of the funds involved in a closing. Often contains a written statement explaining things.

Cloud on title. Term indicating that there is a problem with the title that must be cleared up before closing.

Collateral. Something given as security for a loan. In real estate, it is usually a mortgage or deed of trust.

Commitment. A promise by a lender, in writing, to lend a certain amount of money in exchange for _____, subject to _____.

Commitment fee. A fee charged by a lender for a commitment, usually expressed as a percentage of the amount committed.

Common areas. Areas in a piece of real estate shared by all: parking lots, hallways, sidewalks, and so on.

Consideration. Something given in exchange for something else. Usually it is cash, but it could be services, stocks, or other property.

Contingency. A clause in a contract that states that the contract is subject to something taking place: satisfactory passing of inspection, financing, lease renewal, and so on.

Contract. An agreement. In real estate, due to the Statute of Frauds, to be valid the agreement must be dated, signed, and witnessed, and list all relevant terms including description of property, price, terms, contingencies, and effective or closing date.

Corporation. A form of business (entity) created by law. Considered an individual in the eyes of the law. The corporation (like any individual) is responsible for its own acts. Owners (stockholders) are not responsible for corporate acts or debts. Thus, they get limited liability.

Creditor. Person to whom money is owed.

Deal. An agreement that may be oral or written.

Debtor. One who owes.

Debt service. Payments that must be made on a loan.

Deed. A signed document that is evidence of ownership of property. It shows the name of the seller and buyer, the date of the transfer, and the description of the property.

Default. The breaking of an agreement. For example, not making mortgage payments on a timely basis, as called for in the mortgage agreement.

Depreciation. Reduction in value of property or equipment due to age, use, obsolescence, technological changes, and so on.

Eminent domain. The right of any government to take over a property, but with adequate market value compensation to the owner.

Equity. The owner's net share in the property. For example:

Property value	$100,000
Less mortgage	($ 78,000)
Balance that belongs to owners, or equity	$ 22,000

Eviction. Legal removal of someone from a property, usually a tenant for nonpayment of rent.

Exurb. A rural area just outside of the suburbs of a city.

Fixtures. Items of personal property such as chandeliers or appliances that are attached (not connected) to a piece of real property and thus are considered part of it.

Foreclosure. Legal proceeding by a lender to take the property due to nonpayment of a mortgage.

Grantee. One to whom property is given or sold.

Grantor. One who gives or sells.

Ground lease. A lease for a piece of land.

Ground rent. Rent paid for a ground lease.

HVAC. Heating, ventilation, and air conditioning system in a building.

Infrastructure. The basic common foundation of a city: roads, schools, utility lines, water and sewer lines, transportation systems, hospitals, and so on.

Interest. The price paid to borrow money.

Internal Revenue Code (IRC). The body of laws stating the tax laws of the U.S. federal government.

Internal Revenue Service (IRS). Federal agency responsible for enforcing the IRC and collecting taxes.

Joint tenancy with right of survivorship (JTWRS). Joint ownership of a piece of property with the survivor(s) keeping all of the property if one owner dies.

Judgment. A court order specifying that someone owes a debt to someone else, and the amount of the debt.

Land lease. *See* ground lease.

Lease. An agreement (or contract) allowing one party (the tenant or lessee) to use someone else's property in return for payment, called rent.

Leasehold. Property interest of a tenant (lessee) subject to the terms of a lease.

Lessee. A tenant, someone who gets a lease.

Lessor. A landlord, someone who gives a lease to a tenant (or lessee).

Leverage. The impact of borrowed money.

Lien. A claim against a piece of property, for example a mortgage, judgment, or mechanic's claim.

Liquidity. The speed with which something can be converted into cash.

Lis pendens. Notice of a lawsuit pending against a property.

Loan to value. The percentage of a loan in relationship to the value of the property.

Marketable title. "Clean" title free of liens and so forth. A piece of real estate cannot be sold without a marketable title.

Market value. The price agreed to by a ready, willing, and able buyer and seller in an arm's-length transaction, without undue pressure (duress) on either side to agree.

Maturity date. The date a loan comes due and must be paid off, including interest, if any.

Meeting of the minds. An agreement of two people ready to enter a contract (or formal agreement).

Mortgage. A document from an owner-borrower (mortgagor) giving someone else (the mortgagee) the legal right to place a lien on the property, usually in exchange for a loan (consideration).

Multiple dwelling. A building with more than three apartments.

Net lease. A commercial lease in which the tenant agrees to pay not only the rent, but also the operating costs of the property (real estate taxes, insurance, utilities, repairs, HVAC). It is similar to a ground or land lease.

Offer. A proposal or bid.

Operating costs. Costs of running a property.

Partnership. Two or more people joining for a purpose. In business, it is for profit. Each partner is liable for all of the partnership's acts and debts.

Par value. Face value of a bond or share of stock at the time of issuance.

Payee. One who receives a payment.

Payor. One who makes a payment.

Point. One percent of the amount of a loan, usually charged by a lender or mortgage broker.

Prepayment. Paying back a loan before it comes due (i.e., before the maturity date).

Present value. Current value of payments to be made in the future, allowing for a certain interest rate. The amount of the interest rate affects the discount.

Principal. The amount of a loan owed.

Real estate taxes. (Also called property taxes.) Amounts charged (or levied) on real estate by government bodies to generate tax revenues.

Real property or real estate. Land and anything, including buildings, permanently attached to it, or an ownership interest in such property.

Record. (n.) A document evidencing an event available for inspection, that is, sales of property, mortgages, and so forth. (v.) To put something in the record.

Refinance. To take out a new loan, usually to pay off the previous one, and possibly have cash left over.

Reserves. Money set aside, or allowances made, for future replacement of the parts of a piece of real estate, for example roofs, HVAC systems, elevators, refurbishing, and so on.

Right of survivorship. The principle that in a joint tenancy (joint ownership), if one party dies, the other (survivor) keeps the whole asset.

Second mortgage. A mortgage that is subordinate (or comes after) a first mortgage. The first mortgage must be paid off first.

Self-liquidating loan. A loan with equal payments that include interest and principal (loan payment) over a set period of time.

The interest portion keeps dropping and the principal portion keeps increasing until the loan is paid off.

Settlement costs. Closing costs.

Speculation. Taking high risks (gambling), hoping to get large profits.

Statute of Frauds. A group of laws stating that certain agreements must be in writing and signed by all parties to be enforceable. All real estate agreements fall under this rule, except possibly leases for less than one year.

Sublease. A lease from one tenant to another. Usually, such leases need the landlord's approval unless the original (master) lease says otherwise.

Survey. An exact measurement of the metes and bounds (boundaries) of a piece of land. Usually shows easements, encroachments, and so on.

Tax credit. A deduction from tax owed.

Tax deduction. A subtraction from gross income reported on a tax return. Tax is computed on gross income less tax deductions.

Tenancy in common. Ownership of a piece of property by two or more parties without the right of survivorship.

Time of the essence. A "drop-dead" date, or deadline, by which the contract must be done (closed), or otherwise the contract will be in default and could be automatically ended.

Title. Legal, valid ownership of property and the related documents (deeds, etc.).

Title insurance. A policy issued by a title insurance company that confirms that the buyer is getting good title or ownership of a piece of property.

Title report. Report from a title company as to the ownership and lien status of a piece of property.

Title search. A search of the public property records in regard to the history and current status of the title to a piece of property.

Trust deed. A type of deed given in some states by a borrower to be held in trust instead of a mortgage (right to lien) for a loan.

Usury. Charging more interest than the maximum interest rate allowed by law.

Vendee. Buyer.

Vendor. Seller.

Index